# THE EPISTEMOLOGY OF THE CYRENAIC SCHOOL

The Cyrenaic school was a fourth-century BC philosophical move-ment, related both to the Socratic tradition and to Greek scepti-cism. In ethics, Cyrenaic hedonism can be seen as one of many attempts made by the associates of Socrates and their followers to endorse his ethical outlook and to explore the implications of his method. In epistemology, there are close philosophical links be-tween the Cyrenaics and the Sceptics, both Pyrrhonists and Aca-demics. There are further links with modern philosophy as well, for the Cyrenaics introduce a form of subjectivism which in some ways pre-announces Cartesian views, endorsed by Malebranche and Hume and developed by Kant. This constitutes the philosophical underpinnings of Cyrenaic scepticism, summarised by the thesis that we can only know our own experiences but cannot know anything else, including objects in the world and other minds.

This book reconstructs Cyrenaic epistemology, explains how it depends on Cyrenaic hedonism, locates it in the context of ancient debates and discusses its connections with modern and contempor-ary epistemological positions.

VOULA TSOUNA is Assistant Professor of Philosophy at the University of California at Santa Barbara. She is co-author, with Giovanni Indelli, of [Philodemus] [On Choices and Avoidances] (1995) and author of articles on Plato and on Hellenistic and Roman philosophy.

# THE EPISTEMOLOGY OF
# THE CYRENAIC SCHOOL

VOULA TSOUNA

CAMBRIDGE
UNIVERSITY PRESS

PUBLISHED BY THE PRESS SYNDICATE OF THE UNIVERSITY OF CAMBRIDGE
The Pitt Building, Trumpington Street, Cambridge CB2 1RP, United Kingdom

CAMBRIDGE UNIVERSITY PRESS
The Edinburgh Building, Cambridge CB2 2RU, United Kingdom
40 West 20th Street, New York, NY 10011-4211, USA
10 Stamford Road, Oakleigh, Melbourne 3166, Australia

First published 1998

Printed in the United Kingdom at the University Press, Cambridge

Typeset in 11/12.5 pt Baskerville [VN]

*A catalogue record for this book is available from the British Library*

*Library of Congress cataloguing in publication data*

Tsouna-McKirahan, Voula.
The epistemology of the Cyrenaic School / Voula Tsouna.
p.    cm.
Includes bibliographical references and indexes.
ISBN 0 521 62207 7 (hardback)
1. Cyrenaics (Greek philosophy) 2. Knowledge, Theory of – History.
I. Title.
B279.T76 1998
121'.0938–dc21    97–45022    CIP

ISBN 0 521 62207 7 hardback

*for Jacques*

# Contents

# *Preface*

Cyrenaic philosophy is related to two ancient traditions: the Socratic movement and Greek scepticism. It belongs to the former on historical grounds, since it is one of many attempts made by the intimate associates of Socrates and their followers to endorse his ethical outlook and to explore implications of the principles of his teachings. It fits into the latter by virtue of the close philosophical relations linking the Cyrenaic epistemological views with the two main varieties of scepticism encountered in Greek philosophy, the one reaching back to Pyrrho of Elis in the fourth century BC and the other associated with a particular phase in the history of Plato's Academy.

From the systematic point of view, the Cyrenaic doctrine introduced a form of subjectivism which in some ways appears to pre-announce the subjectivism of Descartes, as endorsed by Malebranche and Hume and developed by Kant. The Cyrenaic conception of subjective knowledge constitutes the philosophical underpinnings of the scepticism of the school, summarised by the thesis that we are unable to know anything at all about objects in the external world. In contrast to the moderns, the Cyrenaics assumed that empirical objects exist and that they act upon us in various ways. Nevertheless, their scepticism, more than any other epistemological position in antiquity, resembles what modern philosophy calls scepticism about the external world.

My main aim in this book is to reconstruct Cyrenaic epistemology in all its interrelated aspects, to locate it precisely in the context of ancient philosophical debate, and to explore its philosophical connections with modern and contemporary epistemological positions.

Before I sketch the main outlines of my argument, I should say perhaps some things about the evidence, which in fact is fairly complex. Since the original writings of the Cyrenaics have perished, we can only reconstruct their epistemological views from what other authors tell us. With few exceptions these are later authors who in most cases did not

make use of the original writings of the Cyrenaic philosophers, but
selected information from secondary sources and presented it in a
context determined by their own philosophical agenda and from a point
of view belonging to their own time. I do not here discuss in detail
problems in the doxographical evidence; however, I provide references
to scholarly treatments of such issues.

My examination of the Cyrenaic doctrine is organised under two
headings, subjectivism and scepticism. A third section is devoted to
discussing the relations between Cyrenaic epistemology and other
ancient doctrines that present important similarities to it. These sections
are preceded by an introductory chapter (chapter 1), in which I sketch
out the connection between the epistemology and the ethics of the
Cyrenaics and thus give a perspective from which we can make sense of
their basic epistemological thesis.

The subjectivism of the school is centred on the notion of the *pathē*,
undergoings produced on a subject by its contact with an object. Crucial
to the analysis of the concept of the *pathē*, which I undertake in chapter 2,
are their physiological and psychological characteristics, as well as their
ontological status. Some of the topics I discuss are the physicalistic
association of different kinds of *pathē* with different kinds of bodily
alterations, their description as states which have no ethical value
beyond the actual time of their occurrence, and the thesis that they are
detected by the so-called internal touch – a notion that I attempt to
clarify by referring to a late Epicurean discussion of the function of the
senses. Regarding the ontological aspects of the *pathē*, I argue that the
Cyrenaic emphasis on the subjective aspects of bodily changes does not
presuppose or entail the mind–body problem as we know it from
Descartes onwards; nevertheless, their conception of the *pathē* primarily
as experiences constitutes a philosophically interesting alternative to
modern conceptions of subjective states.

In chapter 3 I examine the technical vocabulary that the Cyrenaics
coined to refer to the *pathē*. I distinguish between two types of locutions:
verbal expressions such as 'I am whitened' and 'I am sweetened', and
adverbial phrases such as 'I am affected whitely'. Both of these are
autobiographical, i.e., they report the manner in which I am being
affected at a given time, and both are central to the analysis that follows,
since they constitute the only categories of sentences which, in the
Cyrenaic view, are incorrigibly true.

In examining the epistemic status of such reports in chapter 4, I
clarify the sense in which the *pathē* and the reports about them are

attested as the only objects of apprehension and the sole criteria of truth. I compare these claims to the most important uses of the concepts of the criterion, of apprehension and of evidence in Hellenistic philosophy, and maintain that, although it may be anachronistic to attribute these concepts to the Cyrenaics, it is philosophically enlightening to do so. I next study the epistemic characteristics of the sentences describing *pathē*, and in particular the claim that privileged access to our own *pathē* guarantees the truth of sentences reporting them. Subsequently, I raise the question of why the Cyrenaics assumed the *pathē* to be self-evident and I attempt to answer it by interpreting the Cyrenaic position in terms of two twentieth-century foundationalist positions about self-evident propositions and self-evident states. I argue that, on the one hand, infallible awareness of the *pathē* does not amount to direct and immediate perception of distinct mental objects and thus does not conform to the perceptual model suggested by the sense-data theories; on the other hand, the Cyrenaic thesis *is* comparable in important ways to the analysis of perception proposed by other modern foundationalists known as adverbial analysis theorists. I go on to draw a comparison between the Cyrenaics and the Pyrrhonian Sceptics which aims to circumscribe the scope of the claim that only the *pathē* are apprehensible. I compare the position of the Cyrenaics with Sextus' observation that the *pathē*, among other things, constitute the Sceptics' criterion for practical life; my argument is that, while the Sceptics did not assign to the *pathē* a proper epistemic status, the Cyrenaics did. This is precisely what makes their position revolutionary in comparison with those of other ancient sceptics, and what brings them close to modern scepticism.

Chapter 5 completes the analysis of Cyrenaic subjectivism by examining a set of objections levelled against it by Aristocles of Messene, a Peripatetic philosopher who aimed to prove that the Cyrenaic redefinition of knowledge is too narrow to explain all the kinds of knowledge that we have, and also that our awareness of the *pathē* entails or presupposes that we possess knowledge which goes beyond the *pathē*. Aristocles' argument raises important philosophical issues, primarily the question whether the awareness of short-lived internal states is sufficient to explain the conception of oneself as a human being, and whether the possession of subjective knowledge may presuppose that one makes certain cognitive assumptions about objective reality. These points constitute important challenges not only for the Cyrenaics but for most forms of modern subjectivism.

The section on Cyrenaic scepticism examines two main issues, the attitude of the Cyrenaics towards the problem of the external world and their doubts about other minds. In chapter 6, I argue that the expressions used to refer to the external causes of the *pathē* strongly suggest that the Cyrenaics did not question the existence of a reality external to the perceiver. This basic assumption of objectivity corresponds to the limited scope of their scepticism: tbey did not attempt to explain away all empirical knowledge in terms of awareness of subjective experiences, but restricted their discussion to the perception of single empirical properties or qualities. They did not question the existence of concrete objects such as horses and people, but only denied that we can have cognitive access to their properties. Their position, I suggest, invites philosophers to re-examine the force of the fundamental assumption that there is an external world and to compare the circumscribed epistemological doubts of the Cyrenaics with the enlarged scepticism outlined by Descartes in the *Meditations*.

The assessment of their attitude regarding the problem of the external world is important for understanding the nature of the position that the Cyrenaics take with regard to other minds and for distinguishing it from what came to be called in modern philosophy the problem of Other Minds. Chapter 7 maintains that, ontologically, the Cyrenaics assumed that people other than the perceiver experience *pathē* similar in structure to the perceiver's *pathē*, while, epistemologically, they denied that we can gain cognitive access to the content of other people's *pathē*. I argue that their position is weaker than modern versions of the problem of Other Minds, precisely because it is not dominated by the claims and assumptions related to the mind–body problem. Although they posit that we have no access to the *pathē* of our neighbour because they are private, they do not consider privacy the exclusive mark of the mental; and although they contrast our incorrigible access to our own *pathē* with our inability to gain access to our neighbour's *pathē*, they do not apply the concepts of incorrigibility and privileged access to a distinct non-physical realm. These distinctions help isolate what is really distinctive and valuable about the Cyrenaic position and also contribute to understanding the theoretical assumptions behind modern formulations of the problem of Other Minds.

In connection with their position on other minds, the Cyrenaics make some remarks on language. In particular, they draw a contrast between the privacy and incommunicability of our *pathē* on the one hand, and the use of words which we all share on the other hand. In chapter 8, I specify the nature of that contrast and I examine whether it implies that the Cyrenaics find the semantic relationship between words and what they signify inherently problematic. I attempt to clarify the Cyrenaic remarks further by comparing them to the empiricist account of language offered by John Locke.

What is distinctive about Cyrenaic epistemology becomes clearer once it is set against two other epistemological positions that might appear almost identical with it: the Epicurean thesis that all sensations or sense-impressions are true, and the doctrine of the so-called 'subtler' philosophers deployed in the first part of Plato's *Theaetetus*. The third part of the book is centred on these issues.

In chapter 9, I examine the merits of Plutarch's claim that the positions of both the Cyrenaics and the Epicureans entail that infallible awareness of our internal states does not enable us to draw reliable inferences about external objects. I refute this claim primarily by arguing that, while the Epicureans considered the knowledge of sense-impressions knowledge of something physical (an atomic structure with which the perceiver is in contact), the Cyrenaics defined knowledge of the *pathē* exclusively in terms of the awareness of internal states. Thus, in the former case the gap between the sense-impressions and objects is the gap between the films of atoms and the objects emitting them, while in the latter case the gap is defined in terms of the transition from experience to reality. The main philosophical interest of this chapter lies in the fact that the problems raised about the Epicurean theory of perception are found in many representational theories, ancient and modern.

The next parallel which I examine is between Cyrenaic subjectivism and the relativism ascribed to the 'subtler' philosophers in the first part of Plato's *Theaetetus*. This parallel was drawn both by ancient and by modern authors to the effect that the two doctrines amount to practically the same philosophical position. My task in chapter 10 is to clarify the relation between these two doctrines by spelling out their similarities as well as their differences. One philosophically important result is that we can see that the difference between relativism and scepticism is conditioned by the different concepts of truth and knowledge involved in the two approaches.

The autonomy and uniqueness of Cyrenaic epistemology raises questions about its Socratic pedigree. Chapter 11 explores on what grounds the doctrine could have reasonably been considered an offshoot of Socrates' teachings. Following up the interpretation outlined in chapter 1, I argue that the Cyrenaics could present their epistemic analysis of the *pathē* as an effort to obey, like Socrates, the Delphic command 'Know yourself' and to pursue the Socratic example of self-knowledge; they could look to Socrates' avowals of ignorance as legitimating sources of their own scepticism about the knowledge of external objects; and they could inscribe their epistemology in the context of an attempt to ground moral behaviour in some kind of knowledge or understanding, thus appearing to investigate further the implications of Socrates' intellectualism. Such arguments may serve as an example of the ways in which the philosophers and the schools associated with the Socratic movement could have looked to Socrates as a source of inspiration and legitimation. They can be taken to illustrate both how pliable and fluid are the ideas habitually attributed to the historical Socrates and how resourceful the schools who bid for the mantle of Socrates could be in manipulating these ideas, each on its own account.

I append a collection of source materials in translation, parts of which are cited in the main body of my text. It is based on the editions of G. Giannantoni (*I Cirenaici*, Florence 1958), E. Mannebach (*Aristippi et Cyrenaicorum fragmenta*, Leiden/Cologne 1961), and G. Giannantoni's edition of the fragments and testimonies on Socrates and the Socratics (*Socratis et Socraticorum reliquiae*, Naples 1990). However, it differs from previous collections in two ways. I include passages which, although not directly addressing the epistemology of the school, assist in reconstructing and assessing the theory; and I also give more context for the testimonies than previous collections have done, wherever it seems historically or philosophically informative to do so.

My overall interpretation is, by some lights, conservative. On the one hand, I maintain that Cyrenaic epistemology introduces the idea that some kind of truth can be achieved within the limits of subjective experiences, lays claim to knowledge of these experiences, and emphasises the gap between our sense-contents and the things they purport to represent. On the other hand, I resist radical conclusions such as that the Cyrenaics held a Cartesian view of the mind and that they defended a form of anti-realism, and I maintain that their doubts about external objects, about other minds and about the use of ordinary language are less ambitious than they might appear.

The reasons for this restraint are set out in some detail in chapter 1. Here, it suffices to say that my line of interpretation has, I think, considerable historical and textual support. Philosophically, I hope to convince the reader that the study of Cyrenaic scepticism is well worth getting into, both for its own intrinsic interest and for the light it can cast on the presuppositions that we habitually have about subjectivity, objectivity and the nature of sceptical doubts. To give an example, my discussion of the Cyrenaic theory suggests ways in which the privacy of internal states, as well as the infallibility of first-person reports and the accessibility of other minds can be problematised independently of the Cartesian mind–body distinction. And thus it may call for a re-examination of the weight usually assigned to this distinction in formulating epistemological problems.

I shall now come to practical details. Regarding the notes, some are historical, others exegetic, others draw parallels and comparisons between the Cyrenaics and modern philosophers, many of which inform the discussion in the main text without being explicitly mentioned. There is nothing exclusive or normative about these comparisons: they are not the only ones that can or should be drawn. They merely reflect my own interests and train of thought. Regarding the bibliographical references, as well as the bibliography, I have not thought it necessary, or indeed possible, to make them exhaustive. There are several excellent bibliographies on Hellenistic philosophy, and also on the theories of knowledge and on problems in metaphysics and philosophy of mind, with which the readers whom this book primarily addresses are familiar. I cite mainly the scholarly literature to which my argument is indebted, as well as the modern works that have influenced my discussion most.

I have tried to make each chapter as autonomous as possible, and yet to thread each section to the argument in other chapters. This has resulted in numerous cross-references, which I hope will not be too cumbersome.

The book should be accessible to readers with no Greek or Latin. All the texts discussed are given in English translation. I have transliterated individual words and short phrases that readers with no Greek or Latin need to pronounce and use, whereas longer phrases or sentences are cited in the original languages. This is merely a rule of thumb, which I have occasionally abandoned when it seemed appropriate.

Readers will, I trust, forgive me a few words about how this book came into being and what its relation is to my past work on the Cyrenaics. I have been thinking about its subject since working on my doctorate, part of which treated the epistemology of the Cyrenaics. The references to my doctoral thesis, which was completed in July 1988, witness the extent to which I have drawn on it. But this book is another and a very different piece of work. I do not undertake here to spell out and justify the historical and philological assumptions that I make about the Cyrenaic school and doctrine, as I did in my thesis and previous publications. What I am interested in is to raise exegetic and systematic issues and to assess the epistemological views of the Cyrenaics philosophically. I hope I can convince my readers as to the merits of these views.

Relatively few people have seen this work in unpublished form. To those who have, I owe a large debt of gratitude for the gift of their time, for their comments and criticisms no less than for their patience and support. David Blank guided me through intricacies of text, grammar and semantics to help me make sense of the Cyrenaic remarks on language. Richard McKirahan often pointed out what the text says as opposed to what I had wished it to say, and corrected infelicities of language and style throughout the manuscript. From David Sedley's generosity I benefited not once but many times. As an editor for *The Routledge Encyclopedia of Philosophy*, he made me see how to pull loose strings together in my articles on the Cyrenaics and on the Socratic schools and this paid off, I think, in several chapters of the book. Also, he kindly offered to read the entire manuscript and gave me extensive written comments which led me to make, in many places, substantial alterations to my text. It is difficult to thank Myles Burnyeat adequately, partly because my debts to him are so many, and partly because the ways in which he helped me are so very much his own and I cannot readily pin them down. The least I can do is to acknowledge his detailed criticisms on the penultimate draft of the manuscript, which forced me to rethink once again my overall interpretation and, in some cases, to argue my ideas afresh. A debt of another kind is owed to the National Endowment for the Humanities which supported my project with a one-year Research Fellowship in 1994–5.

This book is for Jacques Brunschwig. His work has been a model for me of what scholarly rigour and philosophical strength together can achieve in the study of ancient texts. I have had the gift of his advice and scrutiny of my arguments in this monograph as in much else. And, for many years past, I have cherished his friendship.

# *Abbreviations*

| | |
|---|---|
| Anonymous | Anonymous in *Theaetetum* |
| Aristotle | |
| *De an.* | *De anima* |
| *De int.* | *De interpretatione* |
| *EN* | *Ethica Nicomachea* |
| *Metaph.* | *Metaphysica* |
| *Phys.* | *Physica* |
| Athenaeus | |
| Athenaeus | *Deipnosophistai* |
| *Deipn.* | *Deipnosophistai* |
| Augustine (St) | |
| *Contr.Acad.* | *Contra Academicos* |
| *De civ.dei* | *De civitate dei* |
| Cicero | |
| *Acad.* | *Academica* |
| *De fin.* | *De finibus* |
| *De or.* | *De oratore* |
| *Luc.* | *Lucullus* |
| *Tusc.* | *Tusculanae disputationes* |
| Clement of Alexandria | |
| Clement of Alexandria | *Stromateis* |
| *Strom.* | *Stromateis* |
| Diogenes Laertius | |
| D.L. | Diogenes Laertius, *Vitae philosophorum* |
| DK | H. Diels and W. Kranz, *Die Fragmente der Vorsokratiker*, Berlin 1951 |
| Epictetus | |
| *Epict.diatr.* | *Epicteti dissertationes ab Arriano digestae* |

*Abbreviations*

Epicurus
  *KD*                             *Ratae sententiae* (*Kyriae doxai*)

Epiphanius
  *Adv.haer.*                   *Adversus haeresias*

Eusebius
  Eusebius                  Eusebius Caesariensius, *Praeparatio evangelica*

  *Praep.ev.*                  *Praeparatio evangelica*

Galen (ps.)
  *Hist.phil.*                  *Historia philosopha*

Hesychius
  *Onom.*                       *Onomatologos*

HR                         *The Philosophical Works of Descartes*, translated by E. S. Haldane and G. R. T. Ross, Cambridge 1911, vols. I and II

Jerome (St)
  *Epist.*                       *Epistulae*

Lactantius
  *Divin.inst.*                 *Divinae institutiones*

LSJ                       *Greek–English Lexicon*, compiled by H. S. Liddell and R. Scott, revised and augmented by H. S. Jones, Oxford

Lucretius
  *DNR*                        *De natura rerum*

PHerc.                  Papyrus Herculanensis

Plato
  *Apol.*                       *Apologia*
  *Charm.*                   *Charmides*
  *Phd.*                       *Phaedo*
  *Phil.*                       *Philebus*
  *Rep.*                       *Respublica*
  *Symp.*                    *Symposium*
  *Theaet.*                  *Theaetetus*
  *Tim.*                       *Timaeus*

Plutarch
  Plutarch                 Plutarch, *Adversus Colotem*
  *Adv.Col.*                *Adversus Colotem*

Seneca
  *Epist.*                       *Epistulae*

Sextus Empiricus
  Sextus

  *PH*

  *M*

Strabo

  Strabo

*SSR*


*SVF*


Themistius

  *Or.*

Xenophon

  *Mem.*

Sextus Empiricus

*Pyrrhoniae hypotyposes* (*Outlines of Pyrrhonism*)

*Adversus mathematicos* (*Against the Professors*)


*Geographia*

*Socratis et Socraticorum reliquiae*, ed. G. Giannantoni, Rome 1990

*Stoicorum veterum fragmenta*, ed. H. von Arnim, Leipzig 1903–24


*Orationes*


*Memorabilia*

# CHAPTER I

# Knowledge and the good life: the ethical motivation of the Cyrenaic views on knowledge

What we usually call Cyrenaic 'epistemology' is not an epistemology in the sense that other ancient and modern theories are. It is not a systematic theory exploring coherently and in depth the provenance, nature and structure of knowledge, objective or subjective. Nor, when it comes to scepticism, do we find the Cyrenaics coming to grips with the range of epistemological issues that both Academic and Pyrrhonian enquirers raise in order to cast doubt on the possibility of knowledge. The epistemology of the school basically consists of a two-fold epistemological theme – namely that we have knowledge of our *pathē* but cannot have knowledge of things in the world – and of a number of elaborations upon that theme. Too often in the course of this study we shall see the Cyrenaics in possession of the conceptual tools that would allow them to raise epistemological issues that are recognisably modern, only to realise thereafter that, nonetheless, they do not go much further than their one basic theme. Those who go through the ancient testimonies may experience a sensation not altogether different from bumping their heads repeatedly against a glass door – a feeling that there is an obstacle there, only it is not immediately obvious what it is.

The problem comes down to this. The fact that the Cyrenaics stop short of following up epistemological issues that they themselves raise, and that they do so in virtually every case where we would expect them to develop their position and draw its implications, indicates that we do not get this picture because of gaps in the evidence. We should not assume, I think, that they did not see how they could proceed, for they lack neither originality nor inventiveness so long as they keep to a point of discussion. So we can reasonably infer that, from a given point onwards, they did not have any interest in pursuing matters further, and this seems to imply that they did not act as conventional epistemologists in the sense that they did not explore epistemological questions for their own sake. If so, there are three questions that we need to answer in order to acquire a perspective on their epistemological views. First, if they did not have an intrinsic interest in epistemological questions, why did they take the trouble to make the claim that we can grasp only our own *pathē* but have no grasp of real objects? Second, why do they decide to elaborate somewhat upon that claim? And third, what is it that determines the point where they cut short their remarks on particular epistemological issues – why do they stop where they stop?

The one context that may help us come up with an answer is, I suggest, ethics. The Cyrenaics were hedonists and hence posited pleasure as the supreme good of human life. There are various splits and sects within the members of that school, all of which are over issues in hedonistic ethics. This is not the place to discuss them, but it will suffice to say that, despite their differences, all Cyrenaic philosophers agree that the pleasure that is of supreme positive value is bodily pleasure: not the accumulation of such pleasure over a lifetime, but the bodily pleasure that one is experiencing at present. And conversely, the only thing that is of negative value is pain, defined not as the sum of painful experiences over an extended period, but as the bodily pain that a person is suffering at present.

There is an obvious connection between the ethical thesis that the only things that matter are the *pathē*, pleasurable or painful, that we are experiencing and the epistemological thesis that the *pathē* are the only things we can grasp: our ultimate goal is to achieve pleasure and shun pain, and this goal is perfectly within our reach, precisely because pleasure and pain (as well as other experiences that may be indirectly related to our getting pleasure or avoiding pain) are things we grasp unfailingly and cannot be in error about. Perhaps there is also a further connection bearing upon the very character of pleasure as the moral good, namely that it is vindicated as the moral good precisely in virtue of the fact that we experience it as such; what we grasp unmistakably is not only that our experience is one of pleasure, but also that this pleasurable experience is self-evidently the greatest good.[1]

These links give us an angle from which we are to look at the views that constitute the object of this study. It is not the angle of someone who is particularly interested in analysing *how* we know the things we know and in organising the results into a coherent system. It is rather the perspective of somebody who is mainly interested in *what* we know and makes a series of remarks, some of them fairly elaborate, about the

---

[1] On this see Irwin 1991 and my article 'The Cyrenaics' in the *Routledge Encyclopedia of Philosophy*.

things we do know and those that we do not. The point is not positive, it is negative: the *pathē* are all we can know and are what we want to look at, since at any rate they are all that matters. The philosophical interest of the remarks about our knowledge of the *pathē* lies precisely in that negative point. The Cyrenaics invite us to look within, and to organise our life on the basis of what we find there, namely our experiences. And they set their position deliberately in contrast to the doctrines of other philosophers who urge us to acquire objective knowledge of various further things and lead our lives on the basis of it: we do not in fact need any of that knowledge, since the moral good is found among our *pathē* and can be achieved by attending to them.

Connected to the turn inwards is the physiological and epistemological talk about the *pathē*: for example, the remarks about what kind of states they are, the linguistic ways of expressing them, their epistemological characteristics and the analysis of the manner in which they affect us. The rejections of empirical knowledge and of knowledge of other minds are instances of, and also grounds for, the Cyrenaics' refusal to seek the secret of life outside, in the world around them. Whether they are accumulating positive features in favour of trusting the *pathē* or whether they give epistemological reasons why we should not aspire to information about things and people around us, they follow the same strategy: they pursue questions to the point of vindicating their ethical project, and perhaps to the degree of eliminating any substantial opposition (or so they may hope), and then they drop them. In doing so they act primarily as ethicists, not as epistemologists: they see the exploration of epistemological issues principally as a means to an end, not as an activity that is itself worth practising.

An indication that this is the way they proceed is the conspicuous absence of a distinction that lies at the heart of epistemological doctrines, ancient and modern, namely the distinction between knowledge and belief. Although our sources occasionally mention beliefs, these are always beliefs about *pathē*, true and incorrigible beliefs that amount to knowledge. What we do not find is the full-fledged distinction between knowledge as a cognitive state that has certain epistemic characteristics, such as truth and certainty, and belief as a cognitive condition which bears different epistemic characteristics, notably it can be true or false and does not convey certainty in the way knowledge does. Why is that distinction absent? One answer might be that if we cannot have empirical knowledge we cannot have empirical beliefs either; we have beliefs only about the things of which we have certain knowledge, the *pathē*. But in fact the evidence suggests that the Cyrenaics took a very different line: we may or may not entertain beliefs about various things, but we should not organise our life around beliefs, we should organise it around knowledge. If so, the fully developed epistemic distinction between knowledge and belief is not relevant, I submit, to what the Cyrenaics are proposing: it would not significantly help their ethical project and therefore its epistemological impact is disregarded.

Is there any actual evidence that this is indeed the perspective in which the Cyrenaics placed their study of the nature of the *pathē* and of our knowledge of them? There is, and part of it has to do with the way in which they interpreted the Socratic project and defined the Socratic identity of their school.[2] They adopted to an extent the attitude of thinkers such as Aristo,[3] and also Antisthenes and the Cynics, concentrating on ethics and rejecting intellectual activities such as physics, logic[4] and mathematics.[5] The idea behind this anti-intellectual attitude is one traditionally ascribed to Socrates, namely that we should pursue what helps us to live the good life and we should not worry about matters that are both incomprehensible and useless.[6] On the other hand, the sources inform us that the Cyrenaics left some room after all for logic, epistemology, and even physics: they subdivided ethics into five sections,[7] one of which is on arguments, another on the *pathē* and yet another on aetiology. We shall understand the spirit in which they allow talk about such subjects if we pay attention to the fact that they define these topics as subsections of *ethics*. The moral is clear, I think: we may talk about causes and arguments and *pathē* in so far as this may be of use in helping us to organise our lives with a view to pleasure. But once it becomes clear how this should be done, further enquiry into non-ethical subjects becomes purposeless and wrong.

There is no doubt that this strategy is at times frustrating to the

---

[2] On the Socratic origins and identity of the school, see D.L. II.47, 65; Hesychius, *Onom.* XC.6–9; Strabo XVII.3.22; Athenaeus, *Deipn.* VIII.343c–d; Themistius, *Or.* 34.5; Numenius *apud* Eusebius XIV.5.5; ps.Galen, *Hist.phil.* 3.

[3] See Eusebius XV.62.7 [T8b].

[4] The sources are divided about the study of logic: some attest that the Cyrenaics did away with both physics and logic (D.L. II.92 [T7d]; Sextus, *M* VII.11 [T6d]; and Eusebius XV.62.7 [T8b]), while others inform us that they rejected the study of physics, but kept practising ethics as well as logic in so far as they are useful (D.L. II.92 [T7d] and Sextus, *M* VII.15). If members of the school did do any logic, they probably concentrated on the more practical and less technical aspects of it.

[5] See Aristotle, *Metaph.* B 2, 996a29ff. and M 3, 1078a31ff., and the comments of Alexander and of Syrianus on these passages. See also D.L. II.92 [T7d]; Eusebius I.8.9 and XV.62.7 [T8b]; and Themistius, *Or.* 34.5.

[6] See Xenophon, *Mem.* IV.7.2–8; see also Themistius, *Or.* 34.5 and Eusebius XV.62.7 [T8b].

[7] This is attested by Seneca, *Epist.* 89.12 and by Sextus, *M* VII.11 [T6d].

modern reader. At least it has been for me, partly because I approached the material with the eye of someone interested in epistemology, not only in its history, and partly because I found, and still find, the epistemology of the Cyrenaics so much more interesting than their ethics. However, there are two considerations to take into account here. First, on a general level, the subordination of epistemology and other extra-ethical matters to ethics is not wholly indefensible. For it is part of a concern, which pervades ancient ethical stances, to join the activities, values and goals of each person into a pattern directed to the achievement of whatever each ethical theory defines as the supreme good. Whatever its shortcomings, the model of unifying and giving meaning to human life by relating it to a set of overarching values is not unappealing, I think. Second, the practice of keeping distinct what the Cyrenaics want to achieve from what we might have desired them to have achieved may actually prove philosophically rewarding: in many cases, we may see the point of a remark or assess the force of an argument better if we keep in mind what our philosophers are ultimately driving at than if we do not. This of course is not the only defensible way of approaching the doctrine. For my part, I did not think it wrong also to ask questions that the Cyrenaics might have asked but did not care to, outline answers that they might have given but did not bother to, and occasionally expand on a phrase or on an argument more than the evidence strictly warrants.

So much for the philosophical context. Regarding the historical framework of the doctrine, I only need to identify the main branches or sects of the Cyrenaic school and their leaders, because I shall occasionally refer to them. Readers who are disconcerted by unknown names may skip them altogether, for my argument does not essentially depend upon historical issues.[8]

The founder of the Cyrenaic school was Aristippus of Cyrene, an associate of Socrates and a man of many interests and talents. Around the turn of the fourth century BC, we find as heads of the school his daughter Arete and later his grandson Aristippus the Younger or the Mother-Taught, probably a near contemporary of Aristotle. He is often held responsible by modern scholars for the formulation of the central epistemological views of the school. By the time of Aristotle's death (322 BC), we encounter three new Cyrenaic sects founded by Theodorus,

---

[8] For a comprehensive bibliography on historical and philological problems concerning the Cyrenaic philosophers, see most recently *SSR*. For the arguments defending my claims in this chapter, see Tsouna 1988.

Anniceris and Hegesias. Each of them is identified by the name of its founder (Theodorians, Annicerians, Hegesians) but appears to have kept its Cyrenaic affiliation as well.[9] There seems to have been yet another Hellenistic sect bearing the original name of the school and claiming to represent Cyrenaic orthodoxy.[10] As I mentioned above, these splits are almost entirely over ethics. Very occasionally, they are also over physiological and psychological issues and it is in connection with such issues that the names of individual Cyrenaics and of their sects will turn up in the subsequent discussion. But all branches of the school defend the same epistemological theses – not surprisingly since, despite their variations, they all adhere to the central claim of Cyrenaic hedonism, namely that our experiences are the only things that matter.[11]

[9] See Tsouna 1988, pp. 48–9, and J. Brunschwig, 'La théorie cyrénaïque de la connaissance: quoi de socratique?', in Gourinat (forthcoming).

[10] For an interesting discussion of what counted as canonical Cyrenaic doctrine and what was considered as a deviation from it, see A. Laks, 'Annicéris et les plaisirs psychiques', in Brunschwig and Nussbaum 1993, pp. 18–49.

[11] The last Cyrenaic scholarchs died towards the middle of the third century BC. Assuming that their followers survived them by a few years, the end of the Cyrenaic school should be placed sometime between Arcesilaus' death (242 BC) and the beginning of Chrysippus' career in the Stoa (232 BC).

# I

*Subjectivism*

# CHAPTER 2

# *The nature of the* pathē

## I PHYSIOLOGY

Pleasure and pain are *pathē* (singular, *pathos*).[1] The term *pathos* is related to the Greek verb *paschein* ('to undergo', 'to suffer a change'), and denotes effects upon a subject, usually caused by contact with an external object. Depending on the context, a *pathos* may occur in inanimate substances or in animate beings, and may be an entity or an occurrence of various kinds: a stone heated by the sun undergoes a *pathos* and becomes warm; the diagnosis of a disease is sometimes effected by observing the *pathē* or physical symptoms displayed by the patient; and the pain that the patient feels is a *pathos* as well.

Although the Cyrenaics focused on *pathē* in connection with perceivers, their analysis preserves physicalistic overtones. These are reflected, I believe, in the definitions of pleasure and pain as smooth and rough motions[2] located in the flesh (Sextus, *PH* 1.215 [T6a]) or in the soul (D.L. II.90 [T7c]),[3] which are somehow related to pleasurable and painful feelings. There is little direct evidence about the nature of these motions, but, in my view, 'smooth' and 'rough' designate empirical properties of physical changes in the body and do not refer to the way these changes feel to the perceiver. First, pleasure does not *feel* smooth but pleasurable, and pain does not *feel* rough but painful. Second, most sources agree[4] that the Cyrenaics in fact drew some distinctions between

---

[1] I have left this term untranslated. The English term 'undergoing', which is often used to render *pathos* is, I think, too broad; 'affection' stresses the mental aspects of what the Cyrenaics indicated by *pathos*, but misses its physicalistic nuances. The same holds for 'passion', which may be misleading on account of its uses in early modern philosophy, notably in Descartes and Malebranche.

[2] 'Motion' or 'movement' are convenient translations for *kinēsis*, but they should not be taken to mean locomotion.

[3] Sextus refers to the motions of the flesh by the word *kinēsis*, whereas Diogenes Laertius uses the term *kinēma* for the motions of the soul.

[4] However, some sources identify these bodily alterations with pleasurable and painful feelings. On this view, pleasure and pain *are* physical movements possessing empirical properties, namely

the *motions* associated with pleasure and pain and the *experiences* of feeling pleasure and pain, and they also agree that it is the motions, not the sensations or the experiences resulting from the motions, that are smooth and rough. However, it still remains unclear what precisely is meant by calling physical changes in the body smooth or rough. My speculation is that 'smooth' is an empirical property of bodily alterations that occur in accordance with our natural constitution and therefore find no resistance inside the body, while 'rough' characterises changes that are somehow disruptive of our bodily nature and functions and do not come about without violence to our nature.[5]

Let us now have a closer look at the evidence concerning the physical changes in question and the way they feel to the perceiver. Diogenes Laertius reports that Aristippus of Cyrene defined the supreme good or moral end (*telos*, plural *telē*),[6] i.e., pleasure, as 'the smooth movement that comes forth to *aisthēsis*' (D.L. II.85 [T7a]).[7] And Clement of Alexandria adds that 'the concept of pleasure is a smooth and gentle motion accompanied by some kind of *aisthēsis*' (*Strom.* II.20.106). It seems to me it would be natural to read these passages as making a clear distinction between the physical movement and one's consciousness of it. If so, they suggest that there are smooth motions of the flesh which are sensed, but also some that are not, and that the physical motions counting as *pathē* of pleasure are only those which are sensed.[8]

Aristippus the Younger appears to have drawn a similar distinction and to have applied it not only to *pathē* of pleasure and pain, but also to a third category of *pathē* that he may have been the first to introduce into the Cyrenaic doctrine, the so-called intermediates.

---

smoothness and roughness. For example, in the doxographical presentation of the doctrine of 'those who remained faithful to the teaching of Aristippus and were called Cyrenaics', Diogenes Laertius reports: 'they held that there are two *pathē*, pain and pleasure, the one of them, pleasure, being a smooth movement, the other, pain, being a rough movement' (D.L. II.86 [T7b]), and the same position is attested by the *Suda* (II.553.4f.).

[5] Compare the transmission of *pathē* in naturally mobile substances and their perception by the *phronimon* in Plato, *Tim.* 64b–c. Also, compare the account of pleasure and pain in *Tim.* 64d–65b.

[6] The primary sense of *telos* is end or goal. In ethical contexts, it can mean the goal or purpose of a particular action, and also the overriding goal of a person's life, the supreme good. Yet another sense in which we can speak about the *telos* in an ethical context (and which is particularly relevant to the interpretation of testimonies about the Cyrenaics such as Sextus, *M* VII.199) is 'fulfilment'. See p. 12 and n. 12 of this chapter, and also chapter 10, n. 35.

[7] I discuss the meaning of *aisthēsis* below, pp. 11, 24 and in chapter 4, p. 31.

[8] The use of the term *telos* in this context is anachronistic and the position that pleasure is the *telos* was probably not held by Aristippus; see *SSR* IV A 173. However, Aristippus may well have used the term *aisthēsis* to refer to the experience of pleasure and to differentiate it from the corresponding physical change. Notice that the differentiation between bodily motions and experiences does not imply that the *pathē* of which we have awareness can only be physical – although they may be.

The evidence on the intermediates comes from two main sources, Aristocles quoted by Eusebius (xɪv.18.32 [T5]) and Sextus (*M* vɪɪ.199 [T6b]). The first passage informs us that

> he [sc. Aristippus the Younger] clearly defined the moral end as living pleasant-ly, inserting [into his doctrine] the concept of pleasure related to motion. For he said that there are three conditions (*katastasis*, pl. *katastaseis*) regarding our constitution (*synkrasis*); one in which we are in pain and which resembles a storm in the sea, another in which we experience pleasure and which is similar to smooth sea-waves (for pleasure is a smooth movement comparable to a fair wind);⁹ as to the third state, it is an intermediate condition (*mesē katastasis*), somewhat like a calm sea,¹⁰ in which we feel neither pain nor pleasure. Indeed, he said, we have consciousness of these *pathē* alone (τούτων δὲ καὶ ἔφασκεν τῶν παθῶν μόνων ἡμᾶς τὴν αἴσθησιν ἔχειν). (Eusebius xɪv.18.32 [T5])

This last sentence perhaps reflects the vocabulary of Aristippus the Younger,¹¹ but the passage is ambiguous regarding the intermediates. For although it distinguishes three conditions of our constitution, it does not say that there are intermediate *pathē* occurring in the intermediate condition. Also, while it states that we have consciousness 'of these *pathē* alone', it does not make clear what the word 'these' (*toutōn*) in the sentence refers to, and hence does not specify precisely which are the *pathē* that we are aware of – those that correspond to each of the three states of our constitution, or solely the *pathē* of pleasure and pain alluded to in the previous line.

These ambiguities are removed by Sextus. In the presentation of Cyrenaic ethics in *M* vɪɪ, he attests the tripartition of the *pathē* into pleasant, painful and intermediate and implies that we are fully aware of all three kinds of *pathē*.

> It seems that what is said by these people about the *telē* corresponds to what they say about the criteria. For the *pathē* extend to the *telē*. Some of the *pathē* are

---

⁹ Although the text does not clarify how the states of our constitution are related to the *pathē* corresponding to each state, it suggests that there is a close relation between them. All three states are determined by reference to what we do or we do not feel when we are in them. On the metaphorical level, there is a causal relation between fair wind and smooth sea-waves, and hence between an individual *pathos* of pleasure and a pleasurable condition.

¹⁰ This metaphor need not entail, I think, that in the intermediate condition there is no motion at all in our constitution: a calm sea is not a sea in which there is no movement at all, but a sea in which there are no waves. The author indicates that he does not intend to push this part of the metaphor too far: the intermediate condition is 'somewhat like a calm sea'. On the other hand, a calm sea gives at least an impression of absolute immobility, and it might well be that it is this feature, i.e. the appearance of immobility, that is crucial to the metaphor in Eusebius' text. In either case, this metaphor alone constitutes too slim a basis for inferring either that there is or that there is not motion in the intermediate condition.

¹¹ See chapter 4, p. 31.

pleasant, others are painful and others are intermediate (*ta metaxy*); and the painful ones are, they say, evils whose *telos* is pain, the pleasant ones are goods, whose unmistakable *telos* is pleasure, and the intermediates are neither goods nor evils; their *telos* is neither a good nor an evil, this being a *pathos* between pleasure and pain. Thus, the *pathē* are the criteria and the *telē* of things, and we live, they say, by following these and by attending to evidence and to approval, to evidence regarding the other *pathē* and to approval in relation to pleasure. (*M* VII.199)

Here the intermediates appear as a separate category of *pathē* that have their own special *telos*, negatively described as neither a good nor an evil, but as a *pathos* standing between good (pleasure) and evil (pain).[12] They are also placed on an equal footing with pleasure and pain with regard to our awareness of them: if we are to live by attending to the evidence (*enargeia*) that they yield, we must have consciousness of the intermediates, just as we have consciousness of pleasure and pain. This evidence leaves open the possibility that there are alterations occurring in us of which we do not have awareness; these would not count as *pathē* that could guide us in action.

Eusebius' testimony has often been used as evidence for the thesis that Aristippus the Younger was the first philosopher of the school to associate the *pathē* with movements.[13] The statement that he defined the moral end as living pleasantly, 'inserting the concept of pleasure as motion', is the basis for this claim. However, the sentence does not need to be taken to affirm that Aristippus the Younger was the first to introduce to Cyrenaic philosophy the concept of kinetic pleasure, but may only mean that he introduced it into his own doctrine; besides, independent evi-

---

[12] I have already mentioned that the question whether the intermediate *pathē* are part of the Cyrenaic doctrine has recently become a controversial topic. *M* VII.199 is, I believe, decisive evidence for the existence of the intermediates. However, it has been pointed out to me that the thesis that there is a *telos* for the intermediate *pathē* is problematic for the following reason. The *telos* is that for the sake of which we pursue whatever we pursue and avoid whatever we avoid; since the intermediates are neither pursued nor avoided, how can we say that they have a *telos*, i.e. a thing for the sake of which we pursue or avoid them? I think that this difficulty can be eliminated if we take *telos* here to mean fulfilment. The *telos* of *pathē* such as 'being whitened' is not something in virtue of which you seek to be affected in that way; it is to reach a condition in which you cannot be more 'whitened' than you are now. Also, it seems to me that *M* VII.199 simply differentiates between *pathē* that are morally significant in a direct way and others that are not. Feeling a headache is itself a painful state and eating ice-cream is itself pleasant; seeing blue is intrinsically neither painful nor pleasant, although it may lead to an action that will produce pleasure, for example getting into the sea and having a nice swim.

[13] See, for example, Giannantoni 1958, p. 102 and Humbert 1967, p. 265. Against this hypothesis, see Schwartz 1951, pp. 181ff.; Mannebach 1961, p. 95; and Guthrie, vol. III, p. 494, n. 1. On the relation between pleasure and movement, see also the general discussion of Gosling and Taylor 1982, especially pp. 194–7, 219–21, 225–40, 259ff., 364–96.

dence ascribes it explicitly to the founder of the school (D.L. II.85; Cicero, *De fin.* II.18,39; Athenaeus, *Deipn.* XII.546e).

The thesis that all *pathē* are associated with some kind of movement is crucial to how the status of the intermediates in Cyrenaic epistemology was viewed during the Hellenistic period. Some Cyrenaics appear to have reconsidered the status of the intermediates and the question whether all conditions in which one may find oneself are associated with motions. In particular, Anniceris and his disciples attempted to refine the hedonistic tenet that present pleasure is the moral end by emphasising that pleasure and pain are necessarily related to motions and by arguing that since the mere absence of pain (*aponia*) is not characterised by motion, it cannot be part of the moral end (D.L. II.89 [T7c]). They pressed their point further by comparing the absence of pain to the condition of a person asleep or dead (D.L. II.89 [T7c]; Clement of Alexandria, *Strom.* II.21.130).

Their position might suggest that Anniceris and his disciples held that the intermediate *pathē* are not related to motions, or that they denied the existence of the intermediates altogether. However, it seems to me that their remarks about absence of pleasure (*aēdonia*) and absence of pain (*aponia*) have a very restricted scope and do not constitute adequate grounds for inferring the views of the Annicerians on the classification of the *pathē* in general.

The reason why the Annicerians singled out the states of absence of pleasure and of absence of pain and compared the latter to the conditions of sleep and death was probably polemical. Their claim that the absence of pain cannot be part of the moral end should be set in contrast to the position of the rival school of Epicurus, according to which the supreme moral good is static pleasure, characterised by complete absence of pain: 'this Cyrenaic sect rejected Epicurus' limit of pleasure, namely the removal of what causes pain, calling it a state of death' (Clement of Alexandria, *Strom.* II.21.130). Their point may have been that for the Epicureans absence of pain is unconscious, or almost unconscious, precisely because it is not associated with motions in the flesh or of the soul; but the supreme good must be something that one is conscious of, and therefore absence of pain cannot be the supreme good.[14] If this was roughly the argument, the Annicerians may have drawn an implicit distinction between states in which pleasure and pain do not occur but intermediates do (cf. the reference to the intermediate

---

[14] On the anti-epicurean target of this remark, see *SSR* IVA 185–7. For a different interpretation, see A. Laks, 'Annicéris et les plaisirs psychiques', in Brunschwig and Nussbaum 1993, pp. 43ff.

state as 'somewhat comparable to a calm sea' in Eusebius xiv.18.32
[T5]), and thoroughly apathic conditions in which we feel nothing at all.

One reason why this position of the Annicerians is philosophically
important is that it raises the issue of whether it is possible to feel no
pleasure or no pain at all, and yet to feel something. I shall tackle it by
asking how pleasure and pain, which I shall call the affective (aspects of)
*pathē*, are related to experiences such as seeing white and tasting sweet,
which I shall call representational or informative (aspects of) *pathē*. What
is the connection between one's feeling of pain and the awareness that
one is cut? Or between one's pleasurable feeling and the consciousness
of tasting something sweet? Are the affective and the informative contents two different aspects of the same *pathos* or are they different *pathē*?
And can there be some *pathē* that are purely affective and others that are
purely informative?

The examples of *pathē* cited in the evidence suggest that in most cases
the *pathē* of pleasure and of pain have an informative aspect as well: each
*pathos* of pleasure or of pain is further specified by reference to the *kind* of
pleasure or pain that is being experienced: when I feel pleasure, I am
aware that my pleasure comes from a sweet sensation on my tongue and
not from a soft touch at the tip of my fingers; and when I feel pain, I can
differentiate between the pain of a burn and that of a cut.[15] The only
*pathē* which seem to be determined exclusively in terms of their affective
aspects are the complete absence of pleasure or of pain, and I suggested
above that these constitute special cases which were used by the Annicerians for polemical purposes; but even the Annicerians seem to have
accepted the existence of intermediate conditions of which we are
conscious (and which are associated with motions).

On the other hand, it seems to me that, generically, the intermediates
do not have an affective aspect. Take, for example, warmth: some
tokens of feeling heat may be either pleasant or painful, and some others
may be neither. But feeling heat *as such*, generically, is neither pleasant
nor painful; it is an intermediate.[16]

A further distinction, this time within the categories of pleasurable and
painful *pathē*, has often been used to differentiate the early Cyrenaics from
the Annicerians. Although the Cyrenaics focused on the pleasures of the
body which occupied a central place in their ethics (D.L. ii.87 [T7b];
Cicero, *Luc.* 139; St Augustine, *De civ. dei* xviii.41; Lactantius, *Divin. inst.*

---

[15] See chapter 5, pp. 66, 68.
[16] However, one might wonder what it would really mean to feel heat as such. We say that we feel *a
certain degree of heat* at a given time, but can we really say that we feel *heat as such*?

28.3, 34.7), some of them broadened the scope of the moral goal by emphasising the importance of mental pleasures as well, for example the pleasures deriving from friendship, from honouring one's parents and from serving one's country (D.L. II.89, 90, 96; x.137). The distinction between bodily and mental pleasures does not refer to the organ or to the centre of the perception of pleasures: it need not imply that there are pleasures perceived by the body and others perceived by the soul. It rather applies to two different types of pleasure, both of which are presumably perceived by means of the same psychic capacity.[17]

Mental pleasures may be further distinguished into two sub-categories, those which are ultimately dependent on bodily pleasures and those which are not.[18] The point of this distinction is not entirely clear, but it seems that at least some Cyrenaics believed that the pleasures having to do with the body pertain exclusively to oneself, in contrast to the pleasures which are independent of the body and which focus on objects other than oneself: 'for instance, we feel joy merely on account of the prosperity of our country as if it were our own prosperity' (D.L. II.89 [T7c]). The place of mental pleasures in the doctrine is compatible both with the belief that pleasures experienced in the present are major components of happiness and with the hedonistic thesis that momentary bodily pleasure is the supreme good.[19] Therefore, the genre of mental pleasures may well have been introduced into the Cyrenaic doctrine at an early stage and used by Anniceris at a later stage in a polemic against the pessimistic doctrine of Hegesias.[20] Alternatively, it may have been a late modification of the Cyrenaic doctrine effected by Anniceris and his disciples, partly in the course of an ongoing debate with the Epicureans.[21]

Both bodily and mental pleasures are *monochronoi*. Most scholars render '*monochronos*' by 'short-lived' or 'momentary',[22] but this translation is misleading: there is nothing in the evidence to preclude some

---

[17] See the distinction drawn in Plato's *Theaetetus* 184c–d between perceiving *with* a sensory organ and perceiving *through* it.

[18] Compare Epicurus' distinction between bodily and mental pleasures and his claim that mental pleasures are greater than bodily ones (Cicero, *De fin.* 1.55). On the putative dialogue of the Cyrenaics and the Epicureans regarding this point and on the moral implications of their positions, see Mitsis 1988, pp. 51–8.

[19] It is compatible with this type of hedonism in so far as it can be argued that bodily pleasures are greater than mental pleasures and, when they can be obtained, they are preferable to mental pleasures.

[20] See A. Laks, 'Annicéris et les plaisirs psychiques', in Brunschwig and Nussbaum 1993, pp. 18–49.

[21] See, most recently, Doering 1988, pp. 52ff.

[22] I rendered it in this way in Tsouna 1988, pp. 112–14.

pleasures from being extended in the present and also from being relatively long-lived,[23] and the claim that all pleasures are momentary or of very short duration is philosophically unsustainable. Imagine the pleasure of wearing an extremely comfortable pair of shoes: you may be wearing them for a whole day, and you will be feeling comfortable for as long as you are wearing them. Semantically, the term '*monos*' often indicates unity at a given time as well as singularity, and the first component of '*monochronos*' need imply nothing about the actual *duration* of the time unit in which a pleasure is occurring. All it implies, in my view, is that it is one and the same pleasure that occupies the time unit of its occurrence (unity requirement), and that this pleasure that we are experiencing is unrelated to other times present or future (singularity requirement): it has no prospective or retrospective value, and can only be enjoyed while it is actually occurring.[24] The same must hold of pains, physical and mental.[25] This reading suggests that 'unitemporal' is a better translation of '*monochronos*' than 'short-lived'.[26]

Having approved of the *pathos* of pleasure, Aristippus the Socratic claimed that this is the moral end, that happiness is based on it, and that it is unitemporal (*monochronos*), believing, in the manner of the profligates, that neither the memory of past enjoyments nor the expectation of future ones is important for him, but judging the good by one sole thing, the present, and considering that what he has enjoyed in the past and what he will enjoy in the future are unimportant to him, the former because it exists no more, the latter because it does not exist yet and is not manifest – just like what happens to self-indulgent people, who suppose that only what is present benefits them. (Athenaeus, *Deipn.* XII.544a–b)

The fact that pleasure (and pain) have no prospective or retrospective value is related to their kinetic nature: 'for the motion (*kinēma*) of the soul dies away with time' (D.L. II.90 [T7c]). The point seems to be that when you are trying to recreate a pleasure or to anticipate it, you cannot recreate the movement of the soul that would result in the same

---

[23] On the concept of the 'extended' present (ἐν πλάτει χρόνος), see Arius Didymus fr. 26 in *Doxographi Graeci*, p. 461. Also, see Goldschmidt 1969, pp. 168–210, and M. Schofield, 'The retrenchable present', in Barnes and Mignucci 1988, pp. 329–74.

[24] A good example of a *mono*-adjective is *monoeidēs*, which can mean both 'unique of its kind' (see Plato, *Tim.* 59b) and 'one in kind', 'uniform all through' (see Plato, *Rep.* 612a, *Phd.* 78d, and *Symp.* 211b; and also Sextus, *M* 1.117). Similarly, the noun *monoeideia* can mean singularity as well as uniformity (see Sextus, *M* 1.226 and 117 respectively).

[25] Compare the emphasis that the Epicureans put on the moral value of pleasures and pains experienced in the past or anticipated in the future.

[26] However, a drawback of this translation is that it does not clearly exclude past and future pleasures. 'Unitemporal and extended only in the present' is more accurate, but long-winded. Another possible translation might be 'contemporaneous'.

pleasure. If I am right in maintaining that the intermediate *pathē* also involve motions, they too must be, in a sense, unitemporal: they last as long as the perceptual motions resulting in them last and, as the analysis in the following chapters will show, they can be infallibly known only while they are taking place.

The Cyrenaic thesis that pleasure does not consist in the memory or in the expectation of the good (D.L. II.89 [T7c]) does not entail that the pleasurable *pathē* of the past or of the future were not or will not really be pleasures. The point is rather that such *pathē* did or will count as pleasures *at the time when they are experienced*, but that they are not parts of the pleasure that one is experiencing at present. Thus, one will think of past pleasures as components of one's happiness during one's lifetime, but will not consider them relevant to the present achievement of the supreme good.

Although the three categories of *pathē* correspond to three different kinds of movements, there is no direct information as to distinctions within each kind of movement. For example, it is not attested whether the smooth movement associated with the pleasure of drinking wine differs in any respect from the smooth movement related to the pleasure of warming oneself in the sun.[27] However, it seems probable that phenomenologically different *pathē* would bear different physiological descriptions: for example, being burnt (or the *pathos* of feeling hot) probably corresponds to a different kind of motion from seeing white or tasting sweet. Also, although our sources do not inform us that various *pathē* were differentiated in respect of their duration in time, it is obvious that some pains and pleasures, for example, last longer than others: some headaches last longer than others, and the pleasure of reading a novel lasts longer than that of reading a sonnet.

The Cyrenaics maintained that 'no pleasure differs from any other nor is anything more pleasant than anything else' (D.L. II.87 [T7b]). The motivation for holding this thesis was probably ethical. The term *diapherein* can mean 'differ in moral value',[28] and the argument may be that,

---

[27] This is another reason why it seems unlikely that the Cyrenaics determined the relation between a short-lived physical change and a *pathos* as one of strict identity.

[28] Compare the Stoic use of the term '*adiaphora*', and also the old Stoic doctrine that all sins are equal, that was taken up by Epictetus (Arrian, *Epict.diatr.* 1.7.30–33). Epictetus' point is that each moral failure should be examined in the context in which it has occurred and that, therefore, there is no possibility of comparing one moral fault to another. A person who has committed adultery cannot say that what he did was less evil than a murder, for adultery, not murder, was the sin that he should not have committed at that particular time and in these particular circumstances. Perhaps the thesis of the equality of pleasures points to a similar reasoning: it does not make sense to say that drinking water is less pleasurable than listening to music, because the former pleasure, not the latter, is what corresponds to my feeling thirsty at present.

since unitemporal present pleasure is the *telos*, one such pleasure can
have no greater value than another.[29] For example, the pleasure derived
from drinking wine is the most desirable thing at the particular time and
circumstance in which one wishes to drink wine, and the pleasure that
comes from drinking water is the supreme pleasure when one wants to
drink water.[30]

Alternatively, the (early) Cyrenaics may have meant that no *type* of
pleasure, for example aesthetic or intellectual pleasure, is better than
any other type, for example sensual pleasure. If so, there is one branch
of the Cyrenaic tradition that denies this: the Annicerians, who asserted
that 'bodily pleasures are far better than mental pleasures, and bodily
pains far worse than mental pains; for this reason offenders are punish-
ed through physical pains' (D.L. II.90 [T7c]). The passage implies that,
although bodily and mental pleasures belong to the same category of
*pathē*, i.e., pleasure, they are more or less desirable, depending perhaps
on their different intensity, degree or duration, and that the same holds
for pains. There is no evidence about the way in which this doctrine
originated or about how the Annicerians justified this deviation from
the earlier tradition of the school. Regarding the origin of the doctrine,
it is possible that the belief in the equality of pleasures was abandoned
as new elements, such as the attribution of moral value to mental
pleasures, were introduced into the doctrine.[31] As to its compatibility
with the earlier Cyrenaic thesis that all pleasures are equal, the Annicerians may have divided pleasures into two sub-categories, bodily and
mental, and maintained that all bodily pleasures are equally pleasurable
and all mental pleasures are equally pleasurable as well, but that the
former are more intense than the latter (and the same goes for pains). If
so, their position may have been presented as a development of the
thesis of the equality of pleasures, and therefore as faithful to Cyrenaic
orthodoxy.

Another feature of the *pathē* that bears directly on epistemological
questions is the way in which the *pathē* are detected. According to
Cicero, we register our *pathē* by means of internal touch (*tactus interior*) or
inmost touch (*tactus intumus*).

---

[29] Compare Epicurus' denial that pleasures vary in respect of their intensity and his claim that
infinite time and finite time contain equal pleasure, if their limits are measured by reasoning (*KD*
XIX).

[30] Someone could plausibly maintain this thesis, if they identified pleasure with a desire–satisfac-
tion pattern.

[31] See Giannantoni 1958, pp. 110–11. Mannebach attributes the doctrine to the early Cyrenaics
(1961, p. 45).

In *Lucullus*, after claiming that 'the greatest truth lies in the senses, if they are healthy and powerful and if all obstacles and impediments are removed' (*Luc.* 19 [T4a]), and after appealing to the discerning power of sight and hearing, Lucullus adds:

There is no need to talk at all about taste and smell in which there is a certain power of apprehension, although defective. And why should we speak of touch and, indeed, of what the philosophers call internal touch either of pleasure or of pain in which alone, the Cyrenaics believe, lies the criterion of the true because it is sensed? So, can anybody say that there is no difference between a person who is in pain and a person who is feeling pleasure, or is it that the person who thinks so is clearly insane? (20 [T4a])

Further on, in his retort to Lucullus, Cicero mentions the arguments of eminent philosophers undermining the reliability of the senses, and includes among them the Cyrenaics:

What do you think of the Cyrenaics, by no means contemptible philosophers? They deny that there is anything which can be perceived from the outside: the only things that they do perceive are those which they sense by inmost touch, for instance pain or pleasure, and they do not know whether something has a particular colour or sound, but only sense that they are themselves affected in a certain way. (76 [T4b])

These passages relate the physiological claim that the *pathē* are the only objects of internal touch and the epistemological thesis that they are the sole criteria of the true: the only things known are those perceived by internal touch, and they are known *because* they are so perceived; and, presumably, no external object can be known, precisely *because* it cannot be perceived in that special way.

Although the concept of internal touch is crucial to the formulation of the Cyrenaic views about knowledge, the testimonies offer no further evidence about it. But it seems plausible that the Cyrenaics held with regard to internal touch a position which resembles, in certain respects, a late Epicurean thesis outlined in a Herculaneum papyrus, PHerc. 19/698. The author and the title of the treatise to which the fragments of the papyrus belonged are unknown, but there are grounds for believing that it was a work by Philodemus of Gadara (first century BC). Much of the surviving part is concerned with the objects of the various senses, and focuses on sight and touch.

Touch, so far as its peculiar characteristic is concerned, has as its most peculiar characteristic that of registering no quality at all. So far as concerns its common characteristic of registering the qualitative states of the flesh – a concomitant property of the other senses too – it has as its most peculiar characteristic that of registering qualities different in kind: for as well as discriminating hard and soft things, it perceives hot and cold things, both those within itself and those adjacent to itself. (col. xxvi.3–16)

According to the Epicurean author, the special object of touch is, strictly speaking, body: 'For we hold that vision perceives visibles and touch tangibles, that is, respectively, colour and body, and that one never interferes in the other's sphere of discrimination' (xvii.1–14). But aside from perceiving its special object, touch shares with the other senses the function of registering qualitative bodily changes. Thus, each of the five senses has a double capacity: perceiving its own peculiar object, which cannot be perceived by any of the other senses, and detecting the perceiver's internal condition, which involves awareness of the perceiver's internal states.[32] I think it is probable that like the Epicurean author of PHerc. 19/698, the Cyrenaics distinguished between the fifth sense, touch, which puts us in contact with body, and the common sensory function of 'internal touch', which registers our internal condition and makes us conscious of the manner in which each of our senses is affected.[33]

However, it is important to notice that, on the one hand, the Epicurean distinction between two kinds of touch implies that the senses primarily put us in contact with something external, for example colour, sound or body; the alterations of our sensory organs derive from, and often reflect with accuracy, these empirical properties. On the other hand, the Cyrenaics maintained that the only thing with which our senses put us in contact are the qualitative changes in our body. Thus, the common, 'internal' function of touch is epistemologically secondary for the author of the papyrus: the things we claim to know are not our internal states, but the empirical properties of sensory objects. In contrast, 'internal touch' plays an important epistemological role in the Cyrenaic doctrine, in that it puts us in contact with the only thing that we can apprehend, namely our internal states.[34]

---

[32] A persuasive interpretation of this passage is found in D. Sedley, 'Epicurus on the common sensibles', in Huby and Neal 1987, pp. 123–36.

[33] It is important to stress that, unlike the Epicureans, the Cyrenaics grant a double function to touch, not to the other senses: there is internal touch, but there is no internal sight, hearing, etc. Perhaps their choice of touch is due to some connotation of immediacy; see chapter 4, pp. 44–5.

[34] On this point, see D. Sedley, 'Epicurus on the common sensibles', in Huby and Neal 1987, pp. 130–1.

## II   ONTOLOGY

The Cyrenaics showed no interest in metaphysical issues, and thus did not explicitly determine the ontological status of the *pathē*. However, the physiological features of these entities and the place which they occupy in the epistemology of the school offer some clues about what sort of entities they are.

Neither the motions related to the *pathē* nor pleasurable, painful or sensory experiences are ontologically primary entities. They all depend upon the existence of perceivers. Smooth and rough motions are generated in the flesh or in the soul of individual perceivers – typically human perceivers. They occur only if there is somebody to experience them, provided the sensory apparatus of the perceiver is functional: an alert and normal person is subject to physical and perceptual changes, and will be conscious of his feelings and of the content of his perceptual states at any given time.

The ontological asymmetry between *pathē* and affected subjects is reflected in the metaphysical assumptions that the Cyrenaics appear to make about perceivers. As I shall argue in chapter 10 (pp. 124–37), the Cyrenaics did not relativise the existence and identity of perceivers to the *pathē* affecting them, nor to the time at which each *pathos* is taking place. While they defined the *pathē* in relation to motions, they did not hold that perceivers are constantly changing entities, but assumed that they are beings whose identity persists over time. Each perceiver is assumed to have a stable physiological constitution (*synkrasis*) and to be equipped with a perceptual apparatus which determines to an unknown extent the nature of their experiences (Sextus, *M* VII.197 [T6b]; Eusebius XIV.18.32 [T5]). While one's sensory apparatus may occasionally be wholly unaffected by *pathē*, for example when one is asleep or unconscious, the *pathē* cannot exist independently from the sensory functions of one's constitution. Thus, perceivers and *pathē* are neither interdependent nor ontologically commensurable entities. The former are ontologically prior to the latter, both in the sense that the occurrence of the *pathē* depends on the existence of the perceiver, and in the sense that the motions related to them *derive* from (and are conditioned by) the sensory constitution of each perceiver.

The derivative status of the *pathē* is reflected by the Cyrenaic expressions describing them. These will be the object of the following chapter. Here, it will suffice to point out that, although the Cyrenaics speak generally about the various categories of *pathē* and about their characteristics, when they give examples of individual *pathē*, and especially of internal states related to the perception of empirical properties, they do not use the term *pathos*: the phrasing is not 'I am experiencing a *pathos of white*', but 'I am whitened' or 'I am affected whitely'. The only full-fledged entity indicated by such autobiographical sentences is the affected perceiver, to whom the first personal pronoun refers. The perceiver does not talk about a *pathos* of white, but rather about being affected in a particular manner. This suggests that the undergoing is not conceived as a distinct entity.

Bearing these remarks in mind, we may tackle the question whether the *pathē* are physical or mental entities or occurrences.

It has been suggested that the evidence is ambiguous on this matter and that there is no way of deciding whether the *pathē* are physical or mental.[35] There is much truth in this remark. My task will be, first, to give a partial explanation of this ambiguity by arguing that certain features of the *pathē* cut across the mind–body distinction; and second, to maintain that the Cyrenaics focused primarily on the subjective aspects of the *pathē*, but without presupposing the mind–body distinction.

According to Sextus, the Cyrenaics claimed that the *pathē* are not common to people, but that they are private to the person affected by them (*M* vii.196 [T6b]). The analysis of the context of this passage[36] will indicate that by denying the common character of the *pathē*, the Cyrenaics denied both that the *pathē* are open to observation and that they can be known to be qualitatively alike. Both these denials might create the impression that the Cyrenaics use a post-Cartesian contrast between what is objective and common and what is subjective and private, and that by applying the concept of privacy to the *pathē* they place them in the realm of the mental.

However, such an interpretation would be misleading, I think. I speculated above that, of the motions occurring in the body, some are perceived but others are not. Once perceived, there is the possibility of describing my affective condition at a given time in two different ways: I can use physicalistic language and talk about my pleasure or my pain in terms of smooth or rough motions (*Suda* ii.553.4f.); or I can use mentalistic vocabulary and speak of the *pathē* in terms of my experiences. Thus, there need be no conflict between the texts which define the relation

---

[35] The point is made in Burnyeat 1982, pp.27–9. It is crucial to the author's broader claim that no version of ancient scepticism can be associated with a Cartesian conception of the self entailing the mind–body distinction. I shall return to these claims in subsequent chapters.

[36] See chapters 4 (pp. 41, 44–5), 7 (pp. 89–90, 92–3, 94–5, 100–3) and 8 (pp. 108–9).

between *pathē* and motions as an identity (D.L. II.86 [T7b]; *Suda* II.553.4f.), and those which distinguish between motions and our aware-ness of them (D.L. II.85 [T7a]). These two sets of texts can be seen as complementary in the sense that they offer two different types of accounts of the *pathē*, the one objective, the other subjective.

The reason why the Cyrenaics appear to consider that both types of descriptions can correctly be used of the *pathē* is, I think, that, contrary to Descartes, they did not classify the physical conditions of our body and our awareness of them in different ontological domains: what we are aware of are internal bodily states, not mental objects.[37]

The possibility of giving various types of accounts of the *pathē* is reflected in the examples of individual *pathē* cited in the sources, and also in the vocabulary used in these examples. On the one hand, many *pathē* indicated by first-person present-tense passive verbs may appear best suited to a physicalistic interpretation: 'being sweetened, and bittered, and chilled, and heated, and illuminated and darkened' (Plutarch 1120e [T1]), 'being whitened' (Sextus, *M* VII.191 [T6b]), 'being reddened' (Sextus, *M* VII.192 [T6b]) and 'yellowed' (Sextus, *M* VII.193 [T6b]). But in fact, the locutions themselves are absolutely neutral with regard to the question whether the intermediate *pathē* reported by them are mental or physical. However, an Aristotelian-minded reader may point out that the types of *pathē* expressed by these verbs are more naturally under-stood as physical alterations of the sensory organs occurring at the time of perception.[38] In perceiving an object, my eye is turning white, red, yellow, it fills with light or with darkness; my tongue turns sweet or bitter; and my body turns cold or hot. According to this account, the change which takes place in the sense-organ when it perceives its own peculiar object is comparable to a qualitative change that an inanimate object may undergo: 'we say that a thing is altered by becoming hot or sweet or thick or dry or white; and we make these assertions both of what is inanimate and of what is animate' (Aristotle, *Phys.* 244b7ff.). The difference between physical changes occurring in inanimate substances and those undergone by animate beings lies in the fact that the former are not aware of these changes, whereas the latter are. The Aristotelian-inclined reader could argue that, contrary to Aristotle, the Cyrenaics do not explicitly refer to the awareness of qualitative alterations. Thus, the

---

[37] See S. Everson, 'The objective appearance of Pyrrhonism', in Everson 1991, pp. 121–47, especially pp. 128–35. I shall come back to this point in chapters 6 and 7.

[38] See Aristotle, *De an.* II.6; however, the interpretation of Aristotle's views about what is going on when we perceive is controversial.

natural way of taking their verbal neologisms is to assume that they refer to the alterations themselves: 'being whitened' does not indicate the token mental event of seeing white, but the token physical event of a perceiver's eye becoming white, right now, in perceiving an object.[39]

On the other hand, several examples of *pathē* appear to require a subjectivistic interpretation. Two such cases are reported by Sextus: 'the person who presses down his eye is stirred as if by two objects, and the madman sees (*horai*) Thebes as if it were double and imagines (*phantazetai*) the sun double' (Sextus, *M* VII.192 [T6b]). In the former case, the emphasis is not on the physical act of pressing one's eyes down, but on the mental impression of the perceiver: one is 'doubled' (*dyazetai*: Sextus, *M* VII.193 [T6b]), sees each object as if it were two. In the latter, the physical concomitant of the *pathos* is not apparent at all: the madman 'is doubled' in the sense that he is seeing a 'doubled Thebes' and a 'doubled sun'. Here, the physicalistic account presented above would seem awkward: it is not obvious how a sensory organ, the eye, could become double, whereas it is easy to explain what it feels like to see things double.

The *pathos* of 'being doubled' should presumably be classified as an intermediate, but this does not mean that the examples of *pathē* calling for a subjectivistic account always belong to that category. Although pleasure and pain are standardly associated with physical motions, their role in Cyrenaic ethics is best explained in ethical contexts if they are interpreted primarily as subjective experiences. This point is supported by Diogenes Laertius' testimony that Aristippus of Cyrene maintained that 'the moral end is the smooth motion which comes forth (or: *when* it comes forth) to consciousness (*aisthēsis*)' (D.L. II.85 [T7a]): a smooth motion counts as the moral end only if it is felt.

There are two further features of the Cyrenaic doctrine favouring the view that the analysis of the *pathē* focuses primarily in the awareness of physical states rather than on the physical states themselves. They will be mentioned only briefly, for both will be studied in separate chapters. First, the verbal locutions such as 'being whitened' and 'being sweetened' are not the only expressions reporting the *pathē*. The Cyrenaics also used for that purpose adverbial neologisms such as 'being disposed whitely' (Sextus, *M* VII.192 [T6b]) and 'being affected whitely' (Sextus, *M* VII.198 [T6b]). While many (but not all) verbal locutions can

---

[39] For parallels between Aristotle's analysis of perception and the Cyrenaic theory, see Burnyeat 1982, p. 28, and S. Everson (1991b), 'The objective appearance of Pyrrhonism', in Everson 1991, pp. 130–1.

equally well refer to a physical alteration and to a subjective state, the adverbial expressions cannot: we could say of a piece of iron turning red in the fire that 'it is reddened', but we would not describe a surface painted red as 'being disposed redly'. Thus, the use of these curious neologisms seems intended to mark out the experiences related to the occurrence of physical alterations rather than the alterations themselves.

Second, the Cyrenaic claims that the *pathē* are infallibly and incorrigibly apprehended by the perceiver are incommunicable and are not open to observation indicate that what the Cyrenaics found epistemologically interesting were precisely the subjective aspects of the *pathē*. The reason why they concentrated their attention on them rather than on their physical counterparts has to do, I submit, with the ethical motivation of the Cyrenaic analysis: what matters, and what we must make sure we can grasp, is not the physical changes in our body but how these changes feel to us.

# CHAPTER 3

# The vocabulary of the pathē

The Cyrenaics employed two different types of locution to designate *pathē*. I shall call these types verbal and adverbial.

The verbal expressions consist of present-tense passive verbs. We find them in the testimonies in the first and third persons, singular and plural, and in the infinitive. Colotes attempts to ridicule the Cyrenaics by attributing to them the claim that 'they are themselves being walled (*toichousthai*) and horsed (*hippousthai*) and manned (*anthrōpousthai*)' (1120d [T1]); Plutarch denounces Colotes for intentional inaccuracy, and reports what he claims to be the true letter of the doctrine: 'they say, we are being sweetened (*glykainesthai*) and bittered (*pikrainesthai*) and chilled (*psychesthai*) and warmed (*thermainesthai*) and illuminated (*phōtizesthai*) and darkened (*skotizesthai*)' (1120e [T1]); the anonymous *Theaetetus* commentator attests the locution 'I am being burnt' (*kaiomai*: 65.33 [T3]), and Sextus mentions the expressions 'we are being whitened (*leukainometha*) and sweetened (*glykazometha*)' (*M* VII.191 [T6b]), 'he is being reddened' (*erythrainetai*: 192), 'they are being yellowed (*ōchrainontai*) or reddened (*erythrainontai*) or doubled (*dyazontai*)' (193), and 'being whitened' (*leukainesthai*: 197).

The adverbial formulas are constituted by a present-tense passive verb and an adverb. According to Sextus' testimony in T6b, the Cyrenaics maintained that 'it is probable that one is disposed whitely (*leukantikōs diatethēnai*) even by what is not white' (Sextus, *M* VII.192 [T6b]). They also assumed that 'the person who suffers from vertigo or jaundice is moved yellowly' (*ōchrantikōs kineitai*: ibid.). They reckoned that 'perhaps I am constituted in such as way as to be whitened by the external object which meets with my senses, but another person has the senses constructed in such a way as to be disposed differently' (*heterōs diatethēnai*: 197). And they argued as follows.

It is clear from the cases of people who suffer from jaundice or ophthalmia and from those who are in normal condition that we really are not all moved (by the external objects) in the same way because of the different constructions of our senses. For just as some people are affected yellowly (*ōchrantikōs*), others reddishly (*phoiniktikōs*) and others whitely (*leukantikōs*) by one and the same object, likewise it is also probable that those who are in normal condition are not moved in the same manner by the same things because of the different construction of the senses, but that the person with grey eyes is moved in one way, the one with blue eyes in another and the one with black eyes in another yet different way. (198)

Both types of these curious neologisms designate the intermediate *pathē* alone. The evidence suggests that ordinary language was used to indicate the *pathē* of pleasure and pain. In the testimonies, pleasure is usually denoted by the Greek noun *hēdonē* (Eusebius XIV.19.5 [T5]; Sextus, *M* VII.200 [T6b]) and the Latin *voluptas* (Cicero, *Luc.* 20, 76, 142 [T4a, 4b, 4c]), and pain by the Greek *ponos* (PHerc. 1251 II.9 [T2]; Eusebius XIV.19.5 [T5]) or, more rarely, *algēdōn* (D.L. II.87, 89 [T7b,7c]; Sextus, *M* VII.199 [T6b]) and by the Latin *dolor* (Cicero, *Luc.* 20, 76 [T4a, 4b]). In late Cyrenaic ethics, we occasionally find *chara* (PHerc. 1251 II.13, III.17 [T2]; D.L. II.89 [T7c], 98) and *lypē* (PHerc. 1251 III.16 [T2]; D.L. II.89 [T7c]), which tend to express mental rather than bodily pleasures and pains;[1] Theodorus in particular may have used them for long-term pleasurable and painful situations, rather than unitemporal *pathē*. In one place *hēdonē* is replaced by an unusual term, *hēdypatheia* (Athenaeus, *Deipn.* XII.544a), which may refer either to the collection of individual pleasures constituting a pleasurable life or to a particular *pathos* of pleasure.

Pleasure and pain are referred to by ordinary verbs and verbal phrases, as well as by nouns. The expressions found most frequently are forms of the Greek verbs *hēdesthai*, *algein*, and *ponein*, which seem to have been used by most Cyrenaics. For example, Aristippus of Cyrene claimed that 'whoever has pleasure (*hēdetai*) is happy, while the person who does not have any pleasure (*mē hēdomenos*) is miserable and unhappy' (Epiphanius, *Adv.haer.* III.2.9); Aristippus the Younger specified the two affective conditions of our constitution as 'one condition in which we are in pain (*algoumen*)' and 'another in which we feel pleasure (*hēdometha*)' (Eusebius XIV.18.32 [T5]); his disciples (and/or the Annicerians) 'believed that the experience of pain (*to ponein*) is unwelcome,

---

[1] See D.L. II.98, which attests that, according to Theodorus, the moral ends are *chara* and *lypē*, while *hēdonē* and *ponos* are intermediates. Compare D.L. x.139 (*KD* III) and *SVF* III 431ff. I believe that, in the context of late Cyrenaic ethics, *chara* and *lypē* are distinguished from *hēdonē* and *ponos* not only on account of the fact that they belong to the soul rather than to the body, but also on account of the assumption that they are more long-lasting than the corresponding bodily states.

whereas the experience of pleasure (*to hēdesthai*) is welcome'; and Hegesias claimed that nothing is naturally pleasurable or painful, but that some people have pleasure (*hēdesthai*) and others are in a painful condition' depending on the lack or rarity or overabundance of an object (D.L. II.94 [T7f]).

Although pleasurable and painful states are occasionally indicated by adverbial expressions, these belong to ordinary ways of speaking, unlike the adverbial locutions applying to the intermediates. Their standard form, verb plus adverb, is found only once in connection with individual *pathē*. According to the passage cited immediately above, Hegesias maintained that some persons have pleasure (*hēdesthai*) and others are in a painful condition (*aēdōs echein*), depending on the availability of the desired thing. The adverbial expression *aēdōs echein* probably applies to the particular affection occurring in every particular instance in which the desired object is scarce or too easily obtainable.

It is possible that individual *pathē* of pleasure were also indicated by adverbial formulas, but if so, they are unattested. On the other hand, there is evidence that the Cyrenaics used the ordinary adverbial expression *hēdeōs zēn*, living pleasurably, to denote the particular aggregate of pleasurable *pathē* constituting a pleasurable life; most members of the school considered it the equivalent of happiness and the overall goal of the sage's life (Xenophon, *Mem.* II.1.9–11; D.L. II.91; Eusebius XIV.18.31–32 [T5]; Clement of Alexandria, *Strom.* II.21.127).[2]

Several features about this material require explanation. First, Sextus' text [T6b] makes clear that the two linguistic variants, verbal and adverbial, were used interchangeably.

> That we are being whitened (*leukainometha*) and sweetened (*glykazometha*), we can assert infallibly and truly and certainly and incorrigibly; but that the thing which is producing the *pathos* is white or sweet, that we cannot assert. For it is possible that one is being disposed whitely (*leukantikōs diatethēnai*) even by something not white and sweetened (*glykanthēnai*) by something not sweet. (*M* VII.192–3)

Both types of formula are encountered in the last claim of the passage and both are involved in the explanation of the claim concerning the infallibility of assertions about qualitative *pathē*. Further, adverbial forms and verbal forms are used indifferently in what immediately follows this text: 'the person suffering from vertigo or jaundice is being moved by everything yellowly (*ōchrantikōs kineitai*), and the one who is suffering

---

[2] On the role of happiness in Cyrenaic ethics, see chapter 10, pp. 132–5.

from ophthalmia is being reddened (*erythrainetai*)' (*M* VII.192). Here, the adverbial expression 'he is being moved yellowly' indicates the same type of *pathos* as the peculiar verb 'he is being reddened'; it is replaced later on in the passage by the third-person plural verb 'they are being yellowed' (*ōchrainontai*: *M* VII.193), which still further on is replaced by the adverbial form 'they are being affected yellowly' (*ōchrantikōs paschousin*: *M* VII.198). The intersubstitution of these two categories of neologisms indicates that they are employed in exactly the same way and express the same kind of *pathē*, intermediates related to qualitative alterations in the body and deriving from perceptual events. It is important for our study because it implies that verbal and adverbial reports have similar epistemic characteristics, without precluding the possibility that one type of expression may be epistemically more basic than the other.

Second, although both kinds of locutions are encountered in various grammatical forms, they are properly analysed as autobiographical (first-person) reports – reports of how an individual perceiver is being affected at the time of the occurrence of a particular *pathos*. Thus, in Sextus [T6b], verbs in the third person singular ('he is being reddened': *M* VII.192), in the first plural ('we are being sweetened': *M* VII.191), in the third plural ('they are being reddened': *M* VII.193), 'they are being affected redly': *M* VII.198) and in the infinitive ('being disposed whitely': *M* VII.192, and also 'being sweetened' in Plutarch 1120e [T1]), are briefer ways of illustrating the following claim. Every time that one undergoes a *pathos*, and in particular an intermediate *pathos* such as a *pathos* of red or white or sweet, one's report about oneself at the time of the occurrence of the *pathos* cannot admit of error, but is bound to be true, in some sense of 'true'. I shall discuss this claim in detail in the following chapter.

Third, the verbal neologisms certainly belonged to the original doctrine of the school. They are attested by our earliest source, the Epicurean Colotes, and by later authors, such as Plutarch [T1] and Sextus [T6b], who drew their information from relatively reliable sources.[3] Some doubts might be entertained about the authenticity of the adverbial locutions, since they are reported by Sextus alone. However, I believe that these expressions are authentically Cyrenaic. The fact that Sextus mentions them whereas other authors do not may be due to the degree of detail in Sextus' account of the doctrine and to his philosophi-

---

[3] Scholars agree that this evidence leaves virtually no doubt that the verbal neologisms belonged to the genuine Cyrenaic vocabulary. See, for example, Giannantoni 1958, Mannebach 1961, Doering 1988 and Tsouna 1988.

cal acumen. Other authors may have failed to see the philosophical importance of the adverbial formulas,[4] and may even have failed to notice that they belonged to the technical vocabulary of the Cyrenaics along with the verbal locutions.

Fourth, there are both historical and philosophical reasons why the Cyrenaics may have used ordinary expressions for the *pathē* of pleasure and pain while inventing new terms to report the intermediate *pathē*. Historically, the verb *hēdesthai* and its cognates were always the Greek words signifying pleasure, frequently sensual pleasure. Likewise, the verbs *poneō* and *algeō* and their cognate nouns were always the normal words for bodily toil and pain and for mental suffering. Also, *hēdonē* (pleasure) and *ponos* (pain) were a focus of philosophical debates, notably in the Socratic circle. For example, Plato and Xenophon discuss them in several of their works, Antisthenes stresses the ethical importance of *ponos*, Phaedo may have defended the value of *hēdonē* and may have espoused a moderate hedonism, and, of course, Aristippus of Cyrene makes *hēdonē* a central feature of his ethical outlook. Thus, his successors did not need to invent a new terminology for these categories of *pathē*, for the reasons that there was one available and it had already been used by the founder of the school.

Philosophically, that we are aware of our affections of pleasure and pain was a common assumption of Greek hedonists which was shared by the anti-hedonists as well, so that there was no motive for inventing a new terminology. On the other hand, as I hope to make clear in the following chapter, the Cyrenaic neologisms were forged in order to express an entirely original theory. In the context of that theory, the verbal and adverbial locutions constituted a technical terminology precisely intended to describe perceptual states without making reference to anything beyond the perceiving subject.

---

[4] On the epistemological importance of these locutions, see chapter 4, pp. 47–50.

# *The apprehension of the* pathē

## I THE *PATHĒ* AS OBJECTS OF *KATALĒPSIS* AND AS CRITERIA OF TRUTH

The central tenet of Cyrenaic subjectivism is the thesis that only the *pathē* can be known, in some sense of 'know'. However, it is unclear how this thesis was originally formulated.

It is very likely that the claim attributed to Aristippus the Younger, that 'we have sensation of our *pathē* alone' (τῶν παθῶν μόνων ἡμᾶς τὴν αἴσθησιν ἔχειν: Eusebius xiv.18.32 [T5]) contains the genuine terminology of the Cyrenaic position.[1] This hypothesis is historically plausible, since, by the middle of the fourth century, *aisthēsis* indicates both sensation and perception, and may also refer to certain kinds of knowledge – especially empirical knowledge. According to Diogenes Laertius, the term *aisthēsis* is found in the Cyrenaic definition of the moral end, pleasure: it is 'a smooth motion brought forth (or: when it is brought forth) to consciousness' (*eis aisthēsin*: D.L. ii.85 [T7a]). I argued in a previous chapter (pp. 24–5) that the wording of this testimony appears to suggest a distinction between the physical motions related to the occurrence of pleasure and one's consciousness of feeling pleasure. If so, *aisthēsis* denotes precisely the awareness of the *pathos* as distinct from its physical concomitants. Assuming that *aisthēsis* has this meaning in the definition reported by Eusebius, the thesis that Eusebius attributes to Aristippus the Younger is that we sense our *pathē* alone, and it concerns pleasure and pain as well as the intermediate *pathē*. In what follows, my aim will be to offer a philosophical explanation of this position. I shall start by examining ways in which various authors stated the Cyrenaic claim.

Most of our sources use the verb *katalambanō* (to apprehend) and its derivatives in discussing knowledge of the *pathē*. The formula most frequently attested is that 'the *pathē* alone are apprehensible' (*mona ta pathē katalēpta*: Anonymous 65.30 [T3] and Eusebius xiv.2.4, 18.31, 19.1

[1] See, for example, Mannebach 1961, p. 116.

[T5]); we also encounter the phrases 'only the *pathē* are apprehended' (*mona ta pathē katalambanesthai*: Sextus, *M* VII.191 [T6b]) and 'they said that the *pathē* are apprehensible themselves, not the things from which they derive' (τὰ πάθη καταληπτα: ἔλεγον οὖν αὐτά, οὐκ ἀφ' ὧν γίνεται: D.L. II.92 [T7d]).

While the role of the *pathē* in Cyrenaic ethics suggests that the term *pathē* may safely be attributed to the original doctrine, there are reasons for doubting that *katalambanō* and its cognates belonged to the vocabulary of the early Cyrenaics. The formula that the *pathē* alone are *katalēpta* (apprehensible) is another way of stating that we have *katalēpsis* (apprehension) only of our *pathē*. According to Cicero (*Luc.* 145), the word *katalēpsis* (*comprehensio*) was forged by Zeno the Stoic in relation to the metaphor by which he illustrated the four stages of the cognitive process. Apprehension corresponds to the third stage. It is compared with a fist where the fingers are pressed closely together, and it is called *katalēpsis* in virtue of its similarity to the thing, the tightly closed fist (ibid.). The Stoic analysis suggests that *katalēpsis* signifies the mental *grasp* acquired as the result of assenting to a certain category of impressions, whose propositional content is always true and cannot be false.

It seems fairly clear that if Zeno was indeed the first philosopher to use the term *katalēpsis*, it could not have been part of the doctrine of the early Cyrenaics. Zeno was born about a century after Aristippus of Cyrene (*c*.344 BC) and about forty years after Aristippus the Younger; since Aristippus the Younger was probably the Cyrenaic philosopher who systematised the epistemological views of the school, it is likely that the Zenonian term was not integrated into his epistemology. It seems possible that the original Cyrenaic thesis contained a perceptual or cognitive verb such as *aisthanesthai* ('to perceive', 'to apprehend', 'to sense'), *gignōskein* ('to discern', 'to know', 'to judge') or *gnōrizein* ('to detect', 'to be acquainted with', 'to acknowledge'); if so, the epistemological claim of the early Cyrenaics may have been, roughly, that the *pathē* alone can be sensed, judged or known. The Stoic epistemological terms *katalambanō*, *katalambanesthai*, and their cognates may have been introduced into the doctrine by the Cyrenaic sects of the Hellenistic period, who may have recast the claim that only the *pathē* are known in the current linguistic idiom. But it is also possible that these terms were never taken over by the Cyrenaics and were only attributed to them by later sources.[2]

---

[2] If the terms *katalambanein*, *katalambanesthai* and *katalēpta* were never part of the Cyrenaic doctrine, it is difficult to explain thoroughly the frequency with which they occur in the evidence. Perhaps it would be reasonable to suppose that this terminology was contained in sources which authors

Similar problems arise from the claim that the *pathē* are the criteria of truth and of the true. The term *kritērion* appears several times in Sextus' testimony (Sextus, *M* VII.191, 195, 199, 200 [T6b]). Significantly, it occurs at the very beginning of the presentation of Cyrenaic epistemology in that text (191), and this suggests that Sextus or his source consider it a key notion of the doctrine. It is found again at the end of the passage, where Sextus says that they defined the criterion only in terms of what is evident and in terms of the *pathē* (200).

The only other source testifying that the Cyrenaics had views about the criterion is Cicero. He indicates the criterion by the Latin term *iudicium* and employs it twice in connection with the Cyrenaics. He relates it to the psychological views of the school, in particular to the thesis that the *pathē* are detected by 'internal touch'. 'Why should we speak of touch and indeed of what the philosophers call internal touch,

belonging to different periods used in common, so that they give similar accounts of the doctrine. At least in one case, Sextus Empiricus' testimony in *M* VII.191–200, there is little ground for doubting that his account of the Cyrenaic doctrine originated from the work *Canonica* by Antiochus of Ascalon, who was deeply influenced by Stoic epistemology.

As indicated in the Appendix, the passage on the Cyrenaics is cited in the final doxographical part of *M* VII (141–260), which presents the views of the philosophers who placed the criterion of truth in *enargeia*, a central notion of Antiochus' epistemology related to his claim that some states of affairs are self-evident and self-justified, and never fail to yield non-inferential knowledge. *M* VII.141–260 draws the historical evolution of this concept starting with the Academics, from Plato to Carneades, and continuing with the Cyrenaics, Epicurus, the Peripatetics and the Stoics – a line of succession most of which Antiochus acknowledged as his own. The structure of *M* VII.141–260 suggests that his overall strategy was to show that the epistemological roles attributed by these philosophers to *enargeia* pointed towards the Stoic criterion of *kataleptikē phantasia* which he himself endorsed.

Regarding the integration of the Cyrenaic position in his programme, Antiochus' motive was probably the following. While the sceptical Academy attempted to deny the criteria altogether and was only forced by practical life to concede that some things are *enargē*, the Cyrenaics displayed the tendency to over-emphasise *enargeia* as a criterion at the expense of *logos*. Both the Academic sceptics and the Cyrenaics moved away from Plato, their philosophical relative, in that they both rejected his criterion, which relied on *enargeia* as well as on *logos* and which, according to Antiochus, prefigures the Stoic concept of *katalēpsis*. But despite their sceptical outlook, the merit of the Cyrenaics is that they at least recognised *enargeia* as the sole criterion, thus paving the way towards truth, as Antiochus conceives it. (On this, see Sedley 1992, especially pp. 21–5 and 44–55.) Antiochus interpreted the Cyrenaic position using Stoic concepts such as *enargeia* and *katalēpsis*, and may have influenced some of the subsequent literature on the epistemology of the Cyrenaic school. However, I do not think that Antiochus is a plausible source for *all* the authors who attribute to the Cyrenaics the thesis that the *pathē* alone are *katalēpta* (or some other variant containing *katalambanesthai* or one of its cognates). There is no evidence that his doxography was as widely influential as that of, e.g., Theophrastus. On Antiochus' influence, see Glucker 1978, *passim*; see also J. Barnes, 'Antiochus of Ascalon', in Griffin and Barnes 1989, pp. 51–96.

The frequent occurrence of Stoic terminology in the evidence about the Cyrenaics can also be explained in a simpler way. Stoic terms, such as *katalambanein* and its cognates, were part of a philosophical *koinē* which authors used in order to cite and compare different philosophers' answers to a given problem. To do so they needed a standard vocabulary in which all such answers could be reported.

*Subjectivism*

either of pleasure or of pain, in which alone the Cyrenaics believe lies the criterion of the true (*veri iudicium*) because it is sensed?' (*Luc.* 21 [T4a]). The term also occurs in a purely epistemological context, in which the positions of Protagoras, the Cyrenaics and Epicurus on the criterion are contrasted with that of Plato.

> One criterion (*iudicium*) is that of Protagoras, who considers that what appears to a person is true for him, another is that of the Cyrenaics, who believe that there is no criterion whatsoever except for the inward affections (*permotiones intimas*), another is that of Epicurus, who places the whole criterion in the senses and in the primary notions of things and in pleasure. (*Luc.* 142 [T4c])

Much of the terminology contained in these passages can be traced back to Cicero's sources[3] and was employed in the debates in and between the Academy and the Stoa. It also occurs in cardinal texts of Epicurean epistemology, of which the criterion is a main topic.[4] In contrast, there is no conclusive evidence as to whether the Cyrenaics ever participated in discussions concerning the criterion and whether they used the language of these discussions on their own behalf. It may be that the later members of the school did, but it is also entirely possible, I think, that this terminology was inserted into the Cyrenaic doctrine by later authors.

However, even if *katalēpsis* and *kritērion* are not genuinely Cyrenaic words, their occurrence in the testimonies is philosophically enlightening and may guide our systematic attempts to analyse the epistemological claims of the school.

I shall start with some remarks on the nature and implications of the concept of the criterion in two different contexts, Epicurean empiricism and the Stoic theory of knowledge.[5] The Epicureans conceived of the criterion according to the model of the *kanōn* (D.L. x.129).[6] A *kanōn* is a standard length, a ruler, by means of which other lengths are measured. By analogy, the criterion is itself a self-evident state, whose content is used to confirm the truth of statements about states of affairs which are

---

[3] It is likely that the later part of Cicero's speech was based on Philo's work written in reply to Antiochus' *Sosus*. Other parts of the work may have been based on Antiochus' writings or, conceivably, on Cicero's own notes in class. See, however, Reid 1885, pp. 52ff., who maintains that the doxographical references in *Lucullus* came primarily from a book entitled *On the Sects* (*Peri Haireseōn*) by Clitomachus, Carneades' successor at the head of the Academy.

[4] This terminology is also used by the Middle Platonists. See, for example, Alcinoos' *Didaskalikos*, 154ff., in which the survey of dialectic begins with a section on the criterion.

[5] On the various uses of the *kritērion* in the doctrines of the Hellenistic philosophers, see Striker 1974 and J. Brunschwig, 'Sextus Empiricus on the *kritērion*: The skeptic as conceptual legatee', in Dillon and Long 1988, pp. 145–75 (reprinted in Brunschwig 1994b, pp. 224–43).

[6] According to D.L. x.31, Epicurus' writing which dealt with the criteria of truth was entitled *Kanōn*.

circumstantially or naturally non-evident. Sensations (*aisthēseis*), precon-
ceptions (*prolēpseis*), undergoings or affections (*pathē*), and, in later Epicureanism, mental impressions (*phantastikai epibolai tēs dianoias*) qualify as
criteria primarily because they provide the means by which further
evidence can be tested. The analogy of the ruler illustrates a main
epistemic function of the Epicurean criteria: their application to things
which are not immediately and directly observable *augments* our knowledge about these non-evident things, just as the application of the
standard ruler to unknown lengths increases our knowledge about those
lengths.[7]

Although different Stoics held different views on the criteria, all
members of the school considered the cognitive impression (*phantasia
katalēptikē*) the principal criterion of truth. Cognitive impressions constitute a specific category of impressions, those arising only from what is
(D.L. VII.54), and reproduced exactly in accordance with what is
(Cicero, *Luc.* 77), grasping their objects precisely and stamped with all
their peculiarities (Sextus, *M* VII.248–51), and incapable of deceiving
the perceiver with regard to their content (Sextus, *M* VII.252). Thus,
the cognitive impression is a self-certifiable truth, constituting 'just by
itself' an unchallengeable guarantee that we perceive a real object
precisely as it is (Cicero, *Acad.* 1.41). Provided that one perceives an
external object in a clear and distinct way, one has no choice but to
acknowledge the content of the perception as true; for the faculty of
assent (*synkatathesis*) functions in such a way as to approve, as it were,
automatically of cognitive impressions (Cicero, *Luc.* 38). The outcome
of the process of receiving and assenting to a cognitive impression is a
cognitive grasp (*katalēpsis*) of the object giving rise to the impression
(Cicero, *Acad.* I.41). This concept of the criterion does not fit the model
of the *kanōn*.[8] For the primary criterial function of the cognitive impression is not to test things other than itself, but to establish its own
content as true of the object which the cognitive impression exactly
represents. While the Epicureans considered that the knowledge provided through the use of the criteria is primarily inferential knowledge
about things other than the criteria themselves, the Stoics identified

---

[7] Several scholars relate the conception of the criterion as a *kanōn* to the Epicurean thesis that all
*aisthēseis* are true: their claim is that, according to Epicurus, if *aisthēseis* are among the criteria of
truth, they must themselves be true. However, the generalisation that any criterion of truth must
itself be true is problematic. On this, see C. C. W. Taylor, 'All perceptions are true', in Schofield,
Burnyeat and Barnes 1980, pp. 105–24.

[8] See again Striker 1974 and Brunschwig 1994b, pp. 224–43. See also A. A. Long, 'Ptolemy *On the
Criterion*: an epistemology for the practising scientist', in Dillon and Long 1988, pp. 176–207.

knowledge through the criterion as immediate, non-inferential knowledge. One's knowledge about the world does gradually grow, not because the criterion is applied to non-evident states of affairs, but because one receives an increasing number of cognitive impressions and ascertains an increasing number of propositions as true. (Notice the foundationalist assumptions involved in both the Epicurean and in the Stoic criteria.)

Despite their epistemic differences, both the Epicurean and the Stoic criteria are self-evident representational contents with an infallible cognitive hold on reality. This is exactly what the Sceptics reject in their attacks against dogmatic criteria: they deny that there is any epistemic sense in which it can be claimed that a criterion exists.

But there is a non-epistemic sense in which the Sceptics attend to the criterion, namely they follow non-dogmatically the rules of practical life. In the narrative part of his *Outlines of Pyrrhonism*, Sextus reports:

That we adhere to appearances (*phainomena*) is plain from what we say about the criterion of the Sceptical way of life. The word *kritērion* is spoken of in two ways, namely as a standard regulating belief in existence or non-existence (about which we shall talk in the part concerning refutation), and also as a standard of action by attending to which in practical life we do some things but abstain from others. It is of this that we are now speaking. We say, then, that the criterion of the Sceptical way of life is the appearance, calling by this name what is equivalent to the mental image (*phantasia*) of it. For since this lies in undergoings and involuntary *pathē*, it is not open to enquiry. Thus, perhaps nobody disputes that the underlying object appears such and such. But whether the object is such as it appears constitutes a subject of enquiry.

By attending, then, to the appearances we live without belief (*adoxastōs*) in accordance with the observances of common life, since we cannot be wholly inactive. And it seems that this observance of common life is fourfold and that one part of it lies in the guidance of nature, another in the compelling force of the *pathē*, another in the tradition of laws and customs, another in the instruction in the arts. The natural guidance is that by which we are naturally capable of sensation and thought, the compelling force of the *pathē* that by which hunger leads us to food and thirst to drink, the tradition of laws and customs that by which we accept in common life piety as a good and impiety as an evil, and the instruction in the arts that by which we are not inactive in the arts which we undertake. But we say all this without belief. (Sextus, *PH* 1.22–4)

Thus, according to the Sceptics, the *pathē*, as well as the other observances of common life, are criteria in a non-dogmatic, non-technical sense of the word: they do not regulate beliefs about how things are, but constitute categories of appearances that the Sceptic observes in ordinary life. Regarding the *pathē* in particular, their compelling force lies in 'that by which hunger leads us to food and thirst to drink', hunger and thirst being determined as internal states self-evident to the person in whom they occur (Sextus, *PH* 1.20). Further references to the *pathē* indicate that they are assumed to be processes concomitant with sensation (Sextus, *M* XI.143), more or less permanent (Sextus, *PH* 1.13, 198) and detached from the operations of reason (Sextus, *M* XI.143, 148). Because they are irrational, they are involuntary and unavoidable: we cannot alter the way in which we are affected and we cannot but give our assent to their content (Sextus, *PH* 1.19, 22, 23; *M* XI.143, 144). Acknowledging what moves us 'affectively' (*pathētikōs*) and drives us forcibly to assent is part of acting in accordance with appearances (Sextus, *PH* 1.19). So, the criterial power of the *pathē* lies precisely in the fact that the Sceptic conforms to the constraints that they impose on him and does not attempt to resist them.[9]

Even if the concept of the criterion is not genuinely Cyrenaic, it is philosophically important to decide whether the authors who are attesting that according to the Cyrenaics the *pathē* are the criteria employed this term in a non-technical or in a technical sense. If the former, then the evidence would suggest that the Cyrenaic position is non-epistemic: only the *pathē* can be felt in the sense that only they force us to acknowledge their content and follow their guidance in practical life. On the other hand, if the word criterion is used in its technical meaning, the Cyrenaic thesis should be construed as an epistemic claim: we have *aisthēsis* only of our *pathē* in the sense that only they are self-evident (*enargē*), are apprehensible (*katalēpta*) and establish their own content as incontrovertibly true *of something*. In the following chapter I shall argue for the epistemic interpretation of the *pathē* and I

---

[9] The epistemological implications of the Sceptics' attendance to the appearances are discussed in M. F. Burnyeat, 'Can the Sceptic live his Scepticism?', in Schofield, Burnyeat and Barnes 1980, pp. 20–53 (reprinted in Burnyeat 1983, pp. 117–48). Burnyeat's thesis is further developed and placed within a broad philosophical context in his article 'The Skeptic in his place and time' in Rorty, Schneewind and Skinner 1984, pp. 225–54. An entirely different interpretation is proposed by M. Frede and developed in a series of articles: 'Des Skeptikers Meinungen' (Frede 1979), translated into English as 'The Skeptic's beliefs', in Frede 1987, pp. 201–22; 'Stoics and Sceptics on clear and distinct impressions', in Burnyeat 1983, pp. 65–93; and 'The Skeptic's two kinds of assent and the question of the possibility of knowledge', in Rorty, Schneewind and Skinner 1984, pp. 255–78. A third influential interpretation has been proposed by J. Barnes in Barnes 1982. Other significant articles bearing on the interpretation of the practical criterion are: Stough 1984; J. Annas, 'Doing without objective values', in Schofield and Striker 1986, pp. 3–29 and especially 17–29; McPherran 1987. On the political and practical implications of the Sceptics' criterion, see most recently Hiley 1988, ch. 1. His interpretation has been criticised by Laursen in Laursen 1992 (especially pp. 3–9, 14–93), and by myself in Tsouna-McKirahan 1995.

shall analyse the Cyrenaic position as an epistemological thesis about subjective states.

## II VARIETIES OF PRIVILEGED ACCESS

According to Sextus in *M* VII.191–200 [T6b], the Cyrenaics justified the thesis that the *pathē* alone are apprehended and are the criteria of truth by determining the epistemic features of the sentences describing them.

The Cyrenaics claim that the *pathē* are the criteria and that they alone are apprehended and are not deceitful (*adiapseusta*), but that none of the things productive of the *pathē* is apprehensible or undeceitful (*adiapseuston*). They say it is possible to assert infallibly (*adiapseustōs*) and truly (*alēthōs*) and firmly (*bebaiōs*) and incorrigibly (*anexelenktōs*)[10] that we are being whitened or sweetened; but it is impossible to assert that the thing productive of the *pathos* in us is white or sweet. (Sextus, *M* VII.191 [T6b])

The four epistemic characteristics listed in this passage apply primarily to propositions reporting *pathē*, but at least some of them are used of the internal states as well. This becomes clear at the beginning of the account, where infallibility and incorrigibility are mentioned: both the *pathē* and the propositions about them are infallible and incorrigible. Thus, the claim is both that no *pathos* can yield false information about its content and that no autobiographical report about an individual *pathos* admits of error – provided that it is meaningful and sincerely uttered.[11]

The incorrigibility claim is also reported by Plutarch in connection with opinion or belief. Although Plutarch does not use the term criterion, his account resembles Sextus' presentation in *M* VII.191–200 [T6b], in that it relates the infallibility of the *pathē* to their self-evident character, their *enargeia*. And *enargeia* is a crucial characteristic of the objects of the Hellenistic criteria: if something qualifies as the object of a criterion, it must be evident, *enarges*. A further similarity between the two accounts is that they both employ the Cyrenaic neologisms in connection to the infallibility claim: the reports or beliefs which are claimed to be infallible are formulated in expressions such as 'being whitened' and 'being sweetened'.

They say that we are being sweetened and bittered and chilled and warmed

---

[10] The text is corrupt here. The Loeb editor omitted καὶ ἀληθῶς and so did Mannebach. On the other hand, Giannantoni followed the Mutschmann edition of Sextus and kept the two words in the text. He also kept in the text the adverb βεβαίως and supplied καὶ after βεβαίως, while Mannebach excised the word.

[11] As far as we know, the Cyrenaics did not spell out these conditions, but they seem to be presupposed by their position.

and illuminated and darkened, each of these *pathē* having within itself its own evidence (*tēn enargeian*), which is intrinsic to it (*oikeia*) and irreversible (*aperispastos*).[12] But whether the honey is sweet or the young olive-shoot bitter or the hail chilly or the unmixed wine warm or the sun luminous or the night air dark, is contested by many witnesses (*antimartyreisthai*), (wild) animals and tame animals and humans alike. For some dislike honey, others like olive-shoots or are burned off by hail or are chilled by the wine or go blind in the sunlight and see well at night. So, when opinion stays close to the *pathē*, it preserves the feature of infallibility (*to anamartēton*), but when it oversteps them and meddles with judgements and assertions about the external objects, it often both disturbs itself and fights against other people who receive from the same objects contrary *pathē* and different sense-impressions. (Plutarch, 1120e–f [T1])

An important element of Plutarch's testimony is that it invites a comparison between the evidence intrinsic to each *pathos* and the report that an observer gives about external objects. Plutarch's source borrows the term 'contestation' (*antimartyrēsis*: cf. Sextus, *M* VII.210–16) from the scientific methodology of the Epicureans in order to make the point that empirical reports are fallible. This word evokes the forensic metaphor applying to the kind of criterion that *aisthēsis* is for the Epicureans (D.L. x.146): like reliable witnesses in a court, the *aisthēseis* are trustworthy witnesses providing evidence on the grounds of which we pass judgement about the external objects. The Cyrenaic argument reported by Plutarch may be part of an attack against the criterial power of *aisthēsis* as a basis for forming empirical beliefs: since the reports and beliefs of different observers about the same object are inconsistent, it follows that some or all of them are false (D.L. x.50–1); and since they are or may be false, they cannot provide trustworthy evidence about external objects. If the Cyrenaics employed this argument in defence of their claim that the *pathē* alone are apprehended, they attributed to the *pathē* epistemic features which the predominant Hellenistic schools attached to their criteria of truth: they are self-evident and infallibly true *of something*. But in contrast to these schools, the Cyrenaics denied that the *pathē* are infallibly true *of external objects*.

Infallibility[13] is the strongest epistemic characteristic of the *pathē* and of the autobiographical reports concerning them. It entails that the reports expressing the *pathē* are true, irrefutable and certain: if a report

---

[12] For this translation of *aperispastos*, see Carneades' use of the term attested by Sextus, *PH* I.227–9 and *M* VII.166, 176, 180–82, 184 and 189.

[13] For an informative discussion of the concepts of infallibility, incorrigibility, truth and certainty, see Alston 1971. It is worth noticing that the distinctions that the Cyrenaics drew between different kinds of cognitive access are similar to modern distinctions and are relevant to the issue whether certainty has degrees.

is infallible, it must also be true and cannot be questioned or contested as false. According to the Sextus passage, the Cyrenaics drew these epistemological distinctions. However, it is unclear in what sense the Cyrenaics used the concept of firmness or certainty (if indeed the adverb *bebaiōs* was part of Sextus' text).[14] The word may well indicate a genuine epistemic requirement that the Cyrenaics attached to the awareness of individual *pathē*: if something is to count as knowledge, it must be impregnable to any reasoning that might induce one to believe that one was undergoing one kind of *pathos* instead of another. In that case, the Cyrenaics attributed to the apprehension of the *pathē* a characteristic which several philosophers, notably Plato and the Stoics, attributed to knowledge: firmness is the mark of knowledge (*epistēmē*) as opposed to mere belief (*doxa*)[15] or to single acts of cognition (*katalēpsis*). The Stoics in particular maintained that cognition is a necessary but not a sufficient condition for knowledge: '*epistēmē* is cognition which is secure and firm and unchangeable by argument' (Sextus, *M* VII.151).

Sextus' passage describes a position entailing a very strong epistemological claim: every autobiographical report about *pathē* is incorrigible, true, firm and unquestionable, and every sentence possessing these epistemic characteristics is an autobiographical report about *pathē*. It might be suggested that since Sextus testifies that it is possible to utter such propositions (*dynaton legein*), not that it is necessary to do so, he allows for cases in which propositions about the *pathē* admit of error and can be refuted. However, I think that the force of *dynaton* does not apply to the four adverbs indicating the epistemic features of autobiographical propositions, but to the infinitive *legein*. What is possible, but not necessary, is that one may choose to *say* anything about the *pathē* affecting one: for instance, if I am alone at the time of seeing a white horse, I shall probably remain silent about the event of 'being whitened'. But if I speak sincerely about what I am seeing, then what I say is bound to possess all the features mentioned above.

It seems that according to the Cyrenaics, incorrigibility is not a property which belongs to a certain category of propositions as such. For the incorrigibility claim is valid only for first-person, present-tense sensing reports used by the perceiver himself at the time of perception. For example, the sentences 'He is being whitened' used by someone

---

[14] See above, n. 10.
[15] However, in the *Timaeus* the world Soul has *bebaioi doxai* (37b).

else to refer to me at this moment, 'I shall be affected whitely' used by myself in the past about the present moment, and 'I am being whitened' express the same thing, but only the last of these sentences is expressed in conditions which make it incorrigible. Thus, the incorrigibility thesis amounts to the claim that a sentence is incorrigible only if it is uttered by the affected person himself and reports his present condition. In this respect, the Cyrenaic position concerning the reports of the *pathē* prefigures modern discussions about the indubitability of 'basic' propositions.

The Cyrenaics related the autobiographical character of incorrigible sentences to some remarks about the privacy of the *pathē* and the impossibility of having cognitive access to the *pathē* of people other than oneself.

They say that no criterion is common to mankind but that common names are assigned to the objects. For all people call something white or sweet in common, but they do not have something common that is white or sweet. For each person is aware of his own private *pathos*, but whether this *pathos* occurs in him and in his neighbour from a white object neither he himself can tell since he is not submitting to the *pathos* of his neighbour, nor can the neighbour tell since he is not submitting to the *pathos* of the other person. (Sextus, *M* VII.195–6 [T6b])

I shall discuss this passage in detail in chapters 7 and 8, below. At present, I shall only point out the following things. First, although the concept of privacy, I shall maintain, cuts across the distinction between the objective and the subjective aspects of the *pathē*, the combination of this ontological concept with the incorrigibility claim makes the argument read primarily as one focused on the subjective aspects of the *pathē*. Second, the claim that one infallibly knows one's own *pathē* but has no access to those of one's neighbour confirms that, according to the Cyrenaics, infallible assertions must be autobiographical. Since one is infallibly aware of *pathē* private to oneself, what one *can tell* others (cf. *dynatai legein*: Sextus, *M* VII.196 [T6b]) about one's condition does not admit of error. And precisely because it is definitionally impossible for one to be conscious of other people's *pathē*, one cannot speak incorrigibly about them (*ou . . . dynatai legein*: ibid.).

In the next section I shall discuss in more detail two elements of the view that only the *pathē* are apprehended and are criteria: the self-evident nature of the *pathē* and their compulsory force.

## III  SELF-EVIDENT STATES AND SELF-EVIDENT
## PROPOSITIONS

I mentioned above that, despite their considerable differences, both the Epicureans and the Stoics defined the role of the criterion by reference to reality: the criterion is an immediate, self-evident truth about an object external to the perceiver, whether this is a stream of films of atoms or a three-dimensional object.

In what follows, I shall argue that the Cyrenaic *pathē* too are self-evident states whose content is incorrigibly true, and I shall specify what they are true of. In order to clarify the nature of the connection that the Cyrenaics drew between the self-evident character of the *pathē* and the incorrigible awareness of them, I shall compare their position to modern foundationalist views about the nature of subjective states and the propositions describing them.

In the analytic literature on epistemology of the 1960s and 1970s, we often encounter attempts to determine one or more categories of senten-ces which require no demonstration or justification, and which are epistemically basic with regard to all other propositions.[16] An interesting model of categorisation of basic and non-basic sentences is provided by Roderick Chisholm, who is well acquainted with Greek scepticism; in particular, his analysis of perception presents striking resemblances with the Cyrenaic theory, both on the linguistic and on the conceptual level.[17] I shall focus my argument hereafter on Chisholm's descriptions of subjective states and of 'basic' propositions, as well as on his model of analysis of sensory experience.

The label that Chisholm uses for basic propositions is 'autonomous' propositions.[18] He defines them as 'self-presenting' propositions which refer to self-presenting states of affairs[19] and he proposes to treat these two categories of self-presentation interchangeably on the grounds that they share the same characteristics and their intersubstitution will sim-plify his epistemological argument.[20]

---

[16] For a good general introduction to the assumptions that lie behind foundationalist projects of various kinds, see Dancy 1985, pp. 53–84.

[17] I am not aware of any specific reference of R. Chisholm to Sextus' passages on the Cyrenaics. However, his familiarity with Sextus' writings is apparent in several of his works, and notably in Chisholm 1941.

[18] Regarding justification, the so-called autonomous propositions are those which do not need, and indeed cannot be supported by, any other category of propositions, but which support them-selves or justify other groups of propositions. In the foundationalist picture, the so-called autonomous propositions constitute the basis on which the superstructure of our knowledge of the world is anchored.     [19] See Chisholm 1966, p. 28.

[20] See Chisholm 1966, p. 23 and ch. 5.

Chisholm endorses a widespread foundationalist view according to which a state of affairs is self-presenting to a perceiver *P* only if the state of affairs is necessarily such that, if it occurs, then it is evident to *P*.[21] For example, the sentence 'I am feeling dizzy' expresses a state of affairs which is self-presenting to me: it is necessary that if I am feeling dizzy, it is evident to me that I am feeling dizzy; it would be impossible for me to be feeling dizzy unless it were evident to me that I am feeling dizzy. And the proposition 'I am feeling dizzy' is self-presenting to me only if it is true that I am feeling dizzy.[22] The states which conform to that definition of self-presentation are the so-called internal or subjective states: thoughts, beliefs, desires, hopes, doubts, love, hatred, etc. Self-presenting propositions are propositions referring to these subjective states, i.e. propositions expressing one's inner life and one's awareness of it. My discussion will be centred on perceptual states and on the feelings of pleasure and pain, because these are of prime relevance to an interpretation of the Cyrenaic doctrine.

Sensory foundationalists, including Chisholm, consider propositions about raw feelings and perceptual states basic precisely in the sense mentioned above, that they are self-certifiable and do not need the support of other propositions in order to establish their own content. What justifies my belief that I am feeling pain is simply that I am feeling pain, and what justifies my belief that I am tasting something sweet is that I am tasting something sweet. We can legitimately doubt a proposition *p* if the reasons that can be presented in support of *p* are more persuasive than the mere assertion of *p*. It makes sense to ask whether it is true that the blue colour of the Aegean is due to the lack of plankton, because the truth of that proposition can be demonstrated independently of the assertion of the proposition itself. On the other hand, it is absurd to question the truth of one's utterance that one feels exhausted,[23] for what sort of verification can one bring in order to

---

[21] See Chisholm 1966, p. 28: 'Borrowing a technical term from Meinong [A. Meinong, *Über emotionale Präsentation*, Vienna 1917], let us say that what is directly evident to a man is always some state of affairs that "presents itself to him".' Again, Chisholm defines the directly evident as 'that which constitutes its own evidence and therefore, in the terms of Sextus Empiricus, that which is apprehended through itself [Sextus Empiricus, *PH* 1.6]' (Chisholm 1966, p. 30). Compare Sextus' passages discussing things that are presented *autothen*, without the intervention of a sign or of a criterion. See, for example, *PH* II.7, 107, and *M* II.109, VIII.26.

[22] On the logical relations between what is directly evident and what is self-presenting, see Chisholm 1966, pp. 23–4.

[23] I should make clear that I do not consider this position altogether plausible. It seems to me that room for doubt arises as soon as one undertakes to talk about one's feeling of exhaustion – i.e. as soon as the feeling is translated into a proposition. Consider the following example: 'Yesterday I thought I felt exhausted, but now I realise that I was merely feeling the effects of flu.' Compare *Rep.*

prove that one really feels exhausted? And further, how can one say or do anything *more* efficient in persuading us that it is true that one feels exhausted than simply repeat that one feels exhausted?[24]

In this view, directly evident propositions are also immediately evident, in the sense that they are not inferred from other propositions and their content is grasped by the perceiver non-inferentially. Accordingly, self-presenting states are immediately evident in the sense that, if they occur, they are evident without any mediator or mediation. And since self-presenting states, in particular raw feelings and perceptual states, are directly and immediately evident only to the person who is experiencing them, that person has privileged access to them and is an absolute authority with regard to the truth of first-person reports about them.

The insights behind the epistemic characterisation of the *pathē* as the sole objects of *katalēpsis* and the sole criteria of truth resemble, I think, these assumptions of the foundationalists about self-presenting states and self-presenting propositions. I have pointed out that the Cyrenaics too treated these two categories of self-presentation interchangeably, probably because they believed, as some foundationalists did, that they have similar features. The Cyrenaic thesis that each *pathos* carries within itself its own evidence which is intrinsic to it and inseparable from it recalls the definition of self-evident states as states of affairs concerning which, if they occur, it is necessarily evident to the perceiver that they occur. Both the *pathē* and the self-presenting states are internal to the perceiver – with the difference that the foundationalists classified as internal states other intentional states, such as beliefs and desires, which are not discussed in the Cyrenaic theory. The Cyrenaics too appear to consider reports of one's *pathē* to be non-inferential reports, since they claim that the content of the *pathē* is the only thing which can be sensed and known. Chisholm's definition of directly evident propositions as propositions whose truth is indubitable could equally well apply to the Cyrenaic assertions about

---

580d ff.: Plato distinguishes between three forms of pleasure, corresponding to the three parts of the soul and characterising three classes of people, and argues that, while the lover of victory and the lover of gain may be mistaken as to which type of pleasure is actually the more pleasurable, the lover of wisdom is the best judge of true pleasures. Pleasures other than those of wisdom or intelligence are not entirely real or pure, but are a kind of illusionist shading technique (*eskia-graphēmenē*, 583b), an appearance (*phantasma*, 584a) or jugglery (*goēteia*, ibid.) that has no bearing on the truth of pleasure. Also, compare *Phil.* 36 c ff., where Socrates refutes Protarchus' thesis that no one ever thinks that he feels pleasure but does not really feel it, or thinks he feels pain but does not really feel it (cf. 36e); he draws a distinction between true and false pleasures (36c) and argues that, in the case of false pleasures, you think that you are having pleasure, but in fact you are not.

[24] See L. Wittgenstein's remarks on such propositions in the work *On Certainty* (Oxford 1969), pp. 32e ff. and compare the foundationalist position.

*pathē*, since they too are considered incorrigible. Comparably to the foundationalists, the Cyrenaics may have formed the idea that the *pathē* are immediately evident, in the sense that we are conscious of them without the intervention of any external medium or mediator. This may be indicated by the thesis that the *pathē* are sensed by 'internal touch', which registers the perceiver's internal condition without the interference of any physical medium. Finally, both the self-presenting states of the foundationalists and the *pathē* of the Cyrenaics are private to the perceiver, so that in both cases it can be maintained that the perceiver has privileged access to the content of his affections and is an absolute authority with regard to the truth of propositions referring to them.

IV    TWO WAYS OF INTERPRETING THE CYRENAIC
POSITION: THE OBJECTAL AND THE ADVERBIAL MODELS
OF SENSORY PERCEPTION

The affinities between the epistemic features of self-presenting states and those of the *pathē* have incited a few attempts to construe the Cyrenaic position, that the *pathē* alone can be apprehended, along the lines of foundationalist theories. To my knowledge, two such interpretations have been proposed. One analyses the claim in terms of sense-data theories of perception (I shall call this the objectal model), and the other explains it in terms of the so-called adverbial analysis of appearances (I shall call this the adverbial model).[25] In what follows, I shall outline and argue briefly against the former interpretation. I shall also point out some respects in which the approaches of the Cyrenaics and of the adverbial analysts to perception are remarkably alike, although they belong to very different epistemological contexts.[26]

If applied to the Cyrenaic theory, the objectal model entails that the *pathē* are construed as *sensa*, mental objects directly given to experience

---

[25] For the sense-data interpretation of the Cyrenaic theory, see D. K. Glidden, 'Protagorean relativism and the Cyrenaics', in Rescher 1975, pp. 113–40. I argued against Glidden and I proposed an interpretation of the Cyrenaic doctrine in terms of the adverbial theories in Tsouna 1988, pp. 214–64; I modified my position in Tsouna-McKirahan 1992. To my knowledge, these are the only attempts to discuss Cyrenaic epistemology using current analytic tools.

[26] There is an extensive literature on the problem of sense-data: D. M. Armstrong, J. L. Austin, A. J. Ayer, W. H. F. Barnes, C. B. Broad, N. Brown, R. Chisholm, J. Cornman, R. Firth, H. D. Lewis, G. E. Moore, A. Quinton, B. Russell, and W. Sellars are among the philosophers that appear in various stages of this debate. For discussions relevant to the formulations and criticisms of the adverbial analysis of appearances, see Aune 1967; Chisholm 1957 and 1966; Cornman 1971 and 1975; Ducasse 1949; Sellars 1963 and 1968. A number of articles are relevant to the issues mentioned in this chapter: C. J. Ducasse, 'Moore's refutation of idealism', in Schilpp 1942; Sellars 1964, 1971 and 1975; Heidelberger 1966; Jackson 1975; Tye 1984.

whose phenomenal properties are exactly what they appear to be. In contrast to external objects, *sensa* are defined as objects which are private to the perceiver, last only so long as they are perceived and have no causal properties but can only affect one through being perceived. It has often been stressed by the proponents as well as the critics of the objectal analysis of sensing that *sensa* are somewhat similar to real objects in that these too are distinct and separate from their being perceived. Both the perception of a real object and the perception of a mental object imply the occurrence of a *relational act* between a perceiver and an object: the percipient senses or perceives *something*, whether this is a real object or a *sensum*. In the context of the objectal model, the epistemic claim that we have incorrigible awareness of our *sensa* takes the following form. Since the *sensa* are mental objects private to each perceiver, the perceiver has privileged access to them and is an absolute authority with regard to the description of their properties. The objection standardly raised against this claim (rightly so, I think) has been that, if the *sensa* are mental objects with extensional properties, there is no good reason to grant that the perceiver alone has the final authority to give incorrigible descriptions of these properties.[27] Now, if the Cyrenaics construed the *pathē* in a way prefiguring the *sensa*, it would follow that they conceived of the properties of the *pathē* as extensional properties described in empirical terms. But in that case, they would also be committed to the objectionable thesis that each perceiver alone can offer incorrigible descriptions of the extensional properties of mental objects.[28]

However, the evidence rules out this interpretation of the Cyrenaic theory. First, while the sense-data model involves elaborate discussions of the nature of the *sensa* and their differences from physical objects, the Cyrenaic theory does not sort out the ontological differences between the *pathē* and external objects. Although several passages testify that the former are contrasted to the latter (for example Anonymous 65.30 [T3]; Sextus, *M* VII.191 [T6b]; D.L. II.92 [T7d]), this contrast is set on epistemological rather than on ontological grounds: it does not pertain to the relation between objects of sensory awareness and physical objects, but to the relation between what can be known and what cannot. Second, the Cyrenaics do not provide the grounds for distin-

---

[27] The authority of one's reports about one's own *sensa* and the incorrigibility of these reports are two separate issues. See Cornman 1971, pp. 39ff.

[28] For a devastating criticism of the construction of the phenomenal properties of the *sensa* as extensional properties, see Cornman 1975, pp. 37–91.

guishing between mental objects and physical objects in the way a post-Cartesian philosopher would, since they do not conceive of the *pathē* solely in mentalistic terms. Third, in contrast to the *sensa*, the evidence about the Cyrenaics suggests that the *pathē* do not have properties that could be described as extensional properties. Although modern commentators may for the sake of convenience use expressions such as 'a *pathos* of yellow' and 'a *pathos* of sweet' instead of Cyrenaic locutions such as 'I am being yellowed' and 'I am being sweetened', in fact no *pathos* is attested to be yellow or sweet, nor is a *pathos* yellowed or sweetened; it is the affected person who is being yellowed and sweetened (see, for instance, *M* vii.191–2, 194, 196–7 [T6b]). For these reasons it is misleading to construe the *pathē* in terms of *sensa* and to analyse the claim that we have incorrigible apprehension of our own *pathē* in terms of the incorrigible awareness of our own *sensa*. Consequently, the Cyrenaic position is not vulnerable to the same criticisms as the ones that sense-data theorists have had to face.[29]

The adverbial model of analysis of sensory perception was formed as a result of a controversy regarding the relation between the objects of awareness and the act of awareness itself. In contrast to the sense-data theorists, who maintained that the *sensa* are distinct from our awareness of them, the so-called adverbial analysts held that the act of awareness consists in the awareness of sense-contents which cannot exist (in any sense of 'exist') without being sensed. While the objectal model explains perception in terms of a relation between an act of awareness and an object, the goal of the adverbial model is to eliminate the distance between the perceiver and the perceived object and to analyse perception in non-relational terms, by designating the manner in which one is affected or the kind of affection that one undergoes at a given time. There are several variants of the adverbial approach to perception, but most of them agree on the following points.

First, the explanation of perception in non-relational terms requires extensive revisions of our ways of speaking about perception. These revisions are primarily dictated by the concern systematically to avoid any reference to perceived objects, mental or physical. In order to achieve this, the adverbial analysts tend to eliminate substantival terminology by reformulating statements of the form 'x appears F to me' (where x is an object and F a property of x) into reports of the form 'I am appeared to F' or 'I am appeared to F-ly' (where F and F-ly stand as

---

[29] These arguments have been developed in detail in Tsouna-McKirahan 1992.

adverbs indicating *ways of appearing* rather than *things* which appear to be so-and-so). Chisholm, who is an adverbial analyst and on whose version of this model I shall mainly focus, observes:

'Appear' requires a grammatical subject and thus requires a term that purports to refer not merely to a way of appearing, but also to a thing that is said to appear in that way. However, we may eliminate the reference to the thing that appears if we convert our appear-sentences. Instead of saying 'Something appears white to me', we may say, more awkwardly, 'I am appeared white to by something'. We may then eliminate the substantival 'something' by merely dropping the final clause, saying, 'I am appeared white to' . . . We could say 'I am appeared loud to' and 'I am appeared sour to' just as we have said 'I am appeared white to'. The words 'loud', 'sour' and 'white' in these sentences do not function as adjectives; the sentences do not say of any entity that that entity *is* loud, sour or white. The words are used here to describe *ways* of appearing, or of being appeared to, just as 'swift' and 'slow' may be used to describe ways of running. They function as adverbs and our sentences would be more correct, therefore, if they were put as: 'I am appeared sourly to', 'I am appeared whitely to' and 'I am appeared loudly to'. The awkwardness of the 'appears to' terminology could be avoided if, at this point, we were to introduce another verb, say 'sense', using it in a technical way as a synonym for 'it is appeared to'. In this case, we would say 'I sense sourly', 'I sense whitely' and 'I sense loudly'.[30]

Thus, substantival talk is avoided by replacing the active form of the verb 'to appear' by the passive 'I am appeared to', and then by rearranging the other terms of the sentence according to the traditional rules of grammar and syntax. The revised proposition typically contains an adverb specifying the manner in which the perceiver 'is appeared to' and the whole sentence refers to 'a manner of appearing' rather than to an object's appearance.[31]

Second, adverbial reports are immediately evident and incorrigible. But the account of incorrigibility which they afford is different from the one entailed by the sense-data theories of perception, for the perceiver is claimed to have privileged access, not to a mental object, but to his own experiences; and his reports are not descriptions of the properties of a mental object distinct from himself, but identifications of his own condition. Since such sentences cannot be construed as empirical descriptions of objects separate from the perceiver but only as reports of *how* the perceiver experiences his affections at a given time, it can plausibly be

---

[30] See Chisholm 1966, pp. 33–4.

[31] However, there are considerable differences in the ways in which various adverbial analysts defined the function of adverbially modified locutions. See, for example, Brentano 1924; Chisholm 1957; Cornman's extensive discussion of intensional statements in Cornman 1971; and 'Phenomenalism' in Sellars 1963, especially pp. 92ff.

maintained (or so the adverbial analysts think) that the perceiver has a peculiar authority regarding his reports of his own condition. While in the objectal model several descriptions can refer to the same *sensum* since this is construed as a mental *object*, in the adverbial model each report is supposed to identify one and only one 'way of appearing'.

Third, as mentioned above, adverbial theories are spared the task of developing an elaborate ontology specifying the status of mental objects since they do not consider that *what* is sensed is distinct from *its being sensed*. On the other hand, it is usually assumed that adverbial analyses of perception cannot dispense with the subject of awareness. Indeed, few adverbial analysts would endorse Bertrand Russell's conclusion that the subject of awareness is a logical fiction.

Fourth, most proponents of the adverbial model consider adverbial first-person reports basic and autonomous sentences which constitute the epistemological foundation of empirical claims about the external world.

In what follows, I shall examine whether the adverbial model provides a satisfactory interpretation of the Cyrenaic position, by discussing successively these four points.

I maintained that, while the first-person present-tense passive verbs are equally applicable to perceivers and to inanimate objects and may describe both physical and mental states, the adverbial neologisms are properly used only with regard to perceivers and are coined to express primarily experiences (chapter 2, pp. 24–5). If this is correct, it indicates that the theory focuses on the awareness of internal states rather than on their physical aspects and that the adverbial phrases constitute the basis of Cyrenaic subjectivism. Assuming that this hypothesis is correct, there are grounds for comparing the Cyrenaic theory to an adverbial analysis of appearances.

On the one hand, the conversion of linguistic forms such as 'the fire is burning' and 'the honey is sweet' into phrases such as 'I am being burnt' and 'I am being sweetened' (Anonymous 65.33–6 [T3] and Plutarch 1120e [T1]) eliminate the use of substantival terms referring to physical objects (the fire, the honey), but are neutral with regard to the objectal and the adverbial models of interpretation.[32] For example, the expression 'I am being sweetened' could be analysed as 'I am perceiving a sweet *sensum*' and also as 'I am sensing sweetly'. On the other hand, the adverbial formulas can only be understood in terms of the adverbial model. 'I am being disposed whitely' recalls Chisholm's reports 'I sense

---

[32] I am grateful to David Charles for his comments on this point.

whitely' and 'I sense loudly', and indicates precisely 'a manner of appearing' rather than an object which appears. Thus, the Cyrenaics appear to share the concern of the adverbial analysts: how to avoid references to entities distinct from the perceiver, whether these are substances or objects of sensory awareness.

I maintained above (pp. 42–5) that the characterisation of the *pathē* as the sole objects of *katalēpsis* and the sole criteria of truth entails a conception of the *pathē* similar to foundationalist conceptions about self-presenting states: both are directly and immediately perceived, self-certifiable and incorrigible. A further parallel between the Cyrenaic analysis of perception and the adverbial model might clarify what exactly one is incorrigible about: the *manner* in which one is affected, not the phenomenal properties of what affects one. In both theories, one has privileged access to one's own condition (for example, being disposed whitely or sensing loudly), not to private objects of sensory awareness (for instance, mental images of patches of colour or of sounds). Consequently, neither theory is vulnerable to the objection that the perceiver's reports of what he perceives (sc. *sensa*) are empirical descriptions and therefore can be contested by the descriptions of other observers as well. Instead, the adherents of both theories could argue that adverbial reports are referentially opaque, since they merely identify an internal state without referring to the object that may or may not be involved in it and that, therefore, the cognitive authority of the perceiver remains intact.[33]

In chapter 2, section II, I mentioned that the Cyrenaics did not directly tackle ontological questions. The absence of an elaborate ontology could be the consequence of an assumption which also characterises the adverbial model, namely that an adverbial analysis of perception does not require the support of an elaborate ontological background determining, among other things, the status of the objects of perception.

In these respects, I find the adverbial model suitable for interpreting the Cyrenaic theory in modern terms: it throws light on the insights behind the epistemological enterprise of the Cyrenaics, explains what precisely the apprehension of the *pathē* consists in, and supplies a plausible account of the incorrigibility of autobiographical reports. However, there are fundamental differences between the Cyrenaic doctrine and the modern adverbial theories, principally in their attitudes towards the possibility of acquiring empirical knowledge.

---

[33] Glidden made this claim with regard to the *homo mensura* doctrine of Protagoras in 'Protagorean relativism and the Cyrenaics' (Rescher 1975, pp. 113–40), but he rejected it later in 'Protagorean obliquity' (Glidden 1988).

The foundationalist versions of the adverbial model illustrate an approach to perception which developed initially as a result of objections to the analysis of perception in terms of *sensa*. As mentioned above, the main point at issue was whether a clear distinction could be drawn between objects of awareness and acts of awareness, or whether sensing was really of sense-contents, rather than sensory objects. Notwithstanding this controversy, both versions of sensory foundationalism, as well as the various critiques of them, are encountered in the context of seriously intended attempts to understand and explain reality.

According to most adverbial analysts, the inner episodes, often characterised as 'ways of appearing', are regularly attached to physical objects possessing certain physical properties. Each particular category of such episodes, for example the condition of sensing redly, is causally related to a real property, for example physical redness, which is the power of causing normal perceivers to 'be appeared to redly'. Accordingly, the adverbial locutions referring to these inner episodes derive from recasting a sentence such as 'I sense a red triangle' into sentences such as 'I sense a-red-triangle-ly' and 'I have an (of a red triangle) sensation'. The complex predicates[34] employed in that kind of talk form part of a theory about what it is 'to sense a-red-triangle-ly': it is a state of the kind which in standard conditions is caused in normal perceivers by objects which have the properties of being red and of being triangular.[35] Perceptual states such as 'sensing a-red-triangle-ly' are epistemically fundamental precisely on account of their causal link with the extensional properties of real objects. And the adverbial sentences referring to them are basic in the sense that they provide necessary conditions for empirical knowledge.[36]

On the other hand, the Cyrenaics rejected the possibility of forging epistemic links between the content of the *pathē* and the properties of the objects that may have caused them. Although they considered the *pathē* and the neologisms expressing them self-evident and self-certifiable, they did not consider them foundational to any *further* knowledge or belief claims. The reports of the *pathē* were not intended to support claims and to advance explanations about states of affairs in the world. In contrast to the adverbial analysts who concentrated on sense-

---

[34] See Sellars' definition and use of 'analogical predicates' and 'analogical beliefs'.

[35] Relevant to that idea are issues such as the relation of the technical vocabulary of the adverbial analysts to descriptive discourse, its status with regard to ordinary language and its explanatory power. On this last subject, see 'Empiricism and philosophy of mind', in Sellars 1963, pp. 127–96.

[36] It is precisely this idea that constituted the target of the most vigorous criticisms against various forms of foundationalism.

contents related to the perception of *objects* (for example, a red triangle), the Cyrenaics focused on the manner in which one is affected by the perception of qualities or properties (for example, red) and left unexplored important issues related to the perception of objects.

These differences between the Cyrenaics and the adverbial analysts are further illustrated by their respective uses of the concepts of standard conditions and normal perceivers. While the adverbial analysts employ these concepts in order to draw an epistemological connection between a subjective state, such as 'sensing a-red-triangle-ly' and a thing, such as a red and triangular object, the Cyrenaics appeal to them precisely in order to sever that connection.

That we really are not all moved (by the external objects) in the same way because of the different constructions of our senses, is clear from the cases of people who suffer from jaundice or ophthalmia and from those who are in a normal condition; for just as some people are affected yellowly, others redly and others whitely from one and the same object, likewise it is also probable that those who are in a normal condition are not moved in the same manner by the same things because of the different construction of the senses, but that the person with grey eyes is moved in one way, the one with blue eyes in another, and the one with black eyes in another yet different way. It follows that the names which we assign to things are common but our *pathē* are private. (Sextus, *M* vii.198 [T6b])

According to this passage, the Cyrenaics demolished the credibility of normal perceivers partly on the strength of an analogy between their reports and the perceptual reports of non-normal perceivers who are in peculiar physical conditions. The argument is that, even if various normal perceivers use the same words to express their *pathē* of the same object, it is likely that, in fact, the *pathē* which they receive from the same object are different in content.[37] This point is driven home by comparing what *may* happen in the case of normal perceivers with what *admittedly* happens in the case of people whose perceptual capacity is distorted by disease.[38] For the analogy to work, it must be postulated

[37] The Cyrenaics do not explain the fact that normal perceivers with variously coloured eyes all say, e.g., 'white' in the same circumstances, whereas abnormal perceivers say, e.g., 'yellow'; see chapter 8, pp. 105–11, and also the discussion of the Cyrenaic doubts about other minds in chapter 7, pp. 95–6.

[38] Notice that the claim that perceivers with variously coloured eyes may be affected differently by the same object appears to imply that eyes have an objective colour, and that this colour has a causal influence on the *pathē* that the perceivers receive (although we cannot know what this influence may be). On the Cyrenaic assumption that each perceiver is equipped with a particular sensory apparatus through which he comes into contact with the world, see chapters 2 (pp. 21–2), 7 (pp. 89 ff.), and 10 (pp. 132–3).

that both categories of perceivers are in fact on an equal epistemic footing: none of them possesses the kind of qualifications that would secure the veridicality of their perceptual reports.

These differences exemplify the extent to which Cyrenaic epistemological views are conditioned by the ethical goals of the school. I submit that the Cyrenaics did not work out the foundationalist implications of their claim that autobiographical perceptual reports are infallible, certain and incorrigible, precisely because they were not ultimately interested in exploring possible causal links between perceptual states and empirical objects. The same holds for their reluctance to apply the adverbial model to the perception not only of properties but of physical objects, and for the scepticism that they cast on the concepts of normal conditions of perception and of normal perceivers. Their aim was not to examine whether and in what conditions sense-contents yield information about the world. Nor was it, more broadly, to secure and increase whatever knowledge of reality we have got. They use the adverbial model only in so far as it serves the purposes of eliminating talk about empirical objects and of establishing the infallible awareness of the *pathē*. But once they have accumulated sufficient features in favour of trusting the *pathē*, they are motivated to go no further.

V    THE RESTRICTION OF THE CRITERION

The interpretation proposed above suggests that the *pathē* are epistemologically important in their own right, for their contents are directly given to consciousness and are incorrigibly true. In this section I shall argue that by applying the concepts of truth and cognition to the *pathē*, the Cyrenaics modified the grammar of Greek epistemic terms in significant ways. I shall start by making a few additional remarks regarding the views of the major Hellenistic schools on the criterion and, subsequently, by comparing them to the Cyrenaic position.

Despite their differences, the Epicurean and Stoic theses concerning the criterion[39] presuppose a systematic correlation between the truth of

---

[39] On the Stoic conception of *katalēptikē phantasia* and on the criticisms levelled against it see, for example, F. H. Sandbach, 'Phantasia katalēptikē', in Long 1971, pp. 9–21; J. Annas, 'Truth and knowledge', in Schofield, Burnyeat and Barnes 1980, pp. 84–104, and 'Stoic epistemology', in Everson 1990, pp. 184–203; P. Couissin, 'The Stoicism of the New Academy', in Burnyeat 1983, pp. 31–63, and M. Frede, 'Stoics and Sceptics on clear and distinct impressions' in pp. 65–93 of the same volume (reprinted in Frede 1987, pp. 151–76); Long and Sedley 1987, especially vol. I, pp. 239–41, 249–53 and 256–9.

the criterion and the reality of what it reports. We saw above (pp. 34–7) that the Hellenistic criteria are self-evident and true propositions about objects or states of affairs in the world, and the knowledge achieved through the application of the criteria is objective knowledge. Both the Epicureans and the Stoics then belong to the mainstream Greek philosophical tradition, according to which truth and knowledge are always *of something external to the perceiver.*[40]

It is important to notice that Carneades' attack on the Stoic criterion and Sextus' use of both the Stoic and the Epicurean concepts of the criterion indicate that the Academic and the Pyrrhonian Sceptics also belong to the same tradition. For they too presuppose that truth and knowledge (if they exist) are always of things external to the perceiver.

According to Sextus, Carneades argued that, if the criterion existed, it should be sought in the *pathos* of the soul caused by the *enargeia*, which would be indicative both of its own content and of the evident object causing it (*M* VII.161–2); but although every *pathos* reveals its own content, not every *pathos* is truthful with regard to the external object that caused it (*M* VII.162–5); thus, no impression (*phantasia*) could serve as a criterion and, in fact, none of the proposed criteria secures truths about real objects (*M* VII.159). So, Carneades' conclusion that there is no criterion is established on the assumption that a criterion must be self-evident not only about itself, but principally about things in the world.

Sextus is our main source on the attitude of the neo-Pyrrhonists towards what would count as a criterion. Like Carneades, Sextus appears to assume that if there existed a criterion through which truths could be established, these would be truths about objects in the world. But in addition, he makes clear that representational states whose contents cannot be checked against the reality of the things which they represent do not qualify as criteria. Although the perceiver's appearances (*phainomena*) and *pathē* may be said to have an *enargeia* intrinsic to them, Sextus does not consider that they yield truth or knowledge. This point is illustrated by his comments on the Cyrenaic views about knowledge in *PH* 1.215 and in *M* VII.198.

The principal source of Sextus' presentation of Cyrenaic epistemol-

---

[40] See Burnyeat 1982. Against the position that, in Greek philosophical thought, truth means realist truth and the consequent assumption that what exists exists independently of the perceiver's mind, see Groarke 1990. Chapters 7 and 8 argue against Groarke's central claim that the epistemology of the Cyrenaics is an analogue of modern idealism.

ogy in *M* VII.191–200 [T6b] is probably the work *Canonica* by Antiochus of Ascalon.[41] However, there are parts of this text in which Sextus, I think, is not following Antiochus, but either is making the argument out for himself or is following some other Sceptic (quite likely Aenesidemus, who is Sextus' probable source here and whose sources in turn are Posidonius and Antiochus). The main passage whose source seems to me to be a Sceptic, not Antiochus, starts at *M* VII.193 (ὅθεν ἤτοι) and ends at *M* VII.194 (οὐ φαινόμενον δὲ ὑμῖν) or at *M* VII.195 (παμπληθεῖς αἰτίας). It runs as follows.

Hence we must posit either that the *pathē* are *phainomena* or that the things productive of the *pathē* are *phainomena*. And if we call the *pathē phainomena*, we must declare that all *phainomena* are true and apprehensible. But if we call the things productive of the *pathē phainomena*, all *phainomena* are false and inapprehensible. For the *pathos* which occurs in us reveals to us nothing more than itself. Hence, if one must speak but the truth, only the *pathos* is actually a *phainomenon* to us. But what is external and productive of the *pathos* perhaps exists, but it is not a *phainomenon* to us. (Sextus, *M* VII.194 [T6b])

The Sceptical interpolation may end at this point,[42] or it may extend to the following paragraph, which argues for the thesis that the external object is inapprehensible in a way reminiscent of the Ten Modes. 'We are all unerring with regard to our own *pathē*, but we all err with regard to the external object. And those are apprehensible, but this is inapprehensible because the soul is too weak to distinguish it on account of the places, the distances, the motions, the changes, and numerous other causes' (Sextus, *M* VII.195 [T6b]).[43]

Both the form of the argument in *M* VII.193–5 and the description of the *pathē* in terms of *phainomena* throughout the passages cited above seem to me to support my hypothesis that Sextus or some other Sceptic is trying to make sense of the Cyrenaic position for himself and for his audience. Assuming that this is so, I shall concentrate on the fact that, in these passages, the concept of *pathos* has been replaced by the key

---

[41] See Appendix, p. 154.     [42] See Tsouna 1988, pp. 191–6.

[43] The term *phainomenon* and its cognate verb *phainesthai* reappear a few lines below, in a passage summarising the Cyrenaic views about the inadequacy of language to communicate the *pathē*, which may constitute a brief comment on the semantic views of the Cyrenaics added by Sextus on his own account.

Since no *pathos* is common to us all, it is hasty to declare that what appears of this kind to me (τὸ ἐμοὶ τοῖον φαινόμενον) appears of this kind (τοῖον φαίνεται) to my neighbour as well. For perhaps I am constituted in such a way as to be whitened by the external object which meets with my senses, but another person has the senses constructed in such a way as to have been disposed differently. In any case, the *phainomenon* is surely not common to us all. (Sextus, *M* VII.197 [T6b])

concept of Pyrrhonian Scepticism, the *phainomenon*. Sextus or his source seems to have thought that the term *phainomenon* was an adequate translation of *pathos* due to the self-evident character both of the *pathē* and of the *phainomena*: 'the *pathos* which occurs in us reveals to us nothing more than itself. Hence, if one must speak but the truth, only the *pathos* is actually a *phainomenon* to us' (Sextus, *M* VII.194 [T6b]). The motive for this reformulation may have been to render the Cyrenaic doctrine palatable to a contemporary audience, which presumably was familiar with the terminology of the Sceptics.

The questions which I shall examine are whether the reformulation of the Cyrenaic claim in Pyrrhonian jargon was philosophically success-ful and whether it has any important implications regarding the nature of the Cyrenaic criterion. I shall argue that there are two central features of the Cyrenaic position which are not captured by defining the *pathē* as *phainomena*: that the perception of the *pathē* should be analysed in terms of how one is affected, not in terms of what affects one, and that the Cyrenaic claim that only the *pathē* are true and apprehensible is an epistemological claim.

The problem connected to the first point is apparent at the level of grammar. On the one hand, *pathos* derives from the verb *paschein* ('to undergo', 'to suffer a change') and entails that it is *I* who am affected somehow, rather than *something* which affects me. On the other hand, *phainomenon*, 'appearance', is a cognate of the verb *phainesthai*, whose standard syntactical construction is *phainetai ti moi* ('something appears to me'), which implies that there is something distinct from the per-ceiver which *appears* to the perceiver. While expressions containing the terms *pathos* and *paschō* focus on the condition of the affected subject, expressions employing the term *phainomenon* or a grammatical form of *phainetai ti moi* are centred on what appears to the subject. If I am correct in maintaining that the Cyrenaic locutions formed by *paschō*, or a near synonym such as *diatithemai*, and an adverb should be construed as non-relational reports,[44] then they cannot be adequately replaced by appear-sentences. That is because, in the context of Pyrrhonian Scepticism, appearances may be perceptual or non-perceptual: for example, a wall may appear tall, a woman beautiful, an argument valid, an idea true and a solution practical.[45] But in all cases, the Sceptic speaks of *something* that appears to him to be such-and-such; he

---

[44] See the parallel between the Cyrenaic position and the views of the adverbial analysts in pp. 47–53.
[45] See Annas and Barnes 1985, pp. 23–4.

does not report how he is affected himself when he is receiving an appearance.[46]

The decision to use or to avoid substantival terminology in perceptual reports reflects a deep philosophical difference between the Cyrenaics and the Sceptics. While the Cyrenaic reports of the *pathē* are part of an epistemological position focused on the analysis of internal states and our awareness of them, the appear-sentences of the Sceptics are non-cognitive utterances and do not correspond to any model of analysis of sensory awareness.[47] If the term *phainomena* in Sextus, *M* VII.194 [T6b] is employed in a non-cognitive sense, it is philosophically misleading to attribute to the Cyrenaics the thesis that all *phainomena* are true and apprehensible. That implies either that the Cyrenaics attached no epistemological importance to the *pathē* (which, I have argued, is contradicted by the evidence), or that the Sceptics held the dogmatic position that we have incorrigible knowledge of what appears to us (in which case they would be inconsistent).

Indeed, Sextus' testimony in *PH* I.215 suggests that Sextus or his source used the term *phainomena* in *M* VII.194 in a non-cognitive sense and wrongly applied it to the Cyrenaic theory.

Some people (*tines*) maintain that the Cyrenaic doctrine is the same as Scepticism, since it too (*kakeinē*) says that only the *pathē* are apprehensible. In fact, it differs from Scepticism because the former maintains that the moral end is pleasure and the smooth movement of the flesh, whereas we say that it is tranquillity, wherefore it is opposed to their conception of the moral end. For whether pleasure is present or absent, the person who affirms that pleasure is the moral end submits to troubles, as I have concluded in the chapter about it. Besides, we suspend judgement about the external objects, as far as the arguments go.[48] The Cyrenaics, on the other hand, affirm that the external objects have an inapprehensible nature. (Sextus, *PH* I.215 [T6a])

It is unclear who were the people who maintained that the Cyrenaic doctrine is the same as Scepticism. They may have been philosophers of the first century BC who attempted to undermine the originality of

---

[46] However, it should be emphasised that the Sceptics do not assume that what appears or what is apparent to the perceiver is a peculiar sort of entity, such as a sense-datum. To register appearances is simply to register the way that various things or states of affairs appear, as opposed to the way in which they really are.

[47] Regarding the two models discussed above, the Pyrrhonian's attitude to appearances cannot be understood either in terms of the objectal model or in terms of the adverbial model. A different approach is suggested in Chisholm 1941.

[48] I translated the formula ὅσον ἐπὶ τῷ λόγῳ by the expression 'so far as the arguments go': see Frede 1987, p. 188. For a detailed study and interpretation of this formula, see J. Brunschwig, 'The ὅσον ἐπὶ τῷ λόγῳ formula in Sextus Empiricus', in Brunschwig 1994, pp. 244–58.

Aenesidemus' method by pointing out that it had been invented approximately two centuries before him by a Socratic school, not by
Pyrrho, who was the alleged founder of Scepticism. Alternatively, Sextus may refer to historiographical writings which compared the two
movements.

Also, it is not clear to me precisely what the thesis of these anonymous
thinkers is: the *kai* ('too') included in the word *kakeinē* ('it too', i.e., the
Cyrenaic doctrine) may mean that, in the opinion of 'some people'
(*tines*), the Sceptics also said, in so many words, that the *pathē* alone are
apprehensible, or only that the Cyrenaic position amounts to Scepticism. At any rate, in the passage cited above Sextus contests their claim
by pointing out the respects in which the Cyrenaics are dogmatists.

Sextus seems willing to concede that a common point between the
two groups of philosophers is that they both consider the *pathē* alone
apprehensible, *katalēpta*.[49] *Katalambanō* and its cognates usually occur in
the context of Sextus' dialectical arguments and in connection with
dogmatic theories (see, for example, *PH* 1.126, ii.96, 99, iii.51, 52; *M*
viii.176, x.299). But they are also used occasionally in the expository
parts of Sextus' writings which present the methodology of Scepticism.
In order to specify the sense in which the Sceptic may say that the *pathē*
are apprehensible without committing himself to dogmatism, we must
examine the nature of the Sceptical formulas (*skeptikai phōnai*), as well as
some passages which refer explicitly to the Sceptic's *pathē*.

Sextus records that, although many of the Sceptical formulas exhibit
the character of dogmatic assent or denial, in fact they do not carry their
proper meaning – they are not used *kyriōs* – but are used in an undifferentiated and, as it were, improper sense (*adiaphorōs kai katachrēstikōs*:
*PH* 1.191).[50] In this context, speaking *kyriōs* entails accepting the dogmatic presuppositions of ordinary language, according to which the
Sceptical formulas would be intended as truth-claims (or as parts of
truth-claims) about the states of affairs designated by ordinary linguistic

---

[49] The argument starting with 'since' (*epeidē*) is put forward by 'some people' (*tines*) , the people
whom Sextus is going to criticise. So, one might object that Sextus does not concede their point
that the Sceptics, as well as the Cyrenaics, say that the *pathē* alone are apprehensible (or
alternatively that, by making this claim, the Cyrenaic doctrine amounts to Scepticism). However, notice the beginning of the following sentence: 'in fact (*de*) , it differs from Scepticism, since
(*epeidē*) the former maintains that the moral end is pleasure'. This transition indicates, I think,
that Sextus does not contest that Sceptics and Cyrenaics share a common attitude with regard to
the apprehensibility of the *pathē*; he only contests that this attitude constitutes adequate grounds
for holding that the Cyrenaic doctrine is the same as Scepticism.

[50] On Sextus' conception of what it is to use a term *kyriōs* and what it is to use it *katachrestikōs*, see M.
Burnyeat, 'The Skeptic in his place and time', in Rorty, Schneewind and Skinner 1984, pp. 234ff.

terms. On the other hand, speaking *katachrēstikōs* implies that the Sceptics will use assertive discourse without intending to make any assertion, but simply in order to express, in respect of the Sceptical formulas themselves, their *pathos* (*PH* I.190) and what appears to them (*to phainomenon*: *PH* 1.191).

This distinction between the proper and the catachrestic or improper uses of an assertion applies to all Sceptical formulas, including the phrases 'all things are inapprehensible' (*panta akatalēpta*: *PH* 1.200) and 'I am in a state of inapprehension' or 'I do not apprehend' (*akatalēptō* or *ou katalambanō*: *PH* 1.201). The statement that all things are by nature inapprehensible should be understood *katachrēstikōs*, as the non-assertive report that 'all the non-evident matters of dogmatic enquiry which I have investigated appear to me inapprehensible' (*PH* 1.200). And the statements that 'I am in a state of inapprehension' and 'I do not apprehend' should be construed non-epistemically, as 'indicative of an idiosyncratic condition in which the Sceptic, for the time being, abstains from affirming or denying any non-evident matter of enquiry' (*PH* 1.201).

Thus, it could be argued that the assertion which Sextus acknowledges as common ground between the Sceptics and the Cyrenaics is used not in an assertive but in a catachrestic way, to record that, until now, it appears to both that they have apprehended nothing but their *pathē*. However, one might object that, by conceding that they have apprehended at least as much as their *pathē*, the Sceptics grant that they know some things to be true and, therefore, can be accused of dogmatism. The reason why Sextus does not envisage such an objection is, I suggest, that he does not consider that the apprehension of one's *pathē* or of one's appearances, properly speaking, amounts to cognition.

Sextus' discussion of the question whether the Sceptic dogmatises (*PH* 1.13–15) confirms that the Sceptics did not assign to the *pathē* a cognitive status. Sextus distinguishes between a broad sense of 'dogma', according to which dogma is the approval of or assent to things such as one's *pathē*, and a narrow sense, according to which dogma is assent to the non-evident objects of enquiry (*PH* 1.13). He records that, although the Sceptics assent to nothing that is non-evident, they do give assent to the *pathē* forced upon them by impressions and would not say, for example, 'It seems that I am not feeling hot or cold' when in fact they are feeling hot or cold (ibid.). But as it turns out, the broad or catachrestic sense of dogma is not truly dogma for, in acknowledging 'things which move [them] affectively and drive [them] compulsorily to assent' (*PH* 1.193), the Sceptics simply announce their *pathē* non-dogmatically (*adoxastōs*) without affirming anything about the external objects (*PH* 1.15).

Sextus makes similar remarks about the Sceptics' attitudes with regard to the *phainomena*. They too consist in involuntary impressions forcing assent to their content (*PH* 1.19), are announced non-dogmatically (*PH* 1.15), involve no account of whether the thing which appears is really such as it appears (*PH* 1.19), and dictate a certain line of reasoning pointing to a satisfactory way of living (*PH* 1.17). It seems that the Sceptics did not clarify the relation between the *pathē* and the appearances, the *phainomena*, in the context of the Sceptical method. Some passages indicate that the *pathē* constitute a sub-category of appearances (*PH* 1.17, 23–4), while others suggest that the *phantasia* of each appearance lies in an involuntary *pathos*, in virtue of which the appearance remains uncontested (*PH* 1.19, 22). This ambiguity may be due to the Sceptics' concern to avoid specifications which might be construed as dogmatic. But it may also reflect the assumption that the *phainomena* and the *pathē* can often be mentioned interchangeably, since both are conceived as non-cognitive states.

Such an assumption may lie behind the fact that, in *PH* 1.215, Sextus does not contest the claim that the Sceptics and the Cyrenaics share a common attitude with regard to the *pathē*; and it also may have led him to identify misleadingly the Cyrenaic *pathē* with *phainomena* in *M* VII.194 [T6b]. In both instances, Sextus blurred, I think, what is really revolutionary about the epistemological views of the Cyrenaics. In contrast to the other Greek philosophers, they believed that the only truths that really matter are not of external objects but of internal states. Consequently, they redefined the concept of truth so as to include the awareness of internal states and examined specific problems concerning the nature and apprehension of such states. In this respect, they can be rightly considered, I believe, the forerunners of modern subjectivism.[51]

At this point, we may re-examine the question whether the Cyrenaics and the Sceptics share the same conception of the criterion. The answer is, I suggest, that they do not. On the one hand, in neither case do the *pathē* regulate beliefs about how things really are. On the other hand, the Sceptics suggested that the criterial power of the *pathē* is entirely practical and involves no truth claims at all, while the Cyrenaics held that the

---

[51] Perhaps the relevance of their position to modern epistemology could be put this way: like the moderns, they focused on the subjective aspects of internal states and assigned to them epistemological importance in their own right; unlike the moderns, they did not construe subjectivity in terms of the mind–body distinction.

*pathē* reveal their own content and involve incorrigible awareness of the condition of the perceiver at the time when a *pathos* takes place.

Antiochus of Ascalon appears to have captured this point in his history of the theories of the criterion, if he is indeed Sextus' source throughout the final doxographical section of *M* VII (141–260). The central notion of Antiochus' epistemology, *enargeia*, occurs in the closing paragraph which wraps up the Cyrenaic views about the criterion.

'Such are the teachings of the Cyrenaics who restricted the criterion (*systellontes to kritērion*) more than the school of Plato. For the latter considered it a compound of *enargeia* and reason, whereas the Cyrenaics confine (*horizousin*) it only to the *enargeiai* and the *pathē*' (Sextus, *M* VII.200).

The Cyrenaics did precisely that: they defended an over-condensed version of the criterion by limiting it to self-evident truths about internal states and by severing epistemic references to external objects.

CHAPTER 5

# The criticism of Aristocles of Messene

The restricted scope of the Cyrenaic criterion constitutes the target of the Peripatetic philosopher Aristocles of Messene, whose criticism of the Cyrenaic theory is reported by Eusebius.

At the outset, Aristocles sketches out the theory which he intends to attack in the following terms.

Next are those who claim that only the *pathē* are apprehensible; this was maintained by some philosophers from Cyrene.[1] These philosophers maintained that they know absolutely nothing, just as if a very deep sleep weighs down on them, unless somebody standing beside them struck them or pricked them. For they said that, when they are being burnt or cut they know that they are undergoing something. But whether the thing which is burning them is fire or that which is cutting them is iron they cannot tell. (Eusebius XIV.19.1 [T5])

Aristocles' objections are not targeted against the affirmation that the *pathē* are apprehensible, but against the *restrictive* claim that *only* they can be apprehended.[2] His goal is to show that the Cyrenaic position is inconsistent by arguing that we know many things in addition to our *pathē*, or that our awareness of *pathē* entails (or presupposes) that we know things about external objects.

---

[1] The phrase ἔνιοι τῶν ἐκ τῆς Κυρήνης is ambiguous. If it is rendered 'some of the members of the Cyrenaic school', it implies that the epistemological views of the Cyrenaics varied: some of them held the thesis that the *pathē* alone are apprehensible, while others did not. I did not opt for this translation, because there is no independent evidence that the positions of the Cyrenaic sects differed in matters of epistemology. I translate as 'some philosophers from Cyrene'. The passage distinguishes, I believe, between the Cyrenean philosophers who do not belong to the Cyrenaic school and those who do; only the latter held the position that the *pathē* alone are apprehensible. This interpretation leaves open the possibility that *all* Cyrenaics shared the same epistemological views about the apprehensibility of the *pathē*.

[2] Aristocles' criticism of this claim is doubtlessly motivated by his own epistemological stance, and especially by his unshakeable belief that knowledge can be achieved. See Heiland 1925, pp. 11–70.

## I  *PATHĒ* AND *LOGOI*

Aristocles' first argument is the following:

But then, one would immediately ask those who hold these views whether they know this at least, that they are undergoing and they are sensing something. For if they did not, they would not be able even to say that they know only the *pathos*; but again, if they do know this, then it is not true that only the *pathē* are apprehensible. For 'I am being burnt' is a locution (*logos*), not a *pathos*. (Eusebius xiv.19.2 [T5])

The point is that, whether the Cyrenaics concede that one knows the truth of a sentence concerning an individual *pathos* or not, they are bound to refute themselves: if they do, then they must admit that, in addition to the *pathē*, they know sentences about them to be true; if they do not, then they cannot affirm that they know even the *pathē*. The best way to evaluate the force of this argument is to ask what resources the Cyrenaics can summon in reply.

It is clear that if they denied that we are aware of undergoing a *pathos*, they would indeed be contradicting their thesis that we have incorrigible knowledge of the manner in which we are affected. The only option open to them would therefore be to refute Aristocles' claim that if I accept that I know that I am being burnt, I also must accept that I possess knowledge that goes beyond the scope of the *pathē*.

One way of replying to Aristocles would be to appeal to the peculiar nature of the *pathē* and the locutions (*logoi*) describing them. The Cyrenaics could argue that self-presenting states, such as the condition of my being or feeling burnt, and self-presenting propositions, such as 'I am being burnt', share common features which characterise no other category of states or sentences and which make it permissible to inter-substitute *pathē* and locutions about *pathē*.[3] My awareness of my being burnt entails that I know that my utterance 'I am being burnt' is true of myself; and also, my knowledge of the truth of this utterance entails that I have cognition of the *pathos* expressed by the *logos* in question. In both cases, that of the *pathos* itself and that of the *logos* expressing it, the content of my knowledge is the same, namely that I am being burnt. So the Cyrenaics could claim that, although Aristocles is right in pointing out that, strictly speaking, knowledge of my state of being burnt involves knowledge of the *logos* 'I am being burnt', he is wrong to infer that knowledge of that *logos* goes beyond the limits of the relevant *pathos*.

[3] For a similar claim, see Chisholm 1966, p. 23 and ch. 5.

However, Aristocles' argument could be considerably strengthened by pointing out that there is one *logos* concerning the *pathē* which cannot be known in that way, namely the restrictive assertion that only the *pathē* are apprehensible. This is not an autobiographical locution reporting an individual *pathos* that affects an individual perceiver at a given time, but an epistemological claim which is supposed to be true both of the *pathē* and of first-person reports describing them. This is a philosophically interesting point which, I believe, applies not only to the Cyrenaic doctrine, but also to subjectivism in general: there is something inherently problematic in the assertion that all truth is subjective; for while it purports to demolish the belief in the existence of objective truth, it puts itself forward as such a truth.[4]

The Cyrenaics might retort that the proposition 'only the *pathē* are apprehensible' is itself a subjective proposition, i.e., it states that an individual percipient is being affected in such a manner as to consider that the *pathē* alone can be known. But the idea of the 'meta-pathic' thesis being itself a *pathos* is not very palatable; for it is not clear in this case why anybody should think that the Cyrenaic approach to truth and knowledge is preferable to any other approach. Also, even if the proposition 'only the *pathē* are apprehensible' is intended to report the subjective impression of an individual person, one can argue that it is bound to assert that something is the case, and thus is bound to put itself forward as an absolute, non-subjective truth.[5]

A more promising line of answering questions concerning the epistemological basis of the Cyrenaic thesis is indicated by Sextus.

Just as, in all these cases it is true that people are undergoing this particular *pathos*, for instance they are being yellowed or reddened or doubled (sc. they are seeing an object as if it were double), but it is considered false that the thing which moved them is yellow or red or double, by the same token it is most reasonable (*eulogōtaton*) for us to assume that one can grasp nothing but one's own *pathē*. Hence, we must posit either that the *pathē* are *phainomena* or that the things productive of the *pathē* are *phainomena*. And if we call the *pathē phainomena*, we must declare that all *phainomena* are true and apprehensible. But if we call the things productive of the *pathē phainomena*, all *phainomena* are false and inap-

---

[4] Compare similar criticisms of various kinds of relativism. Regarding ancient relativism, the discussion is naturally focused on Plato's account of Protagorean relativism in the *Theaetetus*, and especially on *Theaetetus* 160e–171e. See, for example, Kerferd 1949, pp. 20–6; Passmore 1961, ch. 4; Burnyeat 1976, pp. 44–69; Waterlow 1977, pp. 19–36.

[5] Compare the remarks on the philosophical pertinence of Plato's avowedly problematic attack against Protagorean relativism in Burnyeat 1990, especially pp. 28–31.

prehensible. For the *pathos* which occurs in us reveals to us nothing more than itself. (Sextus, *M* vii.193–4 [T6b])

This passage suggests, I think, that the Cyrenaics can offer two separate answers. In the first place, their reply runs along inductive-analogical lines: in many cases, we can see that there is a distortion between the particular *pathos* affecting an individual person and the object productive of it as perceived by normal perceivers; therefore, it is very reasonable (*eulogōtaton*) to infer that we can apprehend only our *pathē*. In the second place, they can come up with a categorical or conceptual answer: the *pathos* takes place as an event within ourselves, so it is unable to reveal to us anything in addition to itself.[6]

## II AWARENESS OF THE *PATHĒ* AND AWARENESS OF ONESELF

One epistemological implication of the Cyrenaic position that the *pathē* are unitemporal events located in the present (chapter 2, pp. 15–17) is that one's incorrigible awareness of each *pathos* is strictly limited to the time unit during which it occurs. Aristocles' subsequent arguments aim to show, among other things, that the apprehension of the *pathē* involves knowledge which extends beyond the temporal limits of individual *pathē*. They focus on the identification of the *pathē* and their association with the affected percipient, the awareness of the affected percipient as a living being situated in time and place, and also the knowledge of external objects, including other people.

It is necessary that at least these three things exist together, the *pathos* itself, the thing that produced it and the subject undergoing it. Thus, the person apprehending the *pathos* would certainly sense the affected subject as well. For it cannot be that, if one happens to be warmed, one will know that one is being warmed but will not know whether oneself or one's neighbour is the person who is being warmed. One will also know if this happens now or last year, if it happened in Athens or in Egypt, if one is alive or dead, and further if one is a human being or a stone. (Eusebius xiv.19.3 [T5])

And further:

---

[6] I suggested that this part of the text (starting with *hothen* in *M* vii.193) may be composed by Sextus himself or by some other Sceptic, and that it attempts a philosophically unsuccessful reformulation of certain Cyrenaic claims in Sceptical jargon (chapter 4, section v, pp. 54–61). However, the assumption that the *pathē* are events that occur within individual perceivers is undoubtedly Cyrenaic; see chapter 2, pp. 21–2.

the person who is undergoing a *pathos* must perceive it either as something welcome or as an unwelcome *pathos*.[7] Then, by what means will one be able to tell that this is pleasure but this is pain? Or that one is undergoing something when one is tasting or seeing or hearing? Or when one is tasting something with the tongue, seeing with the eyes or hearing with the ears? (Eusebius XIV.19.5 [T5])

Aristocles appears to interpret the Cyrenaic conception of what it is to be aware of a *pathos* in a very narrow way. And he attempts to prove its inadequacy through two distinct but interconnected lines of arguments: first, that the apprehension of a *pathos* involves more than the plain awareness that a sensory event of a certain kind is taking place and, second, that a philosophically satisfactory conception of self-awareness requires factual knowledge.

According to Aristocles, the apprehension of a *pathos* such as being warmed or feeling pain entails at least the following things. (1) I am able to identify and individuate the kind of *pathos* which I am undergoing: being warmed as distinguished from turning cold, feeling pain as opposed to feeling pleasure, and so on.[8] (2) I can attribute that *pathos* to myself: it is *I* who am being warmed or who am feeling pain, and not my neighbour. (3) I can identify as *pathē* (or presumably, as *pathē* which *I* am undergoing) various sensings occurring through particular sensory channels, such as particular sensations of seeing, hearing and tasting. Finally, (4) I am aware of the sensory organs (eyes, ears, tongue) through which I experience these sensings. The argument seems to be that the apprehension of the *pathē*, as the Cyrenaics define it, covers (1), but not (2), (3) or (4); and since it is absurd to deny that, every time that we experience an affection, we possess knowledge of these elements, it follows that we do not apprehend our *pathē* alone.

To a certain extent, the Cyrenaics can meet that objection. They can agree with Aristocles that it is logically impossible to dissociate one's *pathos* from oneself (2),[9] and that the identification of *what* one is

---

[7] This sentence implies that there is no separate category of intermediate *pathē*. Nevertheless, I do not think that it constitutes an adequate basis for ruling out the existence of the intermediates, for the text suggests that the exclusive division of the *pathē* into pleasant and painful ones should be attributed to Aristocles, not to the Cyrenaics. Here, Aristocles is not presenting the Cyrenaic doctrine, but is drawing its logical implications in order to show that they are absurd.

[8] This is related to the question whether we are conscious of our own internal states. As mentioned above, the Cyrenaics appear to assume that we are. Compare the ambiguity of the Stoic position about the criterion which is reflected in scholarly debates. See, for example, M. Frede, 'Stoics and Skeptics on clear and distinct impressions', in Frede 1987, pp. 151–76, and J. Annas, 'Stoic epistemology', in Everson 1990, especially pp. 189ff.

[9] It is worth noticing that the verbal and adverbial neologisms expressing *pathē* may indicate, precisely, that the Cyrenaics realised the logical impossibility of dissociating a *pathos* from the

sensing (1) implies knowing *that* one is affected in a certain manner (3), and that one's sensing has a certain 'colour' or provenance (4). But they can point out that all these elements are built into the concept of apprehending the *pathē*: the richer that conception becomes, the more difficult it will be to prove that we are aware of other things than the *pathē*.

Aristocles' second line of argument focuses on elements principally related to the affected subject. In the passage cited above, four such features are mentioned: the time when one experiences a *pathos* (e.g., now or last year), the place in which one is located at the moment when a *pathos* affects one (e.g., in Athens or in Egypt), the organic condition of the perceiver (e.g., alive or dead) and the species to which one belongs (e.g., a human being or a stone).

Other similar remarks are spread throughout the critique.

It follows that they are ridiculous every time they say that these things have happened to them, but they do not know how or in what way. For in that case they would not be able to tell even whether they are human beings or whether they are alive. Consequently, neither could they tell whether they say or assert something. At this point, what could one tell to such people? Of course it is surprising if they do not know whether they are on earth or in the heavens. And it would be much more surprising if they do not know whether indeed four is more than three or what one and two make – and yet they affirm that they practise philosophy. They cannot even say how many fingers they have on their hands, or whether each one of them is one or many. Thus, they would not know their own name or their fatherland or Aristippus. They would not know whom they love or hate, or what they desire. Nor will they be able to tell whether they laughed or wept because one thing is funny and the other sad. So, it is obvious that they also do not understand what we are talking about at this very moment. But then, such people would not differ at all from peacocks or flies, although even they know the things which are in accordance with nature and the things which are not. (Eusebius XIV.19.5–7 [T5])

Thus, further elements related to the affected percipient are the knowledge of one's name and country, and the awareness of the parts of one's body (which often involves knowing how to count), of intentional states and their objects, of the time and content of one's discourse. Again, Aristocles appears to defend the thesis that these are pieces of factual knowledge which cannot be packed into the concept of the awareness of

subject undergoing it. In expressions such as 'I am whitened' and 'I am affected whitely', the affected subject is indicated either by the first-person singular personal pronoun or by the first-person singular passive ending of the verb.

individual *pathē*. For example, knowing that one is a living human being
involves a certain familiarity with biological concepts; knowing that
one's two hands have ten fingers implies that one knows how to count
and how to perform elementary mathematical calculations; and so on.

The force of his argument derives partly from the fact that, of the
elements of knowledge mentioned above, several pertain to our sense of
time and our conception of personal identity. The point is that the *pathē*
and the first-person present-tense reports of them involve some sense of
time and a conception of personal identity which transcends the limits of
individual unitemporal *pathē*: my report 'I am feeling pain' involves my
awareness that I am feeling pain *now and not yesterday*, and that it is I, a
human being and not a stone, who am having that feeling.

In reply, the Cyrenaics might claim that these elements are also
momentary *pathē*: at the present moment it strikes me that I am feeling
warm now, not yesterday;[10] and at the present moment, I am aware of
myself as a human being, not as a stone. An alternative (and not very
satisfactory) line of answer could be that the scope of the claim that only
the *pathē* are apprehensible is more limited than Aristocles assumes. It
primarily concerns the awareness of secondary qualities or properties
and what it can reveal about the empirical properties of objects in the
world, and does not cover issues such as one's sense of time and of
personal identity.

### III   AWARENESS OF *PATHĒ* AND APPREHENSION
### OF OBJECTS: THE *PATHĒ* AS GUIDES TO CONDUCT

I shall now turn to Aristocles' claim that the apprehension of a *pathos* also
involves knowledge of the object that caused it.

So one will also know (*eisetai*) what one is affected by, for people are acquainted
with (*gnōrizousi*) each other and they know the streets, the towns and nourishment. Again, the craftsmen know (*oidasi*) their tools, the doctors and the seamen
infer the things to come by means of signs (*sēmeiountai*), and the dogs discover
(*heuriskousi*) the tracks of wild animals. (Eusebius xiv.19.4 [T5])

This passage mentions cases regarding which, the author assumes, one
could not reasonably deny that one possesses information about states of
affairs in the world. The variety of epistemic terms employed makes it

---

[10] Compare the lines of response open to the proponents of the theory of flux in Plato's *Theaetetus*, in
refutation of the thesis that judgements containing predictions about the future cannot reasonably be considered relative to the person who is uttering them (178aff.). On this, see Burnyeat
1990, pp. 39–42.

clear that this information is equated with objective knowledge of various sorts, presumably on empirical grounds: it can be observed that acquaintances greet each other, that people recognise the street and the town in which they live and choose the appropriate kinds of food, that experts are often successful in the practice of their arts, and so on. Aristocles appears to argue that, if one grants that perceivers ordinarily know these things, one must also grant that they possess objective knowledge in addition to the subjective awareness of the *pathē*. Besides, the evidence suggests that he would be prepared to defend the stronger claim that knowledge of real objects is intrinsically connected to awareness of the *pathē*: one cannot be conscious of the latter without learning truths about reality. 'It is necessary that at least these three things exist together, the *pathos* itself, the thing that produced it and the subject undergoing it. Thus, the person apprehending the *pathos* would certainly sense the affected subject as well . . . and one will also know what one is affected by' (Eusebius xiv.19.3–4 [T5]).

The argument is complemented by some remarks suggesting that knowledge of the external causes of the *pathē* is crucial to practical choices.[11] 'And how do they know that they ought to choose this thing (*todi*) but avoid the other? In fact, if none of these things stirred them, they will have no impulse and no desire. But then, they would not be animals either' (xiv.19.5 [T5]). Thus, according to Aristocles, mere experiences cannot offer any practical guidance regarding the objects inciting them: what we choose and avoid are *things in the world*, not private feelings. The remark is intended to apply specifically to pleasure and pain (xiv.19.5) and implies that the epistemological thesis that only the *pathē* can be known undermines the core of Cyrenaic hedonism. If pleasure is the only good to be sought for its own sake, its achievement requires that we possess information about the external objects which may cause it; since the Cyrenaics declare them to be inapprehensible, they eliminate the grounds on which we perform individual choices leading to pleasure. Again, the implication is that in fact we cannot help knowing which objects are pleasurable and which are painful, and therefore it must be concluded that we apprehend other things beside our *pathē*.

These arguments cut to the heart of Cyrenaic scepticism. First, they aim to re-establish the causal link between the content of the *pathē* and the properties of the objects that they are supposed to represent, by

---

[11] Compare the arguments from the necessities of action and of practical life employed to combat ancient Scepticism.

maintaining that the *pathē* go together with their external causes and that the apprehension of the former entails knowledge of the latter. And second, they stress the importance of objective knowledge for practical conduct.

There are two ways in which one could get into position to reply to these criticisms. One way would be to distinguish between knowledge and belief and to claim that we do not have knowledge of people, streets, towns, etc., but merely entertain beliefs about them. One could argue that the cases of people acknowledging their social acquaintances, of crafts-men possessing certain skills and of hunters following the dogs in pursuit of the traces of wild animals are not cases of knowledge: we can have no certainty, but are often mistaken about such things. However, it seems unlikely that the Cyrenaics would take that line, for, as I pointed out in chapter I (pp. 3–4), they did not develop the epistemic distinction between knowledge and belief. And also, given the Socratic aspects of their ethics, they probably would not concede the point that part of our behaviour is organised around uncertain beliefs rather than around knowledge.

In fact, the evidence indicates that the Cyrenaics would take a different line. The point of the claim that only the *pathē* are apprehen-sible is not that we cannot have cognitive certainty about things in the world, but that we cannot have cognitive access to them. Hence, we cannot perform practical choices on rational grounds, but we must reorganise our everyday experience on the basis of our *pathē*: we live in an internal world and we manage as best we can.

Herculaneum papyrus 1251 supports the suggestion that this would be the general line of the Cyrenaic answer to Aristocles' thesis that the knowledge of what causes pleasure or pain is crucial for practical choices. Although the text requires considerable supplementation and the reconstruction of the argument is conjectural, it seems that columns I–III of the papyrus contain an Epicurean attack against various forms of anti-rationalism.[12] Columns II and III appear to focus on the Cyrenaics and other sceptics who, in the view of the Epicurean author, denied that moral choice may be grounded on knowledge or belief.

They claim that in truth no (judgement) takes precedence over any other, being persuaded that the great *pathos* of the soul occurs as a result of pain and that we thus accomplish our choices and avoidances by observing both (sc. bodily and mental pain). It is impossible that the joys arise in us in the same way and all together, in accordance with some expectation. (col. II.5–14 [T2])

---

[12] For the text, translation and interpretation of PHerc. 1251, cols. I–III, see Appendix, pp. 146–7.

Also,

Some people denied that it is possible to know anything. And further, they added that if nothing is present on account of which one should make an immediate choice, one should not choose immediately. Some other people, having selected the *pathē* of the soul as the moral ends and as not being in need of additional judgement based on further criteria, granted to everybody an authority, which was not accountable, to take pleasure in whatever they cared to name and to do whatever contributed to it. (col. III.2–14 [T2])

In column II, the point seems to be that if some judgements were more credible than others, we could use them as guides to, and justifications of, our moral choices; but in fact, no judgement is more probable than any other, including its contradictory, and therefore we are brought to perform our choices simply by following our *pathē*, i.e., in ways that cannot be rationally justified on the basis of knowledge or of probability.

Column III appears to relate the views of the Cyrenaics to the attitude of other sceptics.[13] Both consider that nothing can be known that could serve as a basis for rationally justifying one's actions, and both perform choices by attending to the *pathē*. The anti-rational character of the Cyrenaic doctrine is emphasised by the statement that it turned the hedonistic tenet that pleasure is the moral end into a licence to pursue pleasure indiscriminately and by all means. The text implies that this happened precisely because the Cyrenaics considered the *pathē* the *ultimate* criteria of choice, and rejected the rational calculation of the long-term implications of pleasure and pain (which characterises the Epicurean approach to action).

An anti-rationalistic explanation of practical conduct may also be indicated by the so-called Cradle Argument, which is attested in connection to the Cyrenaic doctrine. It points out that the principle of pleasure governs humans at an age when the will of nature is not yet depraved by non-natural factors, and it suggests that the mere observation of this behaviour proves the soundness of hedonism.

'That pleasure is the moral end is proved by the fact that, from an early age onwards, we welcome it (*oikeiousthai*) without making a deliberate choice (*aproairetōs*) and, once we obtain it, we seek nothing more and avoid nothing so much as its opposite, pain' (D.L. II.88 [T7c]). But 'some people may fail to choose pleasure because of some perversion' (D.L. II.89 [T7c]).

Although this type of argument is often used in Hellenistic philosophy

---

[13] Cf. the expressions 'some people' (*tines:* l.2) and 'some other people' (*tines de:* ll.6–7).

(notably by the Stoics and the Epicureans) in relation to rationalistic ethical theories,[14] it does not presuppose or entail a rationalistic interpretation of choice and action. In fact, the Cyrenaics may have used it to defend a different position: a very young person possesses little or no objective knowledge on the basis of which to deliberate, and yet is successful in seeking pleasure and avoiding pain by following the ways in which things impress him or her. This observation suggests that adults too may choose the right things and avoid the wrong ones merely by attending to the guidance of their *pathē*. If so, knowledge of external objects that produce the *pathē* is not only unreachable, but also unimportant for practical conduct.

[14] On the use of the Cradle Argument by the major Hellenistic philosophers, see J. Brunschwig, 'The Cradle Argument in Epicureanism and Stoicism', in Schofield and Striker 1986, pp. 113–44. For another interpretation of this argument, see D. Sedley, 'The inferential foundations of Epicurean ethics', in Giannantoni and Gigante 1996, pp. 303–39.

# II

*Scepticism*

# CHAPTER 6

# *The causes of the* pathē: *objects in the world*

## I THE ASSUMPTION OF THE EXISTENCE OF THE EXTERNAL WORLD

The thesis that the *pathē* alone can be known, while the nature of external objects is unknowable, raises questions concerning the scope of Cyrenaic scepticism. The most important one is whether the Cyrenaics challenged not only our knowledge, but also the existence, of anything external to the perceiver's *pathē*. If they did, and if they envisaged the hypothesis that each and every individual *pathos* may be a logical construction of one's mind and may have nothing to do with external reality, they prefigured a problem central to the formulation of modern scepticism, the problem of the external world.[1]

In what follows, I shall argue that, although they denied that we can have cognitive access to the properties of the external objects, they do not take the next step of challenging the existence of the objects themselves in a general and systematic way. At the outset, I should like to stress that I do not take a definitive position as to whether the Cyrenaics *need* the assumption that there is a reality external to the perceiver; the point is not so much that they need to presuppose it, but that they do not have a philosophical motive to raise doubts about its existence.

There is no evidence that the members of the school formulated definite views about the existence of external objects. However, the expressions they used to refer to the causes of the *pathē* offer insights into their assumptions regarding the existence of a reality external to the perceiver.[2]

A first group of expressions denoting objects consists of common

---

[1] On the formulation of the problem of the external world, see Descartes, *Meditations On the First Philosophy in Which the Existence of God and the Distinction between Mind and Body Are Demonstrated*, HR I, pp. 131–99, especially Meditations II (pp. 149–57), V (pp. 179–85) and VI (pp. 185–99).

[2] On the assumption of the existence of external reality in Greek philosophy, see Burnyeat 1982. Against the thesis that this assumption permeates Greek philosophy, see Groarke 1990.

nouns. For example, according to the anonymous commentator on Plato's *Theaetetus*, the Cyrenaics questioned the possibility of knowing the nature of fire, namely whether it has the capacity of burning everything that comes into contact with it, but did not question whether there is such a thing as fire: 'I apprehend that I am being burnt, but it is non-evident whether the fire is such as to burn. For if it were such, all things would be burnt by it' (Anonymous 65.33–9 [T3]). Also, Plutarch's testimony, according to which they refused to assert 'whether the honey is sweet or the young olive-shoot bitter or the hail chilly or the unmixed wine warm or the sun luminous or the night air dark' (Plutarch 1120e [T1]), suggests that they did not express doubts about the existence of such things as honey, olive-shoots, and so on. Such passages indicate that the Cyrenaics conceived of the ontological structure of external reality in a fairly conventional way: what they questioned was not whether things or classes of things in the world exist, but only whether they have the properties that an individual perceiver may attribute to them.

A second group consists of expressions which indicate in a general way that the causes of the *pathē* are external to the percipient, but which do not identify these causes by giving them the names of particular objects or classes of objects. The causes of the *pathē* are described as 'the things' or 'the objects',[3] 'the external objects' (τὰ ἐκτὸς ὑποκείμενα: Sextus, *PH* I.215 [T6a]), 'the thing which falls upon [our senses] from the outside' (τὸ ἔξωθεν προσπῖπτον: Sextus, *M* VII.197 [T6b]) and, elliptically, 'the things outside' (τὰ ἔξωθεν: Anonymous 65.31–2 [T3]; τὰ ἐκτός: Plutarch 1120e [T1]). The use of the definite article and the plural suggests that these expressions refer to a reality conceived as a plurality of discrete objects, not as an undifferentiated lump of matter. In any case, according to this group of texts, the Cyrenaics assumed the existence of a world external to the percipient, which may or may not have the ontological structure that ordinary people believe it has.

A third group is constituted by phrases describing the external objects in terms of their effects on the percipient. The causes of particular *pathē* or kinds of *pathē* are indicated by expressions such as as 'that which is burning [us]' (τὸ καῖον: Eusebius XIV.19.1 [T5]) and 'that which is cutting [us]' (τὸ τέμνον: ibid.); also, an external object may be specified in terms of what affects 'some people yellowly, others redly and others

---

[3] On the subject of 'the things' to which the *onomata* are supposed to apply, see chapter 8, pp. 105–7.

whitely' (Sextus, *M* vii.198 [T6b]) and of what moves 'the grey-eyed person in one way, the blue-eyed in another and the black-eyed in another yet different way' (ibid.). Regarding the *pathē* in general, their causes are 'the things productive of the *pathos* [in us]' (τὰ ἐμποιητικὰ τοῦ πάθους: Sextus, *M* vii.191 [T6b]); τὰ ποιητικὰ τῶν παθῶν: *M* vii.194 [T6b]), 'what is external and productive of the *pathos*' (τὸ ἐκτὸς καὶ τοῦ πάθους ποιητικόν: ibid.), 'what moves [us]' or 'what stirs [us]' (τὸ κινοῦν: *M* vii.193 [T6b]), 'what falls upon [us] from the outside' (τὸ ἔξωθεν προσπῖπτον: *M* vii.197 [T6b]). These locutions are entirely non-committal with regard to the identity of external objects: what is burning me may be fire or it may be something else, and the only thing that I can say about it is that it makes me feel burnt. Nonetheless, it does not raise doubts about the existence of things independently of our perceptions of them any more than the other two groups do.[4] The external objects are described exclusively by reference to the *pathē* that they cause.[5] For all these passages tell us, the Cyrenaics might have conceived of external reality as an undifferentiated substratum or lump of matter. But this would still be *something distinct and different* from the *pathē*: what is burning me (τὸ καῖον) is distinct from my being burnt (καίομαι) and does not exist in my own mind, but affects me *from the outside*.[6]

---

[4] This evidence is almost entirely disregarded by Groarke, who claims that 'the only plausible conclusion is that the Cyrenaics question all objects external to our impressions, presenting the problem of the external world in the modern sense' (Groarke 1990, p. 77).

[5] This may presuppose the use of some version of the causality principle: if I am feeling burnt, there is something over there which is burning me.

[6] Compare Descartes' treatment of the belief that nature and the independence of some ideas with regard to my will are good reasons for concluding that these ideas must proceed from objects outside me. He comments:

When I say that I am so instructed by nature [sc. to believe that a certain feeling is produced in me by something which is different from me], I merely mean a certain spontaneous inclination which impels me to believe in this connection, and not a natural light which makes me recognise that it is true. But these two things are very different. (HR i, p. 160)

And further:

As to the other reason, which is that these ideas must proceed from objects outside me, since they do not depend on my will, I do not find it any the more convincing. For just as these impulses of which I have spoken are found in me, notwithstanding that they do not always concur with my will, so perhaps there is in me some faculty fitted to produce these ideas without the assistance of any external things, even though it is not yet known by me; just as, apparently, they have hitherto always been found in me during sleep without the aid of any external objects. (HR i, p. 161)

Notice how Descartes detaches the veridicality of the content of a mental state from the natural inclination to believe that it is true; also, how he casts doubt on the existence of the external objects by introducing the hypothesis that one's ideas of them might be entirely one's own creation, whether one wills it or not.

## II   SOME COUNTER-EVIDENCE

In contrast to the evidence examined so far, there are three passages which might appear to raise doubts as to whether there exists a reality independently of the perceiver.

The first occurs in Sextus' account of Cyrenaic epistemology in *M* VII.191–200 [T6b]. It is found at the close of the passage cited above (chapter 4, p. 55), in which Sextus or his source attempts to reformulate the Cyrenaic thesis that the *pathē* alone are true and incorrigible, replacing the concept of *pathos* with that of *phainomenon*.

'Hence (*enthen*), if one must speak but the truth, only the *pathos* is actually a *phainomenon* to us. But what is external and productive of the *pathos* perhaps exists (*tacha estin on*), but it is not a *phainomenon* to us' (Sextus, *M* VII.193–4 [T6b]).

The crucial word here is 'perhaps' (*tacha*), which applies to the external cause of the *pathos*. The point might seem to be that not only is the external object which produces the *pathos* not self-evident, but it may not even exist; and we have no way of knowing whether it exists, for we have no cognitive access to anything but our *pathos*. The question is whether this sentence offers sufficient grounds for suspecting that the Cyrenaics in fact questioned whether things exist independently of their being perceived.

I do not think it does. First, if I am right in thinking that *M* VII.193–4 is a Sceptical interpretation of the Cyrenaic doctrine which is somewhat misleading,[7] the comment that the external cause of a *pathos* may exist and the implication that it also may not, should probably be attributed to Sextus or, conceivably, Aenesidemus, not to the Cyrenaics.

Second, even if the sentence containing the word *tacha* in VII.194 were attributed to the Cyrenaics, it does not raise the problem of the external world. It can be read, I think, as a sort of dialectical concession: let us admit for the sake of the argument that the external cause of the *pathos* exists, even so, it is not a *phainomenon* to us. Although this appears to suggest that the occurrence and content of an individual *pathos* may have no connection with reality, it is not generalised with regard to each and every *pathos* experienced by all perceivers at all times. On the other hand, the hypothesis that nothing exists outside our own experiences relies precisely on that sort of generalisation: if we are mistaken once in believing that what we perceive is an external object, we may be

---

[7] See chapter 4, pp. 54–61.

mistaken every time in inferring that there exists something external to our experiences.[8]

The remark that the external cause of the *pathos* may (but does not need to) exist concerns primarily, I think, cases of illusions and hallucinations. These constitute stock examples employed by various sceptics in order to shatter the credibility of the senses.[9] Sextus attests that the Cyrenaics used such arguments to illustrate our infallible awareness of the *pathē* and to oppose it to the inapprehensibility of external objects.

> Just as the sufferer from vertigo or from jaundice is stirred by everything yellowly, and the sufferer from ophthalmia is reddened, and the person who presses down his eye is stirred as if by two objects, and the madman sees Thebes as if it were double and imagines the sun double, and in all these cases it is true that they are undergoing this particular *pathos* but it is considered false that the thing which stirred them is yellow or red or double, likewise it is very plausible for us to assume that we can grasp nothing but our own *pathē*. (Sextus, *M* VII.193 [T6b])

Regarding the madman, his *pathē* might or might not be generated by an external object: he might receive them by looking at the city of Thebes and at the sun, or he might have such impressions without actually looking at any object. It is worth noticing that *M* VII.193–4 comes immediately after the examples of illusory and hallucinatory *pathē* cited above and starts with an inferential word, *hothen*. This indicates that the passage in question is some kind of comment[10] explaining further the Cyrenaic position discussed in the previous paragraphs.

---

[8] On the radical character of Cartesian scepticism, see in particular HR I, pp. 149–57 (Descartes' second Meditation). Notice that Descartes' reason for his radical doubt is not that there are some – or even many – things about which the senses are not fully reliable, or that the senses *can* be deceptive, or that suspension of judgement *can* be warranted in specific circumstances. His argument is rather that *every case* of sense-perception can be a case in which we are entirely deceived, and he could not have formed it without an appeal to the possibility of dreaming and to the hypothetical existence of a *malin génie*. It was the purely theoretical and insulated character of Descartes' enquiry that allowed him to take his doubts further than any sceptic before him and thereby raise the problem of the external world as we know it in its modern form. On the kind of examination to which Descartes subjects ordinary beliefs, and on the standards and procedures of his investigation, see Williams 1978, especially chs. 1, 2 and 4.

[9] A representative list of such examples is discussed in 4.324–461: jaundiced persons who see everything yellow, square buildings that look round at a distance, a moving ship that appears to stand still and the surroundings which we sail by to move, separate mountains that seem to be joined far in the horizon, a horse that stands still in the river and yet appears to move sideways, parts of oars submerged under water that seem bent, things that seem double when one presses one's eyeball, and so on. Such examples can be traced back to the early Sceptics, both inside and outside the Academy, and they appear again with the revival of Pyrrhonism. See, for instance, the uses of the example of jaundice in Sextus, *PH* I.44, 101 and 126. On the flaws of the actual arguments, see Annas and Barnes 1985, pp. 42f., 112ff. On the power of the argument from illusion in Scepticism, see most recently Hankinson 1995, pp. 21ff.

[10] See also the uses of the word *hothen* in Sextus, *M* VII.61, 162 and 174.

It might be suggested that in mentioning cases of illusions and hallucinations, the Cyrenaics aimed to cast doubt on the assumption that *pathē* ordinarily derive from our contact with external objects: other *pathē* may resemble hallucinations in that they may be creations of our own minds independent of the existence of anything external.[11] However, a closer look at *M* VII.192–4 will show that, in fact, they intended to bring out a different point, namely that the *pathē* experienced by normal persons are no more revelatory of the nature of external objects than the impressions of people suffering from jaundice, ophthalmia or madness.[12]

The second text that may point to doubts about the existence of external objects is a passage in which Sextus aims to demolish the musical theories and practices of the dogmatists.

The Cyrenaic philosophers claim that only the *pathē* exist (*hyparchein*) and nothing else. Thus, since sound is not a *pathos* but rather something capable of producing a *pathos*, it is not one of the things that exist (*ta hyparkta*). And the schools of Democritus and Plato, to be sure, by denying the existence of every sensory object, deny the existence of sound as well, since sound is taken to be a sensory object. (Sextus, *M* VI.52–3 [T6c])

In this passage, Sextus attributes to the Cyrenaics the thesis that only the *pathē* exist and nothing else.[13] It is clear that he considers it an ontological position, for he infers that the things productive of the *pathē* do not exist precisely because they are not *pathē*. If the Cyrenaics indeed maintained such a position, that would constitute evidence that they raised some form of the problem of the external world.

However, it seems to me that there is a good reason for doubting the credibility of this testimony, namely that the evidence that it gives is inconsistent with the major sources on the epistemology of the school, primarily *M* VII.191–200. While Sextus' main goal in *M* VII.191–200 is to present an accurate and detailed outline of the Cyrenaic doctrine, his purpose in *M* VI.52–3 is dialectical and consists in attacking the implicit belief of the professors of the art of music in the existence of sound. He reasons that if it is demonstrated that sound does not exist, it will be inferred that the musical notes, which are a species of sound, do not

---

[11] The arguments from illusion in their various forms can be truly powerful only if the sceptic can validly move from isolated occurrences of illusions or hallucinations to the conclusion that we may be constantly deluded. On the rationality of forming such a generalised hypothesis, see Putnam 1983, especially ch. 1.

[12] See chapter 7, p. 102.

[13] Compare Plutarch's comment on the Cyrenaic position: τὸ φαίνεται τιθέμενοι, τὸ δ' ἐστὶν μὴ προσαποφαινόμενοι περὶ τῶν ἐκτός (1120d [T1]). Notice that the ἐστὶν in this sentence is predication and not existence, as Plutarch's account in 1120 eff. shows.

exist; and if these do not exist, musical theory, which consists in the study of musical notes, does not exist either. Following the standard strategies of Scepticism, Sextus sets out to demonstrate the first premiss of the argument by opposing to the musicians' dogmatic belief that sound exists other beliefs of dogmatic philosophers which imply the non-existence of sound, namely the views of the Cyrenaics Democritus and Plato. Thus, Sextus had a philosophical motive for attributing to the Cyrenaics the position mentioned in *M* vi.53: while the epistemological claim of the knowability of the *pathē* could not be used as a basis for the inference that there is no such thing as sound, the ontological claim that the *pathē* alone exist could.[14]

The presence of such a motive explains but, of course, does not in itself discredit Sextus' testimony in *M* vi.52–3. What does mar its credibility is Sextus' misconstrual of the positions that he ascribes to Democritus and Plato for the same purpose. It is still disputable how far Democritus intended to go by denying that flavour and colour are 'real' – a denial that must almost certainly cover sounds as well. But at least with regard to Plato, we are on safe ground: although he does explicitly deny that the sensible world has being and argues that it has only becoming, it is a gross oversimplification to say that it is not real, as Plutarch points out (1115d ff.).

The third passage comes from St Augustine's treatise *Against the Academics* and appears to anticipate Descartes' device for generalising doubts about the existence of anything external to the mind.

This I say, that a person, when he is tasting something, can swear with good faith that he knows through his own palate that this is sweet, or to the contrary, and he cannot be brought away from that knowledge through any Greek trickery. Who would be so shameless as to say to me when I am licking something with delight: 'Maybe you are not tasting, but this is a dream'? Do I resist? But that would delight me even if I were asleep. And so, no likeness of false things confuses that which I said I know, and an Epicurean or the Cyrenaics may perhaps say many other things in favour of the senses, against which I have observed that nothing was said by the Academics. (Augustine, *Contr.Acad.* iii.11.26 [T9])

St Augustine's position might be thought relevant to the Cyrenaic attitude regarding the existence of the external world in so far as it introduces some version of the dreaming hypothesis and might appear

---

[14] Again, Groarke takes none of these factors into account, when he uses *M* vi.53 as solid evidence for the thesis that the Cyrenaics raised the problem of the external world in the modern sense. See Groarke 1990, p.77.

to mention the Cyrenaics in this context. However, a closer look at the text removes that impression. St Augustine's argument is that subjective states, such as the condition in which something appears sweet or tastes sweet, yield firm and certain knowledge, *precisely because* they are subjective; this knowledge is immune to scepticism, because it cannot be affected by the possibility that I may be dreaming: the proposition 'This[15] appears sweet' is as true of appearances in my dreams as it is when I am awake.

The idea that subjective states give unshakeable knowledge and the dreaming hypothesis are important steps towards the formulation of the Cartesian conception of the mind and of the radical scepticism which Descartes introduced.[16] But first, we must remember that St Augustine emphasises the unshakeability of subjective knowledge not in order to undermine the capacity of acquiring knowledge of the world, but in order to refute what he characterises as Academic scepticism. And second, he does not mention the Cyrenaics in connection with the dreaming hypothesis, but includes them among the philosophers who defended the reliability of the senses.[17]

### III THE TESTIMONY OF PLUTARCH AGAINST COLOTES

I argued above that, although the Cyrenaics left unquestioned the basic ontological assumption of objectivity,[18] the evidence is divided as to what exactly they took reality to be: an undifferentiated substratum affecting us in various ways (as might be indicated by the phrases of the

---

[15] 'This' refers to a subjective state, not to an object: see St Augustine, *Contr.Acad.* III.24, and Matthews 1977 (also cited by Burnyeat 1982, p. 28).

[16] Compare HR I, p. 153 (Meditation II):

> Finally, I am the same who feels, that is to say, who perceives certain things, as by the organs of sense, since in truth I see light, I hear noise, I feel heat. But it will be said that these phenomena are false and that I am dreaming. Let it be so; still it is at least quite certain that it seems to me that I see light, that I hear noise and that I feel heat. That cannot be false; properly speaking it is what is in me called feeling; and used in this precise sense that is no other thing than thinking.

> On Augustine's conceptions of the mind, knowledge and the self, see G. B. Matthews' articles '*Si fallor sum*' and 'The inner man' in Markus 1972, pp. 151–67 and 176–90 respectively; see also the article of A. C. Lloyd, 'On Augustine's concept of a person', in pp. 191–205 of the same volume. On the ways in which Augustine shifts the focus from the field of objects known to the activity itself of knowing and thus to the self, see Taylor 1989, pp. 127–42.

[17] At any rate, it is unlikely that St Augustine is an independent witness about the Cyrenaics. In the passage cited above, he is almost certainly building on what he has read in Cicero.

[18] Stroud (1984) shows ways in which Cartesian scepticism challenges this assumption. One important issue that Stroud raises in this book is just what relation Cartesian scepticism bears to what we already know about the world.

third group of passages discussed in section 1 of this chapter), or a world of ordinary things or states of affairs, such as fire, iron, honey, night and light (as suggested by the expressions of the first and perhaps the second groups discussed above in section 1).[19] In the former case, their scepticism would affect not only our knowledge of what the objects are really like, but also our beliefs about what kinds of objects they are: it would entail that it is impossible for us to know not only whether the honey is really sweet, but whether the lump of matter that we perceive can be identified as honey. In the latter case, Cyrenaic scepticism would concern exclusively our knowledge of the properties of the objects, but would not undermine our beliefs about their identity: it would assume that what causes an individual *pathos* of sweet is honey, but would declare that it is impossible to know whether the honey is really sweet.

This problem is connected with the question whether the Cyrenaics attempted to analyse in subjective terms both the perceptions of single sensory properties and the perception of sensory objects. The evidence attests that they transformed descriptions such as 'This horse is white' into locutions such as 'I am whitened' or 'I am affected whitely', thus translating the perception of a particular sensory property into the awareness of what I shall call a 'simple' *pathos*, related to a single sensory property such as being white. But empirical objects are usually perceived to have more than one such property. For example, a horse is a four-legged animal; it may be white and tall and slim; it may neigh and gallop or it may stand still. Thus, one may wonder whether the Cyrenaics dealt with the view that a *pathos* deriving from the simultaneous perception of several sensory properties (which I shall call a 'complex' *pathos*) constitutes the entire reality of a particular object, e.g. the horse. If they did, this may point to a conception of reality as something undifferentiated: they could argue that external objects are in fact logical constructions and that the putative objects cannot be denoted by conventional names. On the other hand, if the Cyrenaic theory is restricted to analysing the perception of single properties, it seems consistent with a more conventional conception of reality, according to which the external objects are identified in ordinary ways.

The main evidence in support of the hypothesis that the Cyrenaics proposed a radical subjectivisation of perceptual objects derives from the criticisms of the Epicurean philosopher Colotes against the epistemology of the school. These are reported by Plutarch, who subse-

---

[19] This ambiguity may appear interesting in its own right in the light of contemporary debates concerning the basic structure of reality.

quently undertakes to refute Colotes' testimony by giving what he claims to be an accurate presentation of the theory.

At any rate, after dealing with the philosophers of the past, Colotes turns to the philosophers of his own time without mentioning the name of any of them; yet, the proper thing for him to do would have been to refute them too by naming them, or not to name the philosophers of the past either. And he, who so often criticised Socrates, Plato and Parmenides with his pen, obviously lost his nerve when he was to deal with the living philosophers; he was not moderate in his criticisms because he was respectful, or he would have shown respect to their betters (sc. the philosophers of the past). I guess he intends to refute the Cyrenaics in the first place and the Academy of Arcesilaus in the second place, for the latter were the philosophers who suspended judgement about everything; but the former, placing all *pathē* and all sense-impressions (*phantasiai*) within themselves, believed that the evidence (*pistis*) coming from them is not sufficient regarding the assertions about the external objects (*pragmata*). Instead, distancing themselves from external objects, they shut themselves up within their *pathē* as in a state of siege, using the formula 'it appears' but refusing to affirm in addition that 'it is' with regard to the external objects (*ta ektos*).

This is why, says Colotes, the Cyrenaics can neither live nor cope with things. In addition, he says making fun of them, 'these men do not say that a man (*anthrōpos*) or a horse (*hippos*) or a wall (*toichos*) is (*einai*), but that they themselves are being walled (*toichousthai*) or horsed (*hippousthai*) or manned (*anthrōpousthai*)'. In the first place, he is using these expressions maliciously, just as a professional denouncer would. Doubtless, these consequences amongst others do follow from the teachings of these men. Yet he should have presented the doctrine in the form in which those philosophers teach it. For, they say, we are being sweetened (*glykainesthai*) and bittered (*pikrainesthai*) and chilled (*psychesthai*) and warmed (*thermainesthai*) and illuminated (*phōtizesthai*) and darkened (*skotizesthai*), each of these *pathē* having within itself its own evidence (*enargeia*) which is intrinsic to it and inseparable from it. But whether the honey is sweet or the young olive-shoot bitter or the hail chilly or the unmixed wine warm or the sun luminous or the night air dark, is contested by many witnesses, (wild) animals and tame animals[20] and humans alike. For some dislike honey, others like olive-shoots or are burned off by hail or are chilled by the wine or go blind in the sunlight and see well at night. So, when opinion stays close to the *pathē* it preserves its infallibility, but when it oversteps them and meddles with judgements and assertions about external objects, it often both disturbs itself and fights against other people who receive from the same objects contrary *pathē* and different sense-impressions. (Plutarch 1120b–f [T1])

Colotes is the only source who maintains that the Cyrenaics employed verbal neologisms of the form 'I am being x-ed'[21] in order to express, not

---

[20] See Appendix, p. 145, n. 4.
[21] The verb λέγουσιν has to be understood before αὐτοὺς δὲ τοιχοῦσθαι.

*pathē* deriving from the perception of properties such as white and sweet, but *pathē* of three-dimensional objects such as man, horse and wall.[22] The meaning that they are supposed to have attributed to the expressions 'being horsed', 'being walled' and 'being manned' can be determined by reference to the verbal locutions found in our main sources: 'I am whitened' reports that at the present moment I am undergoing a *pathos* of white; consequently, 'I am horsed', 'I am walled' and 'I am manned' announce, respectively, that right now the kind of *pathos* which I experience is the *pathos* of a horse, a wall or a man.[23]

Colotes' testimony raises two interrelated questions. First, if the Cyrenaics talked about the perception of objects in subjective terms, what would their thesis imply regarding the existence and structure of external reality? And second, assuming that they would grant the existence of *pathē* such as 'being horsed', how would they define the relation between these *pathē* and *pathē* such as 'being whitened'? Is 'being horsed' conceived as one complex *pathos* or as several *pathē* simultaneously affecting the perceiver?

Colotes' statement that the Cyrenaics refused to affirm 'that a man or a wall or a horse is' (1120d) may be interpreted in a variety of ways. The same holds for the contrast between statements such as 'a horse is' and 'I am horsed'. One possibility is that the Cyrenaics questioned the identity of an individual thing causing an individual *pathos*, but not of every thing that may cause a *pathos*. Another possibility is that they wondered whether the *pathos* that I am experiencing right now is caused by anything external to me at all: I can report that I am affected in a horse-like manner, but I cannot tell *whether there is anything out there* that might look like a horse. So long as this observation is not generalised to every *pathos* that one experiences, it does not challenge the existence of external objects or classes of objects. On the other hand, Colotes might suggest that the

---

[22] My inclination is to take *legousin* (1120d) quite literally: Colotes claims, falsely, that the Cyrenaics actually used expressions such as 'being walled' and 'being horsed'. It would be hard to read *legousin* as conveying no more than the embarrassing implications of their doctrine. Plutarch's criticism is that Colotes is being malicious, not careless: the accusation is not that he misunderstands or reports carelessly what he read in Cyrenaic texts, but that he maliciously puts in the mouth of his opponents things that they did not actually say.

[23] I think that Glidden's interpretation of the Cyrenaic theory in terms of a sense-data theory implies that the perception of objects is exhaustively analysed in terms of the awareness of distinct mental objects. See Glidden's remark: 'Colotes' ridiculing objection is effective only if one assumes, as Colotes did, that for the Cyrenaics to sense something as being of a certain kind is to be aware of an appearance which is actually of that kind. This assumes, in modern terms, that such descriptions of appearances are extensional; they purport to refer to actual features of the appearance' (see D. K. Glidden, 'Protagorean relativism and the Cyrenaics', in Rescher 1975, p. 138).

Cyrenaics turned questions regarding the causes of individual *pathē* into systematic doubts concerning each and every *pathos*: they ask not only whether a particular horse is the cause of the horse-like *pathos* of which I am now aware, but also whether *each and every one* of my horse-like *pathē is ever caused* by a real horse, or perhaps even by a real external object.[24]

At first glance, the absence of the definite article in front of 'man', 'horse' and 'wall' (1120d) might appear to favour this last hypothesis. However, on closer inspection, it becomes obvious that Colotes' criticism does not concern the Cyrenaic attitude with regard to the existence of the external world, but is targeted against the epistemology of the school. By assigning to the Cyrenaics the ridiculous expressions 'I am being walled', 'I am being horsed' and 'I am being manned', Colotes aims to stress the following points concerning Cyrenaic subjectivism: first, the Cyrenaic position about the apprehension of the *pathē* implies that one can state absolutely nothing about the external objects – not even that they exist; and second, the Cyrenaics are compelled to talk about objects in the same way in which they talk about properties, namely by using verbal neologisms and by avoiding all substantival expressions.[25]

This last remark is related to the issue of the relation between 'simple' and 'complex' *pathē*, deriving respectively from the perception of single qualities and from the perception of objects. Perceiving a horse might be defined in terms of several simultaneous 'simple' *pathē*: white, tall, four-legged, neighing, galloping, and so on. Alternatively, it might be analysed in terms of one complex *pathos* experienced at a given time, for example a *pathos* of (white and tall and four-legged and neighing and galloping), in which case the Cyrenaics would have to explain how several 'simple' *pathē* are structured so as to constitute a complex one.

There is no evidence that the Cyrenaics faced the problems raised by Colotes' criticism by attempting to give an overall analysis of perceptual processes.[26] Indeed, Plutarch's testimony against Colotes explicitly den-

---

[24] I mentioned above that Plutarch himself reports (1120d) that the Cyrenaics do not assert 'is' of external objects. I think this just means that they feel unjustified in asserting 'It is a man', not that they deny the existence of the man or that they doubt the existence of some external object here.

[25] Here, Colotes anticipates the criticisms levelled against the adverbial analysts for introducing a perceptual vocabulary that is at odds with ordinary perceptual discourse.

[26] A different view is proposed by Hankinson, who comments that 'the barbarous new language of affection satirized by Colotes is an attempt to signal the fact that *all* [my italics] perceptual claims must be interpreted as referring only to their immediate affective contents and not, as the ordinary language of perception implicitly suggests, to anything external which is responsible for them' (Hankinson 1995, p. 58). But he does not explain why the Cyrenaics did not attempt to analyse perceptual examples involving empirical objects rather than single empirical properties.

ies that the Cyrenaics used expressions such as 'being walled', 'being horsed' and 'being manned', and attests that they introduced only locutions such as 'being sweetened' and 'being embittered'. This restricted version of Cyrenaic subjectivism is consistent with the conventional attitude that Plutarch appears to attribute in 1120e ff. [T1] to the Cyrenaics, namely that the external causes of the *pathē* are such familiar objects as horses and men.²⁷

Historically, Plutarch appears justified in rebuking Colotes for inaccuracy. His own version of the Cyrenaic position seems to draw on excellent sources and is corroborated by the rest of the evidence. Philosophically, however, Colotes invites us to think out the full implications of Cyrenaic subjectivism, and in particular the unwarranted character of assumptions concerning the existence and identity of external objects. The acumen of Colotes' criticism is briefly acknowledged by Plutarch, when he observes: 'doubtless, these consequences [sc. the implications drawn by Colotes], amongst others, do follow from the teachings of these men. Yet he should have presented the doctrine in the form in which those philosophers teach it' (1120d–e).

Does then Colotes put his finger on an actual flaw of the Cyrenaic analysis of perception? Are we to count against the Cyrenaics the fact that they do not explore the implications of their position and do not systematically question the existence of the empirical world? The answer depends on the perspective from which this matter is looked at. From one point of view, we may indeed maintain that the theory is severely flawed: it has brought us up to the threshold of a tremendously interesting area in epistemology, only to leave us there to our own devices.

But from another standpoint, we can see that the Cyrenaics would have little to gain and much to lose by radicalising their scepticism about the empirical world. Philosophically, the thesis that we can have knowledge only of our *pathē* receives ample support from their remarks concerning the perception of secondary properties. If all they cared for was, precisely, to lend plausibility to this central thesis (see chapter 1, pp. 1–4), I do not think that they would have achieved much more had they extended their analysis to the perception of three-dimensional objects. In more practical terms, the claim that we are entirely cut off from external objects and that we live in an internal world of *pathē* has a certain amount of plausibility, while radical doubts concerning the

---

²⁷ See above, p. 84.

existence of reality are much less plausible, I believe. If this is correct, the Cyrenaics had a very good reason *not* to question the existence of the external world, namely that they would alienate a considerable part of their audience without any apparent gain at all.

# CHAPTER 7

# Our ignorance of other minds

The subjectivism of the Cyrenaics and their scepticism with regard to knowledge of the real properties of objects are related to the position that they adopted with regard to our knowledge of other people's *pathē*.[1] In connection with their discussion of other minds the Cyrenaics also made some remarks about language. Sextus provides the only surviving piece of evidence on both these subjects, which I shall cite immediately below. In this chapter I shall discuss the evidence concerning other minds, and I shall dedicate the next chapter to the remarks about language.

195. So, we are all unerring with regard to our own *pathē*, but we all make mistakes with regard to the external object. And those are apprehensible, but this is inapprehensible because the soul is too weak to distinguish it on account of the places, the distances, the motions, the changes, and numerous other causes. Hence, they say that no criterion is common (*koinon*) to mankind but that common names (*onomata koina*) are assigned (*tithesthai*) to the objects.

196. All people call something (*ti*) white or sweet in common (*koinōs*), but they do not have something common (*koinon ti*) that is white or sweet. Each person is aware of his own private (*idion*) *pathos*, but whether this *pathos* occurs in him and in his neighbour from a white object (*apo leukou*) neither he himself can tell, since he is not submitting to the *pathos* of his neighbour, nor can the neighbour tell, since he is not submitting to the *pathos* of the other person.

197. And since no *pathos* is common (*koinon*) to us all, it is hasty to declare that what appears to me of a certain kind appears of this same kind to my neighbour as well. Perhaps I am constituted so as to be whitened by the external object when it comes into contact with my senses, while another person has the senses constructed so as to have been disposed differently. In any case, the *phainomenon* is assuredly not common to us all.

---

[1] Throughout this book and elsewhere (Tsouna-McKirahan 1997), I refer occasionally to the Cyrenaic position on other minds by the expression 'doubts about other minds'. I use this expression for brevity's sake, but I should make clear that, properly speaking, the Cyrenaics were not in any doubt about other minds. They firmly believed, first, that other minds exist and, second, that they are inaccessible to us.

198. And that we really are not all stirred in the same way because of the different constructions of our senses is clear from the cases of people who suffer from jaundice or ophthalmia and from those who are in normal condition. Just as some persons are affected yellowly, others redly and others whitely by one and the same object, likewise it is also probable that those who are in a normal condition are not stirred in the same manner by the same things because of the different construction of their senses, but that the person with grey eyes is stirred in one way, the one with blue eyes in another, and the one with black eyes in another yet different way. It follows that the names (*onomata*) which we assign (*tithenai*) to things (*pragmasin*) are common (*koina*), but that we have private (*idia*) *pathē*. (Sextus, *M* vii.195–8 [T6b])

According to Sextus, the Cyrenaics maintained that it is impossible to know the content of other people's *pathē*: one can infallibly tell that one is seeing white or turning white, but one cannot tell that another person is experiencing a *pathos* that has the same content. This tenet is systematically related, on the one hand, to the epistemological thesis that only the *pathē* can be known but the objects cannot be known and, on the other hand, to the linguistic and semantic observation that words (which are used in common and are public) do not denote things (which would also be, in a sense, public), but *pathē* which are private (*idia*) to each perceiver. However, the evidence from Sextus does not make entirely clear the argument by which the Cyrenaics defended their scepticism concerning one's knowledge of other people's *pathē*. This argument should be reconstructed, I believe, as follows.

The constitution of sensory organs is not the same in all people: different people can be affected differently by the same object, in which case their *pathē* are not identical in content. Since they do not have a common *pathos*, they do not possess a common criterion for deciding whether one's *pathē* are identical or similar in content to the *pathē* of other people, or whether they are different. And since such a criterion does not exist, people cannot apprehend the real properties of external objects which the *pathē* are supposed to represent.[2]

In this interpretation, the claim that other people's *pathē* are inapprehensible is supported by a premise which is also found at the core of ancient Scepticism, namely the Trope concerning the different sensory constitution of different perceivers.[3] It is also connected to the Cyrenaic

---

[2] For different ways of reconstructing the inferential links between the premises of this argument, see the final paragraphs of this chapter, pp. 100–4.

[3] See the first Trope in Sextus, *PH* 1.40–79, and especially in *PH* 1.43–7 which concerns humans and other animals and which contains the stock examples of people with jaundice and with ophthalmia, as well as of animals whose eyes have different colours or textures. The second Trope (*PH* 1.79–90), which follows naturally upon the first, focuses exclusively on the differences

remarks on what it is that words denote. The properties of objects are apprehensible neither directly, through the perceptual faculties of the soul, nor indirectly, through the apprehension of the content of other people's *pathē*. Linguistic terms (at least those words indicating properties or qualities), although they are public, are ascribed to private *pathē* precisely because these are the only things that can be apprehended.[4]

These features and implications of the Cyrenaic claim concerning the inapprehensibility of other people's *pathē* suggest that the Cyrenaics faced a problem also raised by Descartes and widely discussed in post-Cartesian philosophy, the problem of Other Minds.[5] Its central question is whether one can transcend the ontological and epistemological barrier between oneself and other people, and whether one can in fact have any kind of access to the mental states of others.[6] Ontologically, the problem of Other Minds is whether people other than myself have any mental states,[7] what these states consist in and

---

between the constitutions of humans – presumably in order to show that even the members of the species that is epistemologically pre-eminent receive conflicting appearances and are committed to suspension of judgement. On the Tropes, see G. Striker, 'The ten Tropes of Aenesidemus', in Burnyeat 1983, pp. 95–115. On the structure of the argument in the first and second Tropes, see Annas and Barnes 1985, pp. 39–53, 57–65. On the notion of appearances and the disagreement between the appearances of various perceivers, see Burnyeat 1979.

[4] On this, see chapter 8, pp. 106–7.

[5] The cases in which ancient philosophers appear to express doubts that might be compared with the modern problem of Other Minds are very few. One such case is a statement attributed to Theodosius, a neo-Pyrrhonian Sceptic about whom little is known. 'In his book *Chapters of Scepticism*, Theodosius says that Scepticism should not be called Pyrrhonism, for if the movement of the mind related to another person cannot be grasped, we shall not know what was Pyrrho's disposition. And since we cannot know that, we should not be called Pyrrhonians' (D.L. IX.70). Theodosius' argument resembles that of the Cyrenaics in that he too appears to consider a category of internal states, namely thoughts, private and incommunicable. On this basis, it has been claimed that Theodosius was Cyrenaic: see Caujolle-Zaslawsky 1982, vol. I, p. 192. However, it seems probable that Theodosius employed the Cyrenaic argument for dialectical purposes and that in fact he did not have a Cyrenaic affiliation. On the issue of our knowledge of other minds in Greek philosophy, see my article 'Remarks about Other Minds in Greek philosophy', Tsouna 1998.

[6] See an example of *philosophical* doubt about other minds (to be distinguished from cases of *natural* doubt) set out by J. Wisdom. Suppose that a man, say Smith, says that he believes that flowers feel. According to Wisdom, what 'the inner–outer doubter' is saying about Smith is the following: even though he knows what Smith's behaviour has been and what it will be in the future and what it would be if this or that were to happen and what it would have been if this or that had happened, and even though all this knowledge is in favour of Smith's believing that flowers feel, still the doubter does not know that Smith really believes that flowers do feel. This is because the extensive knowledge that he has about Smith is about outward and visible things, while the conclusion that Smith really believes that flowers feel is about an inward and invisible state (Wisdom 1952, pp. 1–3).

[7] One form that this question takes in Descartes is whether, when I look from a window and see other men who pass in the street, what I see is really not men, but hats and coats which may cover automatic machines. See HR I, pp. 155–6 (Meditation II).

how they compare with mine. Epistemologically, the problem is how we can tell that other people have any mental states and how we can tell the content of these mental states.[8] An alternative description of the problem is that it appears under two forms, often interconnected. The first, which I shall call the global problem of Other Minds, is the ontological question whether there exist minds other than my own inhabiting bodies which I observe to resemble my own and which I perceive to move, make intelligible noises, change facial expressions, or generally behave in a way similar to mine. The second, which I shall call the local problem of Other Minds, is expressed by a set of epistemological, syntactic and semantic questions and appears in arguments purporting to defend or to refute the possibility of knowing what is going on in other minds. Such are, for instance, arguments which aim to show or to refute the validity of the inference from the behaviour of a body, which is public, to the existence and content of mental states, which are private in an ontological or in an epistemic sense of 'private'. Also connected to the local problem of Other Minds are arguments concerning the meaningfulness of mentalistic terms and the existence of a private language.[9]

The Cyrenaic position appears as an anticipation of modern claims about other minds in the following respects. Ontologically, it involves the assumption that the *pathē* are private, which might be generalised to the thesis that all mental states are private to the perceiver, in a strong sense of 'private'.[10] If the Cyrenaics held this generalised thesis, it would be possible to argue that they left open the question whether people other than myself have any *pathē* or any mental states at all.

Epistemologically, the Cyrenaics connect the concept of privacy with

---

[8] These two sets of questions are often interconnected. Asking whether my neighbour thinks also invites the question how do I know that my neighbour thinks; and when I wonder what my neighbour thinks, I am also inclined to ask how do I know what he thinks.

[9] The literature on the problem of Other Minds in its various forms is extensive. Some of the most interesting discussions appear in this century. They comprise refined versions of the Analogical theory, of the Intuitive theory, of Behaviouristic interpretations and of theories focused on the existence of language and the success of interpersonal communication. Anyone interested in these topics will come across Ryle 1963, especially pp. 13–24, 50ff. 87–8, 148–89, 195–6; Ayer 1954 and 1958, pp. 162–70; Price 1938, pp. 425–56; J. L. Austin's essay 'Other Minds', 1961, pp. 76–116; Wittgenstein's remarks on raw feelings, mental states, criteria, private language, and solipsism, in *Philosophical Investigations*; Malcolm 1958; Wisdom 1952; Hervey 1957; A. Kenny, 'Cartesian privacy', in Pitcher 1966, pp. 352–70; D. Gasking, 'Avowals', in Butler 1962, pp. 154–69; and Strawson 1959, ch. 3.

[10] See again Kenny's article 'Cartesian privacy' in Pitcher 1966, pp. 352–70. An important part of Kenny's discussion is to show how Descartes' introduction of *cogitatio* as the mark of the mental is tantamount to the substitution of privacy for rationality as the defining characteristic of the mind.

the features of infallibility and incorrigibility.[11] According to the Sextus passage [T6b], the Cyrenaic claim is that each person is aware of his *pathos* and that this *pathos* is private (*idion*) to him. And one cannot tell anything about the external causes of one's *pathē* because one 'is not submitting to the *pathos* of his neighbour, nor can the neighbour tell, since he is not submitting to the *pathos* of the other person'. It seems as if the privacy of the *pathē* is a condition of their apprehensibility. And it is also a prerequisite of the infallibility and the incorrigibility of the perceiver's reports concerning the *pathē*: the perceiver is in a position to report the content of his own private *pathos* infallibly and incorrigibly, whereas he has no such epistemic access to the *pathos* of the neighbour.

Semantically, if the Cyrenaics shared the common assumption of the Greeks that the meaning of certain categories of words is determined by their reference, then their claim that people use common linguistic terms to designate empirical properties, but that they have private *pathē* may be taken to indicate the existence of a theory about private language.

Doubtless, these are striking similarities between the Cyrenaic position and the views of the moderns about other minds. However, the nature, the scope and the philosophical importance of Cyrenaic scepticism concerning the *pathē* of other people cannot be fully appreciated without pointing out that this last differs significantly from its modern counterparts.

All modern thinking about other minds is dominated by claims and assumptions which are related to the mind–body problem. The moderns drive a sharp wedge between events in the body, which are physical and therefore observable and public, and mental events, which belong to an ontologically different realm and which are non-observable and private. The perceiver has privileged access to the content of his mental events precisely because these occur in his own mind and, in Cartesian terms, nothing is closer to the mind than the mind itself. By the same token, what makes the perceiver's knowledge of other minds problematic is that he cannot observe them with 'the Eye of the Mind': the perceiver's mind is not identical with the mind of his neighbours and each mind has privileged access only to its own contents.

On the other hand, the Cyrenaic thesis that we can have no knowledge of other people's *pathē* does not presuppose the mind–body problem as we

---

[11] As indicated above, this connection provides the grounds for claiming that, although the Cyrenaics left open the possibility of describing the *pathē* in physicalistic terms, they focused primarily on their subjective features.

know it in its modern forms. I argued previously that, although the Cyrenaics emphasised the subjective aspects of the *pathē* and studied them primarily as experiences, they still conceived of them as ontologically derivative internal states that can be described in both mental and physical terms.[12] Thus, in principle, when the Cyrenaics deny that we can know the content of the *pathē* of our neighbour, they deny both that we can know what it is like to be our neighbour at a given moment and that we can know precisely what physical alteration our neighbour is undergoing at a given time. This does not imply that they suggested that the mental aspects of the *pathē* are ultimately reducible to bodily changes or that they can be described exclusively in physicalistic terms. So, it would not be correct to attach to their theory the naive implication that, if somehow one could observe the smooth or rough movement of the flesh that affects one's neighbour, then one would know what the *pathos* of one's neighbour is.[13] Their emphasis on the subjective aspects of the *pathē* strongly suggests that they would not consider any account of the *pathē* of other people adequate unless it dealt explicitly with their subjective character. The point is rather that the nature of the *pathē* is such that, at least in principle, the knowledge of other people's *pathē* can or should contain physicalistic as well as mentalistic elements. In that sense, the Cyrenaic position cuts across the mind–body distinction involved in modern discussions of our knowledge of other minds.

I suggest that, precisely because the concept of the *pathē* cuts across that distinction, the Cyrenaic claim that one perceives infallibly one's own private *pathos* but cannot tell the content of the *pathos* of one's neighbour is weaker than similar claims found in modern discussions about other minds. First, the Cyrenaic concept of privacy does not apply exclusively to the ontological realm of the mental, but simply to the internal states of the perceiver. It is not the case that our neighbour's *pathē* are private to him if and only if they are mental. They are private because they are his experiences rather than ours; because they occur in him rather than in us; and because 'no *pathos* is common to us all'. While the interpretation of the modern notions of privacy relies, at the bottom

---

[12] See chapters 2 (pp. 9–25), 3 (pp. 28–30) and 4 (pp. 31, 38–53).

[13] In that respect, the Cyrenaic doctrine is not vulnerable to the criticisms levelled (and rightly so) against contemporary reductionist analyses of mental phenomena and mental concepts in the context of some varieties of psychophysical identification and of materialism. For more or less successful attempts to explain the relation of mind to brain in reductionist terms, see Lewis 1966, pp. 17–25; Smart 1963; Armstrong 1968; and Dennet 1968. A most forceful argument to the effect that reductionist theories miss what makes the mind–body problem unique and uniquely difficult, explaining why we have at present no conception of what a physicalistic explanation of a mental phenomenon could be, is found in Nagel 1974.

line, on the distinction between the mental and the physical, the Cyrenaic concept of privacy can be best understood by using partly different, albeit overlapping, distinctions: *pathē* versus objects, states or events internal to the perceiver versus occurrences external to him, things or conditions which are common to many perceivers versus others which are not common.

Second, according to the Cyrenaics, the perceiver perceives his own *pathē* 'infallibly, truly, certainly and incorrigibly' because they are his and because he perceives them 'by internal touch'. On the other hand, those modern philosophers who claimed that one has privileged access to one's own experiences considered the epistemic features of infallibility and incorrigibility to be the exclusive mark of the mental.[14] The Cyrenaic position concerning privileged access to one's own internal states is weaker than the modern position, in so far as it applies to the problem of apprehending other people's internal states. It is weaker, I suggest, in that the epistemic notions of infallibility and incorrigibility, like the metaphysical notion of privacy, are not applied to a separate ontological realm, the realm of the mental.

This last claim is supported, I think, by the Cyrenaics' remarks about language. I mentioned above that, according to the Cyrenaics, it is impossible to establish a direct correspondence between certain categories of linguistic terms, which are used by all people in common, and the things which these terms are supposed to denote. However, although expressions such as 'I am sweetened' are attached to private referents and although this might seem to imply that the Cyrenaics had a rudimentary conception of a private language, in fact they did not question the meaningfulness of terms whose reference is private and they did not challenge the efficiency of language on the level of interpersonal communication. On the other hand, the belief of some modern philosophers that mental states are private because they are mental led to the idea that private experiences are incommunicable and raised puzzles concerning the meaningfulness of mentalistic sentences. Again, this difference is due, I submit, to the fact that Cyrenaic semantics operated with a much weaker notion of privacy than modern theories of language and meaning.[15]

---

[14] Recall the position endorsed by Descartes, and no less by Locke, Hume and Berkeley, that mind is better known than body: what is subjective is better grasped than what is objective, what is private is epistemologically prior to what is public.

[15] In the context of the Cartesian tradition, 'pain' in the private language connecting words to sensations refers to something private in a specific sense: it refers to an inner state whose occurrence and nature the owner can know with certainty while other people cannot, the owner

The absence of a sharp distinction between the mental and the physical determines a series of further points with regard to which the Cyrenaic doctrine differs from post-Cartesian discussions about other minds. As mentioned above, Cyrenaic scepticism does not concern, properly speaking, other people's minds, but rather other people's *pathē*. While the Cartesian mind is ontologically basic in the sense that its existence does not depend upon the existence of other entities such as other minds or other bodies, the *pathē* are ontologically derivative since they are conceived as internal states of spatially and temporally located perceivers.[16]

The fact that the scepticism of the Cyrenaics concerns ontologically derivative entities is partly responsible, I suggest, for the most important difference between Cyrenaic scepticism and modern scepticism about the internal states of people other than ourselves. The ontological component of the problem of Other Minds, that is, the question whether there exist minds other than my own or whether my neighbour has a mind, is widely discussed by the moderns, whereas it is not envisaged by the Cyrenaics.[17] The Cyrenaics did not doubt, I think, that everybody's *pathē* are generically the same type of entity. And precisely because they did not face the ontological problem, they also did not ask the epistemological question how we know that other people have *pathē*. They simply assumed that other people do have *pathē* because they defined them always as *the pathē of some person*,[18] events which occur in a person's body and/or are a person's experiences. Since they left unquestioned the existence of ontologically primary entities, and in particular of other persons, they were bound to assume that the *pathē* exist as well.

Moving a step back, one might wonder why the Cyrenaics did not express doubts about the existence of other persons as persons endowed with sensory faculties and undergoing *pathē*. One answer is that the Cyrenaics had no philosophical motive to question the existence of other people. While their thesis that we cannot know the content of

---

cannot doubt while other people can. It is this notion of privacy that constitutes the target of Wittgenstein's devastating criticisms against private languages. Notice the dependence of the concept of private language on Descartes' ontological distinction between the mind and the body: sensation-words *must* refer to immediately graspable *private* entities in order to have meaning, for they are supposed to be used at a stage where doubt is cast on the existence of any body at all.

[16] On this, see chapter 2, section II (pp. 21–5).

[17] To my knowledge, no ancient philosopher asked the ontological question whether other people have minds or mental states similar to one's own.

[18] In principle, it is possible to define the *pathē* as being necessarily the *pathē* of some person and yet to remain a solipsist: the *pathē* must be someone's *pathē* and I am the only entity that exists and that has *pathē*. In fact, however, the Cyrenaics did not entertain that possibility, for reasons that should be obvious by now.

other people's *pathē* has plausibility, the further step of doubting whether other people have *pathē* has none.[19] If they had taken it, their theory would have lost much of its appeal without gaining anything in return.

Another answer (which is related to the previous one) can be provided by comparing, again, the Cyrenaic position to modern formulations of the problem of Other Minds. In modern philosophy, the problem of Other Minds often appears as a natural accompaniment of the problem of the external world.[20] Just like the problem of Other Minds, the problem of the external world occurs both in a local and in a global form. Locally, the principal question is whether the world is what it appears to be to one, many or all observers, or whether in fact reality is entirely different from what our appearances suggest it to be. Globally, the question is whether our appearances correspond to any reality at all. Thus, modern philosophers often consider the two problems as parallel cases of scepticism.

Besides, although usually the problem of Other Minds is generated independently of the problem of the external world, occasionally it is also generated from the problem of the external world. The problem of Other Minds can emerge as follows. I observe somebody's movements, facial expressions and general behaviour and I conclude that he feels pain. Later on, he tells me that he was pretending and that he acted as if he felt pain although in fact he did not. I conclude that my observations misled me: the other person did not in fact experience the mental state which I believed that he did experience. Generalising, I infer that I may be wrong in many cases when I believe that other people undergo certain experiences judging by their external appearance or behaviour. Generalising further, I wonder whether I may be deceived in all such cases, and indeed in all cases involving the mental states of other people. If such a logical procedure is followed, the formulation of the problem of Other Minds is reached independently of any doubts that one may or may not entertain about the external world.

But a different procedure can be followed as well. I base my judgements concerning the existence of mental states animating a foreign human body and concerning the content of these mental states on the way in which that body appears to me to look or act. But my appearances may be misleading. Locally, I may be wrong to infer that Denis feels pain for he may simply be pretending that he feels pain. Globally, I am possibly wrong to believe that Denis has any feelings at all or even that

---

[19] Compare chapter 6, pp. 87–8.     [20] See Mates 1981, pp. 109ff.

there is a body that is Denis' body: my perceptions of Denis' body may be logical constructions or hallucinations created by my own mind. What I call Denis' body may not exist anywhere but in my mind. And if so, then I can appeal to no factual basis for inferring anything about Denis' mind from observing Denis' body and behaviour.

Constructed as parallel cases, both problems in modern philosophy amount to a radical scepticism. Concerning the problem of the external world, if there is an external reality at all, it is impossible that I can ever come to know it. And if there is not, I still may have the very same reasons to believe that there is as I would have if such a reality existed. Concerning the problem of Other Minds, if other bodies are animated by minds, I shall never come to know it. And if they are not, I may still have the same reasons to believe that other bodies have mental states as I would have if they in fact did have mental states.

Now if the Cyrenaics conceived of the existence and knowledge of other persons or of the *pathē* of other persons in a way parallel to the way in which they conceived of the existence and knowledge of the external world, then we should indeed not expect to find the ontological component of the problem of Other Minds in Sextus' testimony. As I argued in the previous chapter, they do not face the ontological problem of the external world. Thus, they do not envisage the possibility that objects external to the perceiver, people other than the perceiver, or both, may exist nowhere but in the perceiver's mind.

There are two further considerations that may be relevant to the fact that the Cyrenaics questioned the knowledge but not the existence of other people's *pathē*. Looking again at modern treatments of the problem of Other Minds, we shall not fail to notice that many of the arguments supporting the belief in the existence of other minds are instances of analogical reasoning. For example, by analogy with the links between my own mental states and my outward demeanour, of which I am conscious, I infer that such links hold in all cases of creatures that have bodies like mine and behave like me.[21] Or, judging by the connection between my use of language and my thoughts, I infer that other beings which have intelligible and intelligent speech also have mental states expressed by that speech.[22] Many philosophers have found such arguments unpersuasive, and one of the reasons why they have criticised them was their analogical form. For example, one may chal-

---

[21] J. S. Mill put forward such an analogical argument defending the belief in the existence of other minds.

[22] See Price 1938.

lenge the legitimacy of the established analogies, the soundness of the archetypes or primary examples of the analogies and the circularity that lurks in some of the premises. These criticisms are derived partly from the fact that, although analogical arguments are still very much in use, they have been discredited on various accounts in modern times.

On the other side, arguments from analogy were widely respected in Greek thought, although their shortcomings were occasionally pointed out, and they were used both in philosophical and scientific contexts, as well as in ordinary conversation.[23] Now the assumption that other people have *pathē* just as I do may well rely, I believe, on the obvious analogies that can be drawn between two or more human beings. The point is not that the Cyrenaics did face some form of the ontological problem of Other Minds and answered it by using an analogical argument. The point is rather the following: one reason why the Cyrenaics did not question the existence of other people's experiences is that they thought it is obviously true that other people do have experiences. And one reason why they considered this obvious is that they found reasoning by analogy, which could be used to ground the belief in the existence of other minds, for the most part unproblematic.

Another consideration that may be pertinent to our subject is that the hypothesis that human or animal bodies may be inanimate automata goes against a fundamental belief that many Greeks shared, namely that there is causal interaction between the body and the soul of all animal beings, and therefore a close relation between their physical features and their inner character.

This belief constitutes the fundamental principle of the science of Physiognomy, formalised and codified in a number of handbooks.[24] However, it is not found only in technical writings, but also in several domains of intellectual activity, e.g. literary genres as varied as epic, elegiac, iambic and lyric poetry, satire and fiction, tragedy, history, biography and rhetoric. Perhaps it is not an exaggeration to suggest that the ancient authors display a general 'physiognomic consciousness',[25] which does not usually derive from an acquaintance with the science of Physiognomy, but simply from the shared common conviction that the psychic and the physical states of people are interrelated and that descriptions of physical features are an important tool in the analysis of character.

---

[23] For a comprehensive study of the forms and uses of analogical reasoning in classical antiquity, see Lloyd 1966.
[24] See Evans 1969.   [25] The expression is borrowed from Evans 1969.

If the Cyrenaics left this conviction unquestioned, it seems unlikely that they would raise ontological doubts about the existence of other people's *pathē*. The idea that one's body is the mirror of one's soul blocks the way to forming the hypothesis that there may be bodies which are automata and are not animated by a soul.[26] It is important to notice that the acceptance of the governing principle of Physiognomics, namely that the soul and the body interact causally, presupposes that there is no radical ontological gap between these two entities.

At this point, the nature of the Cyrenaic position on our knowledge of other people's *pathē* and the ways in which it differs from the modern problem of Other Minds must have become clear. Next I shall try to determine the Cyrenaics' motive for denying access to other minds by examining the place which this position occupies in the argument reported by Sextus.

Depending on how we reconstruct the inferential links between the parts of the argument in Sextus, we may endorse either of the two following interpretations. One possibility is that the position that other people's *pathē* cannot be known is intended to support the claim that external objects are inapprehensible. Each person perceives only his own *pathē*, *therefore* there is no common criterion (οὐδὲ κριτήριον εἶναι κοινὸν ἀνθρώπων (*M* VII.195) . . . ἕκαστος γὰρ τοῦ ἰδίου πάθους ἀντιλαμβάνεται *(M* VII.196)); since there is no common criterion, one cannot compare the content of one's own *pathos* to the content of the neighbour's *pathos* deriving from the same object (ibid.); on the widespread ancient assumption that if something were really F, it would appear F to everybody,[27] since nothing can be known to appear F to two different perceivers and intersubjective comparisons are impossible (*M* VII.197), it cannot be decided whether the content of one's *pathos* truly reflects a property of an object in the world.

Thus, the Cyrenaics may appear to reckon that one way of establishing the epistemic link between the content of one's *pathos* and the object which it is supposed to represent might be to apprehend the content of other people's *pathē* deriving from that object and to compare it with one's own. If so, their point is that if I could verify that the content of my own *pathē* about the properties of an object x is qualitatively identical with the content of everybody else's *pathē* about the properties of x, then

---

[26] However, neither the professional physiognomists nor anyone else in antiquity considered that Physiognomy might provide a kind of answer to doubts about other minds. On this, see Tsouna-McKirahan 1997.

[27] See below, pp. 101ff.

I could infer that the object x really has the properties represented by the contents of our *pathē*.[28]

This is where the denial of access to other people's minds comes into the argument: there is no way of deciding whether my own *pathos* and my neighbour's *pathos* both come from, e.g., a white object, because there is no way to test the content of my neighbour's *pathos*, and thus affirm that it is the same as mine or that it is different. To this, one might raise the objection that the use of the same word, e.g. 'white', by different perceivers to indicate the real property of an object suggests, in fact, that the *pathē* of different perceivers are caused by a white object and that they have the same content. But the Cyrenaics would retort that this use of the word 'white' is improper; there is no criterion by which we can determine the meaning of 'white' in empirical assertions such as 'The snow is white'.[29]

This reconstruction of the argument suggests that the epistemological doubts that the Cyrenaics raise about the knowledge of other people's *pathē* are secondary and subordinate to the project of defending their scepticism about the possibility of knowing the real properties of objects in the world. The Cyrenaics are interested in other people's subjective states only in so far as these might be instrumental to the aim of learning truths about reality. They do not enquire into the subject of the nature, content and communicability of subjective experiences for its own sake.

The problem with this interpretation is that it attributes to the Cyrenaics a position which contains a variant of the semi-rhetorical argument from *consensus omnium* and which is obviously incoherent.[30] Suppose that we had cognitive access to the *pathē* of other people about an object x and that we found them identical in content with our own *pathē* about x. It still does not follow that our common *pathē* reflect the real properties of x.[31] All that the common character of our *pathē* would need to imply is that the same object produces *pathē* identical in content to all the members of the human species. But the human perceivers could have a physical and psychological constitution such that it always yielded representations of objects which are distorted in the same way in

---

[28] Again, the Cyrenaics may have thought that one could draw this inference only if they shared the widespread assumption mentioned above, namely that if something were really F, it would appear F to every perceiver.

[29] See chapter 8, pp. 106–10.

[30] On the origins and uses of this argument, see Oehler 1961, Schian 1973 and, most recently, Obbink 1992.

[31] For everyone's *pathē* to agree is certainly not a sufficient condition of their being true of x. However, it might be considered a necessary condition – on the principle that if x were really F, it would appear F to everybody.

all cases. They could be collectively enclosed in an illusory *pathos* that has absolutely no connection with reality. Scepticism with regard to the qualities of objects in the world does not entail a negative answer to questions concerning the knowledge of other minds. But also vice versa: the position that we cannot know the content of the internal states of other people does not entail that the properties of real objects cannot be known in a some direct, non-inferential way.

This problem can be avoided if the argument in Sextus is reconstructed in a different way. It could run, roughly, as follows. We cannot know anything about the external objects, because of distances, changes, and so on (*M* VII.195). Hence (*enthen*) what we share is only a vocabulary, i.e. words such as 'white' and 'sweet', not a criterion for discovering inter-subjective truths about our perceptions of white and sweet (*M* VII.195–6). While we all use these same words, we cannot pool the contents of the corresponding *pathē* so as to arrive at a shared criterion, for each of us apprehends his own *pathos*, and neither of us can tell whether or not you and I are both having a *pathos caused by* something, e.g. white, or *representing* something white (*apo leukou*).[32] Since we do not share any *pathos*, I cannot be sure that what appears F to me appears F to you (*M* VII.197). It may be that, because of our different constitutions, what F-ens me G-ens you (*M* VII.197). Therefore the way things appear to us is not something we share (*M* VII.197). The experiences of the sick confirm that even between healthy people there are likely to be perceptual differences (*M* VII.198). Hence, while we have a shared vocabulary, our *pathē* are private to each of us (*M* VII.198).

This interpretation avoids the difficulty of the argument from *consensus omnium*: it does not suggest that, if I could test the content of other people's *pathē* and determine that they are the same as my own, I could then infer truths about external objects. On the other hand, it leaves us with two questions that are very difficult to answer. First, what does the

---

[32] My initial tendency was to take ἀπό + gen. to indicate causal derivation. David Sedley pointed out to me that it is more likely that ἀπό gives the representational properties of a *pathos*, not its external cause. Of the many parallels for this use of ἀπό that he brought to my attention, I shall cite two. First, the Stoics claim that the cognitive impression must be 'of such a kind as could not arise ἀπὸ μὴ ὑπάρχοντος' (*M* VII.248). If this ἀπό indicated causal derivation, it would produce nonsense, since according to the Stoics nothing, not even a false impression, can be caused by something non-existent. The point is rather that the cognitive impression is such that it cannot represent a non-actual state of affairs. Second, the Stoics illustrate impressions that are both true and false by the example of a dreamer, who experiences in his sleep a totally vacuous image 'ἀπὸ Δίωνος ζῶντος' (*M* VII.245): not 'caused by the living Dion', but 'representing Dion as alive'. How we take the expression ἀπὸ λευκοῦ in *M* VII.196 is crucial to the overall interpretation of the argument. I shall try to show why it is crucial in what follows.

absence of a shared criterion follow from, from what precedes *M* VII.195, or from what follows, or both? And second, what is this shared criterion? Is it a shared means of judging external truths or is it a yardstick for internal truths about *pathē*?

If the absence of a common criterion follows from the argument preceding *M* VII.195, then the point is that, since there cannot be *any* criterion of external truths (*M* VII.191–5), there also cannot be any *shared* criterion of external truths (*M* VII.195–8). One problem that this would raise (although not an insuperable one) is that the argument in *M* VII.195–8 would seem redundant. On the other hand, if the thesis that there is no common criterion follows from the premises set out from *M* VII.195 onwards, then the argument may be as follows. If we had cognitive access to externals, that would have been sufficient to ensure shared *pathē* and a shared criterion, since we would all alike be experiencing things as they really are. But since we have been shown to have no cognitive access to externals (down to *M* VII.195), the only other way we could have shared *pathē* and a shared criterion would be by intersubjective comparisons, and this can be ruled out on independent grounds (*M* VII.196–8).

On the first of these alternatives, the common criterion turns out to be above all a shared yardstick for judging external truths. On the second, it is, primarily at least, a yardstick of internal truths. Which of these we take it to be will largely depend on how we interpret the expression *apo leukou* in the following sentence:

For each person is aware of his own private (*idion*) *pathos*, but whether this *pathos* occurs in him and in his neighbour from a white object (*apo leukou*) neither he himself can tell, since he is not submitting to the *pathos* of his neighbour, nor can the neighbour tell, since he is not submitting to the *pathos* of the other person. (*M* VII.196).

If *apo leukou* indicates causal derivation (i.e. that a *pathos* is being produced by a white object which acted upon me), then the remark in *M* VII.196 is that each of us apprehends his own *pathos* and neither of us possesses a shared criterion enabling both of us to decide whether the object that causes our *pathē* is truly, e.g., white. On the other hand, if *apo leukou* designates the representational properties of a *pathos*, then the point is that we cannot get by intersubjective comparisons a common criterion of truths about our respective *pathē*.

On either of these readings, we have available an interpretation which avoids the pitfalls of the *consensus omnium* version. Whatever the

merits of an interpretation along these lines might be, it leaves us with no
direct evidence regarding the motivation of the Cyrenaics for denying
the knowability of other minds. Perhaps we should turn again to their
ethics. They may have intended to drive home the point that, since we
cannot have a common, agreed standard for what things are pleasant
and what things are painful, each of us must fall back on his own *pathē*.
Or alternatively, a possible motive for denying a shared criterion of
internal truths could be this: I cannot know what *pathē* are pleasant or
painful *for you*, so I should focus on recognising and pursuing what is
pleasant for me alone.

# CHAPTER 8

# Some remarks on language

It seems that the Cyrenaics did not have detailed linguistic and semantic views. However, the Sextus passage (T6b) cited in the previous chapter (pp. 89–90) indicates that some Cyrenaic positions are relevant to language. These are the following: (i) the *pathē* are private; (ii) nobody has access to the *pathē* of anyone else: in that sense the *pathē* are incommunicable; (iii) there is no common criterion, which on one interpretation entails that no proposition is evidently true of an object or state of affairs in the world, but on another interpretation (outlined at the end of the previous chapter) entails that we cannot establish truths about shared experiences. On the other hand, (iv) the *onomata* which we use are *koina*, commonly shared; also, the text suggests that (v) there is a disparity between the lack of a common criterion and the use of commonly shared *onomata*. The point appears to be that, when I and my neighbour both use the word 'white' in relation to the same thing, we tend to assume that the content of our *pathē* is qualitatively identical; yet we should not assume this, because of (i), (ii) and (iii).

In what follows, I shall first specify what the expression 'common names' (*koina onomata*) may mean, what entities are 'the things' designated by these 'names', and what semantic relation is indicated by the statement that common names are 'assigned' (*tithesthai*) to things. And second, I shall try to determine the scope and purpose of the Cyrenaic remarks on the use of 'names'.

The Cyrenaics justify their claim that *koina onomata* are applied to things by appealing to the fact that all people (presumably, all those who speak the same language) commonly call something white or sweet (Sextus, *M* VII.195–6). These examples, which correspond to the immediate contents of *pathē*, suggest that the *onomata* with which the Cyrenaics are primarily concerned are adjectives indicating sensible properties or qualities: they are neither proper names such as 'Socrates' nor common names such as 'horse'. (Adjectives fall comfortably within the scope of *onomata*.) As the text makes clear, these *onomata* are called *koina* to indicate that people use them *koinōs*, i.e., they share the same linguistic expressions.

The next matter to clarify is what are 'the things' to which the *onomata* are supposed to apply. This question is complicated for textual reasons: it is controversial whether the dative after the infinitive *tithesthai* in *M* VII.195 is *chrēmasin* (as Natorp suggested, followed by Mannebach), or *pragmasin* (as Kayser proposed on the grounds that almost the same phrase seems to occur both in *M* VII.195 and in *M* VII.198), or *krimasin* (the MS reading defended by Bekker) or the emended form *synkrimasin* (as Mutschmann suggested, followed by Giannantoni).

The word *krimasin*, which occurs in the manuscripts, often means 'object of judgement';[1] its correlation with *kritērion* (*M* VII.195) makes it, I think, a very plausible reading in the Sextus passage. This term may refer to sensory objects or to any other object judged, be this a physical object, a *pathos* or anything else. The same holds for the conjectures *chrēmasin* and *pragmasin*[2] if they are adopted instead of *krimasin*: they too could indicate 'things' of various sorts: sensory objects, states of affairs, etc.

The fact that *krimasin* (or *chrēmasin*, or *pragmasin*) can in principle refer either to external objects or to *pathē* bears on the question whether, when we are using a name, we are using the name of our *pathos* or that of an object. There is no reason, I think, why it should be one of those to the exclusion of the other, for conversations are both about external objects and about *pathē*. Look at the examples of *koina onomata* assigned to *krimata*, i.e. the words 'white' and 'sweet'. Suppose we disagree as to the whiteness of the snow. If we disagree about whether the snow is white, we disagree about the object. On the other hand, if we disagree about whether the snow appears white, we disagree about our *pathē*.[3]

This brings us to the next issue, namely, what the Cyrenaics mean when they claim that words are assigned (*tithesthai*) to things. Again, this expression could have a technical meaning: it could indicate some kind of theory about the origin or the correctness of language, in the former

---

[1] LSJ is quite wrong, I believe, to translate *krima* primarily by 'judgement'. There is good evidence that the work often indicates the content or object of judgement: see, for example, PHerc. 19/698, and also Plutarch 1121e.

[2] Both these conjectures are possible, I think. On the other hand, Mutschmann's *synkrimasin* is unlikely; on this, see Tsouna 1988, pp. 208–13.

[3] The advantage of this interpretation is that it explains why the Cyrenaics would have chosen the word *krimata* rather than, say, the more ordinary *pragmata*, which would unambiguously refer to external objects.

case determining whether language is established by convention (*thesei*) or by nature (*physei*),[4] in the latter case concentrating on the relation between words and things.[5] Indeed, the contrast which the Cyrenaics draw between the private content of sensory *pathē* and the public denotation of their external causes by linguistic terms could be employed in support of the thesis that they held some version of a 'conventional' theory about the origin or use of words: the fact that there are things that we share, namely the *onomata*, could mislead us and make us assume that what the *onomata* denote is shared as well; in fact, we have agreed not to compare our experiences (for they cannot be compared),[6] but to assign names to things arbitrarily. If so, what the Cyrenaics have in mind when they claim that names are *assigned* to things are, I suggest, linguistic acts or habits of assigning an *onoma*, i.e., an adjective, by convention to what is perceived as a quality. The act of assigning *onomata* to *krimata* is what goes on when we agree, conventionally, that what we believe to be one and the same colour is what we will call 'white', whenever either of us comes across it.[7]

There is no evidence that the Cyrenaics discussed the legitimacy of the names people use in a systematic way. Nonetheless, the testimonies of both Plutarch and Sextus indicate that they marked out as problematic a specific category of sentences, namely empirical descriptions of the form 'x is F' in which the subject-expression stands for an external object and the predicate-expression signifies a sensory property attributed to that object. Thus, according to Plutarch, Colotes' satirical remark is that 'these men do not say (*ou legousin*) that a man or a horse or a wall is, but instead (*de*) that they themselves are being walled or horsed or manned' (Plutarch 1120d [T1]); but setting the record straight, Plutarch reports that the Cyrenaics 'say (*legousi*) that we are being sweetened and bittered', and so on, and sets these utterances in contrast to statements such as 'The honey is sweet' and 'The olive-shoot is bitter'

---

[4] This debate is traced back to the philosophers before Socrates and became particularly lively among the Sophists. It is reflected and ramified in Plato's *Cratylus*, where Cratylus maintains that the correctness of names is a matter of nature, while Hermogenes maintains that it is a matter of convention. The debate was protracted into the Hellenistic period: two important contributions are the arguments of the Dialectician Diodorus Cronus in support of the convention thesis, and the Epicurean theory of language. On the problems and ambiguities involved in the debate about the naturalness or conventionality of names, see Denyer 1991, especially pp. 68ff.

[5] On the distinction between the question of the origin of language and the question of its correctness see Boissonade 1820, p. 8.

[6] The goal of comparing our experiences would be to find out the natures of things and capture them in names; since we cannot do that (the argument goes), we name things arbitrarily.

[7] The expression *onoma tithesthai* is standardly used for naming – giving a thing its name. See, for example, Aristotle, *De int.* 18a18ff. and 20b16.

(1120e [T1]). The same goes for Sextus: 'it is possible to assert (*legein*) infallibly and truly and firmly and incorrigibly that we are being whitened or sweetened, but it is impossible to affirm (*apophainesthai*) that the thing productive of the *pathos* in us is white or sweet' (*M* VII.191 [T6b]). These texts seem to me to indicate that the neologisms of the forms 'I am being F-ed' or 'I am being affected F-ly' are intended to replace the empirical statements in question: we should not assert 'The snow is white', but only report 'I am being whitened' or 'I am being affected whitely'; and we should not state 'The honey is sweet', but announce 'I am being sweetened' or 'I am being disposed sweetly'.

The reason why the Cyrenaics found empirical descriptions of the form 'x is F' problematic seems to be epistemological. Assertions of the form 'x is F' attach an external quality F to an external object x and imply that x really has that quality. The Cyrenaics could object that, although you and I may have agreed arbitrarily to call 'F' a particular colour whenever we perceive it, we cannot tell whether our *pathē* of F have the same content, let alone decide whether x truly possesses the quality F. In order to assert justifiedly that x is F, we would need a common criterion. As it is, we possess only a private criterion, i.e. our *pathē*, securing private, not shared truths. The tensions that the Cyrenaics diagnosed between the use of common *onomata* and the absence of a common criterion, and between the public character of the *onomata* and the private nature of the *pathē*, are emphasised in the Sextus passage by the constant opposition of the notions of *koinon* and *idion*.[8]

An important question is how the neologisms of the forms 'I am F-ed' and 'I am affected F-ly', which were invented to report *pathē*, are better fitted to the task of indicating private entities than ordinary linguistic forms are. It is possible that the Cyrenaics thought of first-person present-tense verbs and adverbial expressions as somehow less public or less common (*koina*) than the terms of ordinary language. But in what sense could they maintain that the neologisms are not common and publicly shared? Surely not in the sense that only one person can say 'I am being whitened', for different people can say truly of themselves 'I am being whitened' in the same or in different circumstances. Perhaps the neologisms were thought less public and therefore more appropriate for expressing private *pathē* on account of their technicality and their autobiographical character: they were coined exclusively in order to

---

[8] See the contrasts marked by the expressions ἔνθεν οὐδὲ . . . δὲ (ἔνθεν οὐδὲ κριτήριον κοινὸν . . . πάθη δὲ ἴδια (*M* VII.195 [T6b]) and μὲν . . . δὲ (λευκὸν μὲν καλοῦσιν κοινῶς πάντες . . . κοινὸν δὲ τι λευκὸν οὐκ ἔχουσιν· *M* VII.196, 198 [T6b]).

express internal conditions, each private to an individual perceiver; and every time that the locution 'I am whitened' is used, it is uttered by the same or a different perceiver to describe his own condition at that given time. In contrast with the terms of ordinary language, these neologisms are not *meant* to refer to things which are common and open to observation, and hence might not create the misleading impression that they capture the nature of external properties.

We should rule out, I think, the possibility that the Cyrenaics made similar remarks about the use of nouns, proper names, pronouns, verbs, and so on. First, Plutarch 1120d–e [T1] explicitly denies that the Cyrenaics used locutions of the form 'I am F-ed' in order to reformulate sentences involving reference to physical objects. And this precludes that the neologisms in question were intended to serve as paradigms for recasting most kinds of sentences that are found in ordinary language.[9]

Second, a radical interpretation according to which the Cyrenaics would have systematically challenged the legitimacy of our linguistic practices is inconsistent with the ontological and epistemological assumptions that they make about the external world and other minds. We saw (chapters 6 and 7) that they left unquestioned the existence of external objects and other minds, assuming that there exist entities which, in some sense, can be considered common and public. If so, they can assume that *koina onomata*, such as 'this horse' and 'horse', are legitimately used because their referents are, in some sense, *koina*: I may be mistaken in believing that the horse which I now see is white, but I assume that the cause of my *pathos* is a horse.[10] A similar remark may apply to terms denoting perceivers. It could be maintained that the use, e.g., of personal pronouns and proper nouns is legitimate on the grounds that they are *koina onomata* whose referents are also *koina*: I may

---

[9] Indeed, if we try to apply the remark about the use of *koina onomata* across the board, we shall find it a hard task. Locutions of the form 'I am F-ed' are inadequate to recast sentences such as 'Piety ought to be reserved for the gods, not for men' and 'Did you go to the theatre yesterday? If you did not, you missed the performance of Theodorus as Antigone. Of course, he got the prize!'

[10] One could object that, from the Cyrenaic point of view, the assumption that this is a horse is as problematic as the assertion 'This horse is white'. However, cautiously compare the Cyrenaic assumptions concerning the external causes of the *pathē* with Locke's supposition of the essential unknowability of the substance or the substratum or the support of the discoverable qualities of things, which Locke relates to the distinction between nominal and real essences. See *An Essay Concerning Human Understanding*, II.23.3, IV.12.12, and, on the names of substances, II.6.1–49. All that Locke and the Cyrenaics need to postulate is that there is an external entity causing me this particular batch of various perceptions or *pathē*; we cannot know the real qualities of this entity, we simply assume that it exists. It seems to me that this assumption in itself does not make the positions of the Cyrenaics or of Locke incoherent. I am grateful to Victor Caston for his remarks on this subject.

be wrong in identifying the human figure which I now see as Socrates, but in fact there is at least one entity that the term 'Socrates' designates.

Finally, notice the fact that the Cyrenaics do not doubt that ordinary language assures communication. Even if they problematise to an extent the use of *koina onomata*, they do not seem to think that this makes men unable to understand one another: 'white' in the assertion 'The snow is white' is not meaningless; and the assertion 'The snow is white' may be epistemologically vulnerable, but it is not unintelligible. A similar point can be made with regard to the neologisms: although their referents are both private and incommunicable, utterances of the forms 'I am F-ed' and 'I am affected F-ly' are considered meaningful as well as truthful.[11]

The fact that the Cyrenaics refrain from saying more about linguistic and semantic matters may lead to the thought that they did not have any particular theory about language in the way that, for example, the Epicureans clearly did.[12] Perhaps the primary purpose of their remarks about the use of *koina onomata* is not to express a semantic position, but to back up their thesis that we lack a common criterion through which we could gain cognitive access to reality. Although the fact that we use language in common with other people might make us believe that we possess such a criterion, a closer look at our use of words and at what these words signify will remove that illusion and turn us back to our private *pathē*.

Be this as it may, we shall appreciate better the philosophical potential of the Cyrenaic remarks on *koina onomata* by comparing them to the views of the British empiricist philosopher John Locke on the use of words. According to Locke, language is an instrument for communicating thought, and thought is a constant stream of ideas that succeed each other in a person's consciousness and are private to the perceiver. Ideas can be expressed by words, and the meaning of words is defined in terms of the ideas that they represent. Communication obtains if and only if the linguistic expression of the idea that was in the mind of the speaker evokes the same idea in the minds of his interlocutors.[13]

The relation that the Cyrenaics appear to draw between neologisms

---

[11] I suggested that the fact that the Cyrenaics did not question whether language assures communication is partly due to their notion of privacy, which is weaker than the Cartesian concept of privacy in significant respects; see chapter 7, pp. 94–5. However, the evidence does not clarify how terms such as 'whitened' can be meaningful (and in what sense of 'meaningful').

[12] See Epicurus' *Letter to Herodotus* 75–6. For discussions of this passage, see Bollack, Bollack and Wissmann 1971, especially pp. 235ff.; Sedley 1973; Brunschwig 1977; and Long and Sedley 1987, vol. I, p. 97.

[13] See Locke, *An Essay Concerning Human Understanding*, III.2.1–6.

such as 'I am whitened' and the *pathē* which these neologisms report may bear some resemblance to the relation that, according to Locke, holds between words and ideas. In both cases, language expresses something subjective and private to the perceiver, the *pathē* in the case of the Cyrenaics, the ideas in the case of Locke;[14] language is public and commonly used, as opposed to the *pathē* or to the ideas which are private to the perceiver; and although the meaning of at least certain categories of linguistic expressions depends on the private entities to which they refer, intersubjective communication is considered possible.

However, while Locke admits that there is a criterion for deciding whether the word used by the speaker calls to the mind of the listener *the same* idea that the speaker intended to express, the Cyrenaics explicitly deny that such a criterion may exist. On the one hand, Locke suggests that we can judge whether the speaker and the listener mean the same things by the same words, by observing how they converse with each other: if they appear to understand each other and continue to speak on the same subject, this is proof that the words which they use in common evoke the same ideas in their minds.[15] On the other hand, the Cyrenaics claim that access to the content of other people's *pathē* is structurally and definitionally impossible. Any two interlocutors may use the same expression and yet report qualitatively different *pathē*; or they may employ different expressions and yet refer to *pathē* that are qualitatively identical. If they were faced with Locke's argument, they would probably retort that a successful talk between two people might only prove that the mapping, as it were, of the *pathē*–objects *relations* is identical for both the speaker and the listener; but the fact that they are talking to each other cannot prove that their *pathē* are identical in content. I cannot know that the *pathē* that make you say either 'red' or 'blue' are the same as the ones that make me say either 'red' or 'blue'. But we both realise that we use 'red' or 'blue' without disagreement in the same circumstances, assuming that we are normal perceivers.

---

[14] See Locke's statement: 'Words in their primary and immediate signification stand for nothing but the ideas in the mind of him that uses them, how imperfectly soever or carelessly those ideas are collected from the things which they are supposed to represent' (*An Essay Concerning Human Understanding*, III.2.2).

[15] Further, men are so fashioned by nature as to be able to frame articulate sounds, to use them as signs of internal conceptions and to suppose that their words are marks of ideas in the minds also of other persons with whom they communicate (*An Essay Concerning Human Understanding*, III.1.1–2, III.2.4).

# III

*Subjectivism, empiricism, relativism: Cyrenaics, Epicureans, Protagoreans*

# CHAPTER 9

# Cyrenaic subjectivism and the Epicurean doctrine that all perceptions are true: Plutarch, Adv.Col. *1120f–1121e*

In the two subsequent chapters, I shall turn to the parallels drawn by ancient authors between the Cyrenaic position on the one hand, and the doctrines of Epicurus and of Protagoras in Plato's *Theaetetus* on the other hand. My aim is to show where the Cyrenaic position approaches certain varieties of empiricism and relativism, and also where it diverges from either of these positions. If this is achieved, we may reach a better understanding of the bounds and limitations of the Cyrenaic doctrine.

I shall start with Plutarch [T1], who raises the issue of the relation between Cyrenaic scepticism and Epicurean empiricism. Plutarch's testimony [T1] consists of two parts. In chapter 6 I discussed the first part of the testimony (1120c–f), in which Colotes comes out as an unreliable and even malicious historian, but as a good philosopher.[1] This picture changes in the second part of Plutarch's passage (1120f–1121e), in which Colotes is accused of philosophical naivety on two accounts. First, Plutarch maintains that Colotes fails to see that he is attacking the very tenets which, as an Epicurean, he is bound to endorse.

It would seem that Colotes has the same trouble as boys who are just starting to learn how to read. While they are used to spelling the characters on their tablets, when they see these characters written on other things outside the tablets, they are doubtful and confused. And so with him: the views which he follows eagerly and treats with respect when they occur in the writings of Epicurus, he neither understands nor identifies when they are asserted by others. (1120f–1121a)

And second, in Plutarch's view, Colotes does not realise that the Cyrenaics are more consistent than the Epicureans in defending a thorough scepticism with regard to the objects of the external world.

---

[1] Colotes' critique of the Cyrenaics in the context of his overall aim of refuting scepticism is explored by Vander Waerdt 1989, pp. 225–67.

In what follows, I shall set out the arguments by which Plutarch supports the claim that in some respects the Epicurean doctrine amounts to the same thing as Cyrenaic subjectivism, and I shall discuss whether this claim is philosophically plausible. Subsequently, I shall turn to the question of the consistency of the Epicurean doctrine and I shall maintain that, contrary to what Plutarch thinks, it is not true that a radical scepticism is the logical implication of Epicurean empiricism. I shall discuss both points by comparing Epicureans and Cyrenaics in matters of epistemology and by pointing out the relevant differences between the two theories.

Colotes' critique is mainly targeted against the Cyrenaic thesis that while we do have infallible awareness of our own internal states, this awareness provides no grounds for inferring truths about any object external to the perceiver. Plutarch attempts to assimilate that thesis to the controversial Epicurean doctrine that all *aistheseis* are true.[2] On Plutarch's interpretation, this doctrine states that in all cases of perceptual acts, the things which stimulate *aisthesis* are real, physical things, namely films of atoms (*eidōla*) emanating from the surfaces of three-dimensional atomic structures (1123b–c); while we have knowledge of these films of atoms that impinge on our senses, we do not know the properties of the objects emitting the films of atoms. Plutarch's argument is that this doctrine commits the Epicureans to a view that is essentially the Cyrenaic view, namely that we have infallible awareness of our own internal states (*pathe* in the case of the Cyrenaics, *aistheseis* in the case of the Epicureans), but cannot draw inferences about anything external to the perceiver. Thus, Colotes' own position does not differ from the position that he is attacking.

Those who maintain that when a film of atoms (*eidōlon*) rounded at the corners, or again one which is bent, comes into contact with our senses, our sensation (*aisthesis*) is truly imprinted, but who do not allow us to affirm as well that the tower is round or that the oar is bent, do establish as true their own *pathe* and sense-appearances but do not want to concede that the external objects have these characteristics. (1121a)

The question is whether Plutarch interprets correctly the Epicurean

---

[2] The original formulation and the meaning of this thesis have been the subject of various interpretations. See de Witt 1943, pp. 19–32 and de Witt 1954, especially pp. 138ff.; Long 1971b; Striker 1977; and C. C. W. Taylor, 'All perceptions are true', in Schofield, Burnyeat and Barnes 1980, pp. 105–24. I discuss the meaning of *aisthesis* (pl: *aistheseis*) below, pp. 121–3. My interpretation of the Epicurean doctrine owes very much to Taylor's discussion in the article mentioned above.

doctrine that all *aisthēseis* are true as positing no more than the infallible awareness of one's own sense-contents.

> As to the fact that they (sc. the Epicureans) protest aloud and are vexed on behalf of *aisthēsis*, which is to say that they do not affirm that the external object is warm but only that the *pathos* inherent in *aisthēsis* is warm, is that statement not the same as the [Cyrenaic] statement about taste, i.e., that [the Cyrenaics] do not say that the external object is sweet but that a *pathos* or a movement of this kind related to taste has occurred? (1121b–c)

Is Plutarch right to identify the two theories on these grounds?

It should be obvious that he is wrong to do so. According to his own testimony, the awareness of a Cyrenaic *pathos* implies no commitment to the veridicality of its content, whereas the content of an Epicurean *aisthēsis* represents a state of affairs precisely as it is in reality. The question, then, which I shall examine here is why Plutarch does not see this difference.

First, there are some striking affinities between the Cyrenaic conception of the *pathē* and the Epicurean definition of the nature and role of the *aisthēseis*. Both involve the occurrence of subjective states such as individual acts of sensation, individual acts of perception, and feelings. Both presuppose that the perceiver is aware of the condition he is in when such an event happens.[3] In both cases, the role of the perceiver remains entirely passive since the perceiver can do nothing to alter the contents of his perceptual states. The Epicureans emphasise the passive character of the *aisthēseis* by claiming that they are irrational, *alogoi* (D.L. x.31; Sextus, *M* vii.210),[4] and therefore they are receptive of the things presented to them, but cannot alter them in any way whatsoever (Sextus, *M* vii.210).[5] In the Cyrenaic view, the role of the perceiver or of the perceiver's mind in receiving a *pathos* is passive as well: *pathos* is what one undergoes, what one suffers; and one cannot change in any way whatsoever the fact that one feels pain or sees white. A last relevant

---

[3] I think the Cyrenaic *pathē* and the Epicurean *aisthēseis* entail awareness of their content, not simply because they are criteria, but because of the kind of criteria that they are. However, notice that Lucretius suggests that it can be very hard to tell the difference between, for example, a circular impression and a many-sided polygonal one (*DNR* 4.353–63). On this point, see Scott 1989.

[4] Compare the dogma, shared by all modern empiricists, that in perception the mind is passive and merely reproduces data without processing them. However, as Taylor notices, while empiricists such as Locke talk about the passive reception of mental impressions, the Epicureans talk about the passive reception of physical *eidōla* (Schofield, Burnyeat and Barnes 1980, p. 119).

[5] See Solmsen's article 'Αἴσθησις in Aristotelian and Epicurean thought', in his *Kleine Schriften* (Solmsen 1968–82), vol. i, pp. 612–33; Detel 1975; Long and Sedley 1987, vol. i, pp. 78–90; and C. C. W. Taylor, 'All perceptions are true', in Schofield, Burnyeat and Barnes 1980, especially pp. 119–24.

similarity between the two theories is that both the *aisthēseis* and the *pathē* always tell the truth and never lie. On the epistemic level, the differences between the two become obvious once one presses the question what the *aisthēseis* and the *pathē* are true of. But if one does not ask that question, one can easily assimilate the *aisthēseis* with the *pathē* on account of the fact that they are both infallible. This confusion is made all the more easy since both notions are defined as criteria of truth.

Second, Plutarch puts his finger on a problem of the Epicurean theory of perception which, incidentally, is a problem for most representational theories: the relation between the representational content of the *aisthēsis* and the three-dimensional object that the *aisthēsis* is ultimately supposed to provide evidence for. The Epicureans acknowledge that the relation is complex and potentially problematic, since they claim that the fact that a tower looks round or an oar looks bent does not suffice to establish that the tower is really round or the oar is really bent. This looks very much like the difficulty that lies at the roots of Cyrenaic scepticism and that is brought out by the doubts concerning one's knowledge of other people's *pathē*. For the Cyrenaic argument is that, since we can have no access to the representational content of other people's internal states and since we cannot compare it with our own, we can establish no epistemic link between the content of subjective states and the real properties which this content is supposed to represent.[6] The similarity in question may have led Plutarch to believe that Epicurean empiricism is faced with the same difficulty that forced the Cyrenaics to resign themselves to scepticism, and that it is faced with it for very similar reasons.

Third, the Epicureans propose a way of circumventing the problem of the epistemic relation between *aisthēseis* and objects. They claim that it is the business not of *aisthēsis* but of judgement to decide by using the evidence from several perceptual acts whether the tower is really square or the oar is really bent (Sextus, *M* VII.209–10).[7] But we shall see later in this chapter that Plutarch rejects this solution on the grounds that it is inconsistent with the Epicurean tenet that all *aisthēseis* are equally trustworthy. On account of that objection, Plutarch did not perceive, I think, one more fundamental difference between the Cyrenaic and the Epicurean doctrines: that knowledge of the *aisthēseis* is already knowledge of something physical with which the perceiver is in contact, whereas in

---

[6] See chapter 7, pp. 89–91, 100–3.

[7] Again, compare the contrast that modern empiricists drew between the passivity of the mind in perception and its active role in forming concepts and making judgements.

knowing the *pathē* the perceiver is only in contact with himself. Thus, in the case of the Epicureans, the gap between the *aisthēseis* and the objects is merely the gap between the films of atoms and the objects emitting them. On the other hand, in the case of the Cyrenaics, the gap between the *pathē* and the objects is defined in terms of the unbridgeable gulf between experience and reality.[8]

Plutarch's confusion is also noticeable in a series of auxiliary arguments which he brings in support of his main point. One such argument concerns belief: 'Since the *pathos* differs from the object, it is necessary for belief either to stick to the *pathos* or to be refuted whenever it asserts how things are in addition to how things appear' (1121b). The argument is that the *pathē* and the objects are not the same thing, and beliefs are either about the former or about the latter; since the Epicureans, in fact, 'establish as true [only] their own *pathē* and sense-appearances but do not want to concede that the external objects have these characteristics' (1121a), it follows that beliefs are true and irrefutable only when they are about *pathē* (or sense-appearances), but that they can be convicted of falsehood when they are about objects.

The answer to this argument is given above: the reason why the Epicureans founded inferential beliefs about the world on the evidence offered by the *aisthēseis* and considered such inferences both safe and legitimate is, precisely, that the *aisthēseis* themselves accurately report external information.

Another argument concerns the linguistic and philosophical implications of both doctrines.

Just as those philosophers (sc. the Cyrenaics) are committed to speaking about being horsed or being walled and not about a horse or a wall, so these philosophers (sc. the Epicureans) must say that the eye is rounded or with rough angles, and not that the oar is bent or the tower is round, for the film of atoms from which the eye has been affected is bent, whereas the oar from which the film of atoms has come is not bent. (1121a–b)

Here Plutarch turns the tables on Colotes by applying to Epicureanism the derogatory remarks that Colotes made about the Cyrenaics (1120d). Driving home the point he made in the first part of his testimony (1120d), Plutarch maintains that the logical consequence not only of the Cyrenaic doctrine (as Colotes suggested) but also of Epicureanism is, on the linguistic level, the wide application of neologisms of

---

[8] On the difference between the Epicurean thesis that all *aisthēseis* are true and the thesis that we have incorrigible awareness of our sense-contents, see C. C. W. Taylor, 'All perceptions are true', in Schofield, Burnyeat and Barnes 1980, pp. 117–19.

the form 'I am x-ed' and, on the philosophical level, a radical subjectivisation of our perception of objects.

The drive of Plutarch's remark is that neither theory, as it stands,
offers any criteria for drawing a line between the perception of properties and that of objects, such that it would allow one to analyse properties in terms of *pathē*, and yet to assume throughout that the perception
of a wall or a horse is something over and above collections of one's
*pathē*. In chapter 6 (pp. 82–8), I discussed the extent to which the
Cyrenaics might be vulnerable to this objection.[9] But the objection does
not hold, I think, for the Epicurean theory. The films of atoms reflecting
the structure of, e.g., a round tower have the objective property of being
round.[10] And what the *aisthēsis* reports is not that one is being affected so
as to see round, but that one is seeing something real which is round.[11]

In the last part of his testimony, Plutarch argues that the Cyrenaic
doctrine is more consistent than Epicureanism.[12] His purpose here is to

---

[9] Compare criticisms levelled against Locke with regard to his notion of substance, as it occurs, for
instance, in the *Essay Concerning Human Understanding*, II.23.2–6 (an account which he refined in his
*Letter* and *Replies* to the Bishop of Worcester). One such criticism is that, since Locke maintained
that all our meaningful concepts originate in experience and since he defined substance as
something 'obscure and relative', which by definition cannot be experienced, his views about
substance constitute a strange counter-example to his own epistemological theory. Another
criticism is that he follows Descartes in assuming that attributes must inhere in substance, without
submitting this belief to any rigorous examination or providing in support of it any proof.

[10] On atomism, atoms and minimal parts see, for example, Bailey 1928; Furley 1967; Solmsen 1977;
Konstan 1982 and his article 'Problems in Epicurean physics', in Anton and Preus 1983, vol. II,
pp. 431–64; Leone 1984; Long and Sedley 1987, vol. I, pp. 25–78, and especially pp. 37–57; and
D. Sedley, 'Epicurean anti-reductionism', in Barnes and Mignucci 1988, pp. 297–327.

[11] Notice that the Epicurean examples cited by Plutarch refer only to spatial properties such as
shape, and not to secondary properties such as colour and taste. On a reductionist interpretation, the Epicureans chose the examples of the round tower and of the bent oar to illustrate the
thesis that all *aisthēseis* are true, precisely because they attributed to the atomic components of the
films of atoms size, weight and shape. On the other hand, examples such as the perception of a
white wall or of the sweet taste of honey could be problematic, if the Epicureans assumed that
the atomic components of the films of atoms have no other intrinsic properties: if no impercep-
tible structure of *eidōla* has secondary qualities, it is difficult to maintain that the *aisthēseis* of the
whiteness of a wall and of the sweetness of honey are true of the films of atoms that we perceive in
these cases. For an anti-reductionist approach, see Sedley's 'Epicurean anti-reductionism', in
Barnes and Mignucci 1988, pp. 297–327.

[12] The beginning of this section runs as follows.

The person who says that he is receiving a man-like sense-impression (*phantasia*) but is not
sensing whether there is a man – from where has he got his original idea? Was it not from the
philosophers who claim that they receive a curve-like sense-impression but that the sight does
not go further to affirm that something is curved or round, but rather a sense-appearance
(*phantasma*) or an imprint of round form related to sight has occurred? (1121c)

On the strength of the examples that Plutarch employs, I take it that the first sentence refers to
the Cyrenaics, while the second one refers to the Epicureans. If this is right, Plutarch's argument
is problematic, for it is Plutarch who insists that the epistemological views of the Cyrenaics do
not apply to entities such as men and horses, but only to properties commonly attributed to such

force an imaginary Epicurean interlocutor into conceding, again, that Cyrenaics and Epicureans maintain some of the same tenets. The fictional interlocutor grants a close affinity between the two doctrines, but argues that nonetheless they differ significantly. 'Most certainly, one will answer. But for my part, after I come close to the tower or after I touch the oar, I shall assert that the oar is straight and the tower is angular. But this other man, if he gets close, will admit what seems to be the case and what appears to him, but nothing more' (1121c). The remark is very much to the point. The Epicurean will finally allow himself to form judgements about external objects and about their real properties, whereas the Cyrenaic will not.

This answer prompts Plutarch to press his second charge against Colotes and the Epicureans, namely that their view that all *aisthēseis* are true but that their content is not necessarily true of real objects is inconsistent with other tenets of Epicurean epistemology.

Indeed, my dear friend, he (sc. the Cyrenaic) better than you observes and defends the logical consequences of his doctrine, that all sense-impressions alike are trustworthy about themselves and no sense-impression is trustworthy about anything else but all are equally good witnesses. And here is the end of your doctrine that all sense-impressions are true and none is unreliable or false, if indeed you think that this category of sense-impressions must state additional truths about external objects, while you refused to trust that other kind of sense-impressions in anything beyond the *pathos* itself. If sense-impressions have an equal claim to trustworthiness, no matter whether they occur when we observe an object closely or at a distance, then it is only fair either to confer on all sense-impressions the power of making additional judgements about how things are, or to subtract that power from the former category of sense-impressions as well as from the latter. But if there is a difference in the *pathos* affecting one when one is at a distance and when one is close at hand, it is false to assert that no sense-impression and no sensation is more evident than another. Likewise, what they call attestation and contestation have nothing to do with sensation but rather with belief. Thus, if they urge us to make assertions about the external objects by following these, they transfer the object of judgement from what is unfailingly true to what is often false. (1121d–e)

In this passage, Plutarch gives two arguments in support of his thesis that the Epicurean doctrine is inconsistent in ways in which the Cyrenaic doctrine is not. First, he claims that the Epicurean analysis of how

entities (1120d–f). Also, Plutarch seems to maintain that the Cyrenaics got the original idea for their theory from the Epicureans, but his claim is historically anachronistic. Actually, ancient authors sometimes suggest the contrary. On the historical and philosophical relations between the two schools, see Gosling and Taylor 1982, pp. 365–96, and especially 394–6.

perceptual judgements are formed belies the thesis of the truth of all *aisthēseis*; and he suggests that this inconsistency arises precisely because in fact the Epicureans step outside the bounds of the *aisthēseis* and make claims about reality. The Cyrenaics are more consistent precisely because they do not transcend the limits of the *pathē*: they treat all *pathē* as equally true and reliable about themselves, and they consider them all as equally unreliable with regard to external objects. The implication that we are expected to draw is that if the Epicureans maintained consistently the position of the truth of all *aisthēseis*, they should be committed to radical scepticism, as the Cyrenaics are.

Regarding the Cyrenaics, his observation is obviously correct. But regarding the Epicureans, the accusation that their theory is inconsistent is supported by false premises. The *aisthēseis* reveal truths about physical structures and not only truths about themselves. And although all *aisthēseis* are equally true and reliable,[13] not all films of atoms which imprint themselves upon the *aisthēseis* have the structure and the properties of the aggregates from which they are emitted. It is opinion, not *aisthēsis*, which will decide what kind of films of atoms affected the eye in each case. Thus, the Epicurean claim is not that, although some *aisthēseis* suggest that the tower is round, the evidence from other *aisthēseis* suggests that, in fact, the tower is square. The claim is that opinion should discriminate between these two kinds of *aisthēseis* and realise that they do not represent the same object.[14]

Plutarch's second argument is that since the processes of confirmation (*epimartyrēsis*) and contestation or refutation (*antimartyrēsis*) 'have to do with' belief rather than *aisthēsis*, and since we form our judgements about external objects by following these processes, judgement 'is transferred' from what is always true to what is either true or false.

The claim that confirmation and contestation or refutation 'have to do' with belief probably refers to the Epicurean position that beliefs about external objects are confirmed or refuted by appealing to the evidence offered by the *aisthēseis*. A belief is established as true if it is witnessed for (*epimartyreisthai*) or if is not witnessed against (*ouk antimartyreisthai*) by the *aisthēseis*, and it is established as false if it is witnessed

---

[13] On the arguments defending the thesis that all *aisthēseis* are true and no *aisthēseis* can be false, see primarily Lucretius, *DNR* 4.469–521; D.L. x.31–2; Epicurus, *KD* xxiii; PHerc. 19/698, cols. xvii, xviii, xxiii, xxv, xxvi. On the fallibility of opinion, see Sextus, *M* vii.211ff., viii.63; D.L. x.34. How the Epicureans explained the truth of *aisthēseis* related to phenomena such as optical illusions is explained in Lucretius, *DNR* 4.353–63, 379–86, Sextus, *M* vii.206ff. Translated texts on these subjects are found in Long and Sedley 1987, vol. i, pp. 78–83, 87–8, 90–4.

[14] On this, see Sextus, *M* vii.210.

against (*antimartyreisthai*) or if it is not witnessed for (*ouk epimartyreisthai*) by them.[15] Thus, the first premiss of the argument is that confirmation and refutation are *of beliefs*, not of the content of *aisthēseis*. The second premiss recalls the Epicurean position that we form our judgements about external objects on the grounds of the evidence offered by the *aisthēsis* and through the processes of confirmation or refutation mentioned above.

The force of Plutarch's objection is difficult to determine, mainly because it is unclear what he means by the phrase that the Epicureans 'transfer judgement' from what is always true to what is sometimes true. If he is accusing the Epicureans of obliterating the criteria of judgement by allowing room for error, then he is plainly wrong, for what confirm or refute our beliefs about external objects are *aisthēseis*, and these are always true, not sometimes true. On the other hand, if Plutarch is accusing the Epicureans of placing judgements in the realm of belief and thus allowing room for error, then it is unclear why he considers this a liability of the theory. It could be objected that, in this respect, the Epicurean doctrine fits the facts: it is the case that sometimes we are mistaken in our assertions about external objects.

Thus, Plutarch does not succeed in his attempt to show, first, that Cyrenaic scepticism and Epicurean empiricism are based on a common position concerning the truth of all sense-impressions and, second, that the former doctrine is more coherent than the latter. The examination of the evidence indicates, I think, that Plutarch has a good understanding of the Cyrenaic doctrine, but an inadequate understanding of Epicureanism. In locating his mistakes, we may have learnt something about the kinds of objections that representational theories of perception have to face, and also something about the relations between empiricism and Cyrenaic scepticism.

[15] See Sextus, *M* vii.211–16; D.L. x.34. The procedure of verification or falsification of beliefs about facts is discussed in Asmis 1984, pp. 141–66, 190–6, 227ff., and in Long and Sedley 1987, vol. i, pp. 94–7.

# CHAPTER 10

# Cyrenaic epistemology and Protagorean relativism: some considerations

The next parallel, between the epistemology of the Cyrenaic school and Protagorean relativism, was attempted both in ancient and then in modern times. However, there is little evidence as to how precisely the relation between the two theories should be determined.

Cicero clearly considers that there are differences between the two schools since he reports that they have different positions concerning the criterion of truth.

One criterion is that of Protagoras, who holds that what appears to a person is true for that person, another is that of the Cyrenaics, who believe that there is no criterion whatsoever except the inmost feelings, another is that of Epicurus, who places the whole criterion in the senses and in the primary notions of things and in pleasure. On the other hand, Plato believed that the whole criterion of truth and truth itself lies merely in reasoning and in the mind, detached from belief and from the senses. (Cicero, *Luc.* 142 [T4c])

A similar statement is made by Eusebius.

Aside from the philosophers that were set forth by us, in this gymnastic contest the stadium will also contain, stripped of all truth, those from the opposite side who took up arms against all the dogmatic philosophers put together (I mean the school of Pyrrho), and who declared that nothing amongst men is apprehensible, and also the school of Aristippus who maintain that only the *pathē* are apprehensible, and again the schools of Metrodorus and Protagoras, who hold that we must trust only the sensations of the body. (Eusebius XIV.2.4–7 [T8])

However, neither author clarifies whether the differences between the doctrines of the Cyrenaics and the Protagoreans are significant, or simply a matter of emphasis and degree. Both authors suggest that the common points of these doctrines lie in their anti-rationalism, their empiricist elements and their emphasis on the importance of the senses, but do not pursue the matter any further.

These limitations of the ancient testimonies are partly responsible for the fact that there is considerable variety amongst the views of modern scholars on the relationship of Protagoras and his followers to the Cyrenaics.

Some have attempted to determine that relation by using fragments and testimonia concerning the historical Protagoras.[1] However, I shall not discuss their views here. I shall turn instead to another group of commentators, who try to determine the relationship between the relativism of Protagoras and the epistemology of the Cyrenaics by focusing their discussion on the first part of Plato's *Theaetetus*. In this case, the debated issue is whether the views of the Platonic Protagoras, and in particular those attributed to the 'subtler' philosophers (*hoi kompsoteroi*), are historically and philosophically related to Cyrenaic epistemology.[2] Most scholars belonging to this group agree that the epistemology of the Cyrenaics closely resembles the Protagorean ingredients of the secret doctrine in the *Theaetetus*; and they appear to assume that, if the metaphysical elements of the latter could somehow be accommodated within the context of the Cyrenaic doctrine,[3] there would be no major obstacle to identifying the two theories.[4]

My approach to the problem is this. There is a deliberate mystique surrounding the doctrine of the 'subtler' philosophers: it is a 'hidden truth' (155e), a set of 'mysteries' (*mystēria*: 156a) to which only the initiated must listen (155e). This may indicate that there are no such philosophers;[5] but it may also suggest that there is an actual group of people,[6] but that Plato cannot give them a name without making the dramatic setting of the dialogue implausible: if the *kompsoteroi* are philosophers of the fourth century BC, Socrates could not have known them. My aim will be to construct as strong a case as I can in defence of this last alternative and then criticise it.

The theory of the 'subtler' philosophers is presented in connection

---

[1] See, for example, Guthrie 1969, vol. III, pp. 496ff.; Grote 1865, vol. III, pp. 560ff.; Glidden 1975 and my discussion of his views in chapter 4, pp. 45–7.

[2] The three leading interpretations are the following. (1) The *kompsoteroi* are a historically identifiable school, the Cyrenaics, and the theory developed and refuted in the first part of the *Theaetetus* is a version of the Cyrenaic theory: so Schleiermacher, *Platons Werke*, II, 1, pp. 183ff.; Dümmler 1889, pp. 173ff.; and Mondolfo 1953 and 1958. (2) The *kompsoteroi* have no historical reference, and the doctrine that Plato attributes to these thinkers is his own creation: see Burnet 1914, Cornford 1935 and W. D. Ross 1951. (3) This matter cannot be settled because of the inconclusiveness of the evidence: so Natorp 1890. See also the extensive bibliography on this subject in Giannantoni 1958, pp. 129–45, and Giannantoni's concluding comments in p. 142 of that volume.

[3] Zeller, for example, questioned whether the Cyrenaics could consistently maintain both that the nature of things is inapprehensible and that it is in perpetual flux.

[4] This is the line of argument followed in Mondolfo 1958.

[5] See note 2.     [6] See note 2.

with Theaetetus' second attempt to determine what is knowledge, in which knowledge (*epistēmē*) is defined as sense-perception (*aisthēsis*).[7] Theaetetus' thesis is complemented by two other doctrines. First, there is Protagoras' doctrine that 'Man is the measure of all things, of things that are, that they are, and of things that are not, that they are not' (152a)[8] which, according to Socrates, amounts to claiming that 'as each thing appears to me, so it is for me, and as it appears to you, so it is for you – you and I each being a man' (152a). And second, there is Heraclitus' theory that

there is nothing which in itself is just one thing: nothing which you could call anything or any kind of thing . . . What is really true is this: the things of which we naturally say that they 'are' are in process of coming to be, as the result of movement and change and blending with one another. We are wrong when we say that they 'are', since nothing ever is, but everything is coming to be. (152d–e)

So, the question 'What is knowledge?' is answered by means of a threefold theory which consists of the thesis that knowledge is sense-perception, the Protagorean position defending the relative truth of appearances, and a version of Heraclitean metaphysics of eternal flux.

The 'subtler' philosophers offer an explanation of sense-perception by appeal to the last of these positions, namely the metaphysical claim that everything is motion or moves. The relevant passage is 156a–157c. According to this passage, 'the mysteries' of the 'subtler' philosophers consist in denying the independent existence of perceivers and perceived objects or properties, and in replacing them by processes which *are* perceivers and perceived objects or properties *only at the moment of perception*. The perception of an object possessing a certain property, e.g., of a white stone, occurs as a result of twin pairs of motions which arise in the space between the sense-organ and the object which is commensurable with the sense-organ. On the side of perceiver, what is generated is a sense-organ which is perceiving something at that moment, e.g., a seeing eye. On the side of the thing perceived, what is generated is a object possessing the property which came into being from the contact of the sense-organ with something commensurable with it, e.g., what

---

[7] My understanding of Plato's argumentative strategy in the first part of the *Theaetetus*, and a great deal more about philosophical relativism in general, owes much to Burnyeat 1990 (especially pp. 7–65). References to specific pages aim to guide the reader rather than to record my own debts, which will be obvious to all those familiar with Burnyeat's analysis.

[8] The passages of the *Theaetetus* cited in this chapter come from M. J. Levett's translation, revised and printed in Burnyeat 1990.

comes into being is a white stone.⁹ This analysis entails, first, that all perceptions arise from motions. Second, in every perceptual act, the perceiver and the object perceived are ontologically relative to each other and they are tied together necessarily.¹⁰ Third, the theory suggests that a new language, a language of becoming, should replace the language of being: verbs such as the verb 'to be', substantival terms such as 'something', pronouns such as 'I', pronominal adjectives such as 'mine', expressions denoting individual things such as 'this man', and perhaps even some classes of things,¹¹ should be eliminated, because they bring things to a stop. Their use implies that the things to which they refer are not in perpetual motion but at rest, and that they are in themselves, not through association with one another.

Three important implications of the doctrine are drawn. First, no perceiver and no thing perceived have an identity which persists beyond the moment of perception. Socrates ill is a different percipient from Socrates well, and the perception of wine that Socrates has when he is ill is a different perception from that which he has when he is well (159c). Second, the Heraclitean analysis of perception implies that each perception is an event private to the perceiver. It is private to me primarily in the sense that it is 'that being which is peculiarly mine' (160c); it belongs uniquely to me and could not belong to anyone else. The privacy of perceptions is mainly connected to the thesis of the ontological relativity of perceptions to individual perceivers: 'Since that which acts on me is for me, and not for anyone else, it is I who perceive it too, and nobody else' (160c).

Third, perceptions are infallibly known by the perceiver *precisely because* they are events private to him: 'My perception is true for me – because it is always a perception of that being which is peculiarly mine (*tēs emēs ousias*); and I am judge, as Protagoras said, of things that are, that they are, for me; and of things that are not, that they are not'(160c). The position that the knowledge of one's own percepts is

---

⁹ See Burnyeat 1990, pp. 10–19 on the exposition of the triple theory. More insights into the Heraclitean component of the theory are offered in pp. 42ff. (Burnyeat's discussion of the refutation of Heraclitus' theory in *Theaet.* 179c–183c).

¹⁰ See 160a–b. The thesis that perceivers and objects are ontologically commensurable is defended in Burnyeat 1982, pp. 11ff.; the symmetry between perceivers and objects is contrasted with the ontological primacy that Berkeley assigns to the perceiving mind over the objects perceived.

¹¹ It is not entirely clear that all expressions denoting classes of things are banned here: because Socrates' interlocutor still defends the thesis that man is the measure, he may not want to say at this stage of the argument that there is no such thing as man or we cannot speak about it. The conclusion that, for the proponents of the triple theory, language would be entirely impossible is finally reached in 182a–183b.

infallible[12] is crucial to the development of the argument in the first part of the dialogue. It supports Theaetetus' claim that sense-perception and sense-perception alone guarantees knowledge. It determines the nature of knowledge as the infallible and incorrigible awareness that the perceiver has of how things appear and are for him. And it constitutes part of the reasoning defending the position that all sense-perceptions are veridical and no sense-perception can be false to what is perceived.

These features might appear to coincide with central features of the Cyrenaic position. On the ontological level, like the perceptions of the 'subtler' philosophers, the *pathē* of the Cyrenaics are events whose occurrence depends upon the existence of a perceiver;[13] they are private to the perceiver; they are related to motions; and they can be short-lived, although they often are not.[14] So it might be argued that the Cyrenaic theory has the same metaphysical background as the threefold doctrine of the 'subtler' philosophers: it relativises perceptions with regard to perceivers and it defines them as constantly changing phenomena which are identifiable only while they are taking place.

On the epistemological level, the Cyrenaic theory may appear similar to the doctrine of the *kompsoteroi* in that it excludes the possibility of obtaining objective knowledge. Like the *kompsoteroi*, the Cyrenaics claim that it is the *pathē* and the *pathē* alone that provide knowledge and certainty; they define this knowledge as infallible and incorrigible awareness; they contrast one's unerring awareness of the *pathē* with the fundamental incapacity of any person to know what other people know about their own internal states; and they draw a connection between the incorrigibility and the privacy of perceptual states.

Both doctrines face the question of how far they can go without introducing the notion of objective truth – a challenge faced by modern versions of relativism and by subjectivistic theories alike.[15] In the *The-*

---

[12] This position should not be analysed, I believe, in terms of a sense-data theory of perception. However, see G. E. Moore, 'A defence of common sense', in Muirhead 1924, p. 218, and Warnock 1967, p. 8.

[13] Taken in itself, this assumption could hardly be a criterion for identifying the Cyrenaics, for every Greek philosopher makes it.

[14] See chapter 2, pp. 15–16, where I argued that *monochronos* does not mean 'momentary' or 'short-lived', but 'unitemporal': the point is that a *pathos* can only be enjoyed while it is occurring – whether it lasts for a few minutes or for longer periods. Notice that if *monochronos* is understood as 'momentary', it increases the similarity between the two doctrines.

[15] For elucidation of problems raised by various kinds of relativism, see Williams 1972, ch. 3; Williams 1981, especially the chapter 'The truth in relativism', pp. 132–43; and Williams 1985, especially ch. 9: 'Relativism and reflection', pp. 156–73. See also Harman 1975, which attempts to develop a kind of relativism that avoids the standard problems.

*aetetus*, it takes the form of asking whether Protagorean relativism is compatible with the presence of certain kinds of knowledge or expertise, which prompts a broad-ranging discussion of the doctrine culminating in the famous self-refutation argument.[16] We encounter another form of the problem in the Aristocles passage [T5], when Aristocles argues that Cyrenaic subjectivism is either too narrow or too broad to be consistent, and that in fact the apprehension of the *pathē* must involve factual knowledge.[17]

Finally, on the linguistic and semantic level, it might appear that the Cyrenaic neologisms serve the same end as the language of becoming proposed by the 'subtler' philosophers, i.e., avoiding reference to external objects and reporting only how things appear and are for the perceiver at a given time.

This is the strongest case that I can make for identifying the *kompsoteroi* with the Cyrenaics. It was important, I believe, to produce it, for it bears on larger issues concerning the nature of subjectivist and of relativistic approaches to truth, knowledge and reality. These issues will emerge more clearly if we turn to the objections that can be raised against identifying the two views in question.

Aside from historical considerations, even if we assume that the 'subtler' philosophers were philosophers active in the fourth century BC,[18] there are philosophical reasons why we must reject both the thesis that the 'subtler' philosophers *are* the Cyrenaics and the weaker thesis that these were different groups of thinkers who, however, held essentially the same doctrine.

---

[16] See the analysis and discussion of this argument in Burnyeat 1976 and Waterlow 1977.

[17] See chapter 5, pp. 62–72.

[18] If my chronology of the Cyrenaic school is roughly correct (see Tsouna 1988, pp. 15–37), then only the doctrine of Aristippus of Cyrene or, perhaps, of his daughter Arete, could have been known by Plato. The prologue of the *Theaetetus* is situated in 369 BC and the actual year of its composition was probably close to that date. Euclides tells Terpsion that Socrates had a talk with the young Theaetetus very shortly before Socrates' death in 399 (142c), which Euclides wrote down in conversational form soon afterwards (143a–c). Both the dramatic date of the dialogue and the date of its composition suggest that the doctrine of the *kompsoteroi* must have been fully formed before the mature years of Aristippus the Younger, who was born around 380 BC and who is usually considered the first epistemologist of the Cyrenaic school. Thus, if one maintains that the doctrine of the 'subtler' philosophers is the Cyrenaic doctrine, then one must infer that the doctrine was fully formed by Aristippus of Cyrene or by his daughter (see, for example, Giannantoni 1958, p. 118). In that case, we would need to account for the testimonies which attribute the main tenets of Cyrenaic epistemology to Aristippus the Younger (see Eusebius XIV.18.32 [T5]), and for the passages creating the impression that the founder of the school was mainly concerned with ethics. Also, the *kompsoteroi* need not be an actual group of thinkers. As I mentioned above (p. 125), we cannot exclude the possibility that they are not: the deliberate mystery with which Plato surrounds them may be taken to point in that direction.

From the ontological point of view, the fact that the Cyrenaics associated the occurrence of the *pathē* with motions of the flesh or of the soul does not, by itself, indicate that they held the metaphysical doctrine of perpetual flux. In fact, the analysis of internal states or experiences of various sorts in terms of motions seems to have been quite common in antiquity, and occurs in medical and philosophical passages.[19] For example, it is found in the tradition of the natural philosophers[20] and in Plato.[21]

Another point of difference between the ontological commitments of the two positions is found in their views on the temporal identity of objects and perceivers. The Heraclitean account of perception in the *Theaetetus* entails that no perceiver and no thing perceived has a stable identity over time.[22] The identity of the perceived object, for example sweet wine, is relativised to a single perceiver, for example Socrates healthy, and to the moment when Socrates is tasting the sweet wine. But also, the identity of Socrates is relativised to a single perception, his perception of sweet wine, and to the time at which that perception occurs. It follows that 'when a thing mixes now with one thing and now with another, it will not generate the same thing each time but different things' (159a), and this same statement applies to objects as well as to persons and to the concept of the self (159a–160a). The correct use of 'the language of becoming' would involve realising that words such as 'Socrates', 'man' or 'stone' designate aggregates of many momentary perceptions which we add together (πολλὰ ἀθροισθέντα, 157b).

It is important to emphasise that the non-identity thesis is vital to the relativisation of all perception and all knowledge proposed by the

---

[19] Afflictions or diseases are often attributed to changes brought about by factors internal or external to the body. It should be stressed that the Greeks did not think that *perpetual* movement within man is normal. On the contrary, in several contexts, the outward signs of continuous or violent movement within indicate that something is wrong. On the ambiguous nature of inner movement, both as source of suffering and as the focus of varied experience and knowledge, see Padel 1992, pp. 65ff.

[20] See, for example, *Theaet.* 152e which lists Empedocles among the partisans of the doctrine of flux; the anonymous *Theaetetus* commentator (70.44ff.) informs us that he is included among them because of his theory of effluences.

[21] See, for example, *Tim.* 86a, where Plato seems to espouse a version of the theory of humours and he explains both bodily diseases and mental afflictions in such terms. Notice, however, that in the *Timaeus* Plato has some sort of commitment to physical flux.

[22] The earliest challenges to ordinary assumptions about identity are found in Heraclitus (DK 22 B 91) and Epicharmus (fr. 170 Kaibel); in Plato, aside from the *Theaetetus*, see also *Symp.* 207d. However, it was not until the emergence of the Stoic school that the issue of temporal identity was systematically explored. On the nature of the debate focused on the so-called Growing Argument between the Stoics and the Academics, see Sedley 1982. On the nature of puzzles such as the Growing Argument, see Sedley 1977. As he points out, the Growing Argument can be compared to the argument put forward by Locke in *An Essay Concerning Human Understanding*, II.27.3, and reiterated by Hume in the *Treatise of Human Nature*, 1.4.6.

'subtler' philosophers. If perception is to yield knowledge, it must be certain and incorrigible. If it is to be incorrigible, it must be confined within the limits of single perceptual acts, in which whatever is perceived is true for the person who perceives it. For this to obtain, there must be no independent standard through which or against which the content of individual perceptions can be measured. But if objects or perceivers had a stable identity, there would exist such standards and they would allow the confirmation or refutation of individual perceptual reports.[23]

The question is, then, whether the Cyrenaics were committed to holding a form of the non-identity thesis. The sources do not offer direct evidence on this point. However, one obvious place to look for indirect evidence on this topic is the Cyrenaic analysis of perception in subjective terms. Here is a rough outline of an argument supporting the hypothesis that the Cyrenaics met the 'subtler' philosophers more than halfway in entertaining doubts about the temporal identity of objects as well as of perceivers.

Suppose for a moment (against chapter 6, pp. 82 ff.) that the Cyrenaic analysis of perception in terms of how the perceiver is affected is intended to apply not only to properties, such as white and sweet, but also to objects, such as wall and honey. Since they pronounce only the *pathē* deriving from the perception of properties true and irrefutable, we might then infer that they consider the *pathē* coming from our perception of objects less trustworthy and liable to refutation. The reason why they would consider this second category of *pathē* epistemologically vulnerable could be that they involve assumptions about collections or aggregates of different impressions: for example, a wall-like *pathos* involves a number of assumptions and judgements about how to collect individual *pathē* of white, nine feet tall, smooth, cool, and so on. But all sorts of problems can be raised regarding collections related to the existence of objects and their continuing identity over time[24] and, as readers of the *Theaetetus* are well aware, the same goes for perceivers.[25] So, supposing that the Cyrenaics analyse our perception of objects in terms of 'complex' *pathē* (i.e. aggregates of impressions to which terms such as 'wall' apply), and supposing that they consider these *pathē* less reliable than the

---

[23] On the place that the universal non-identity thesis occupies in the argument, see Burnyeat 1990, pp. 15ff.

[24] One set of such problems is raised by the so-called Growing Argument: every increase or decrease of a subject constituted by the collection of qualitatively identical components (e.g. heaps) involves the loss of identity of that subject and the coming into being of a new one.

[25] See *Theaet.* 159a–160a: Socrates ill is not the same person as Socrates well, and the bitter wine which Socrates is tasting, at the time when he is ill, is not the same wine as that which Socrates tasted yesterday, when he was well.

*pathē* of single properties, it might seem to follow that they acknowledge the difficulties concerning collections and hence that they cast doubts on the temporal identity of objects and perceivers alike.[26]

Perhaps the most important feature of this argument is that it implies a radical rejection of eudaemonism. The search for happiness arguably presupposes both that happiness is something extended in time and that one's conception of oneself is that of a person persisting in time. Both these presuppositions involve belief in collections. If the Cyrenaics have exposed such beliefs to doubt, and if they have implicitly denied that there is such a thing as a temporally extended self, they have a powerful motivation for rejecting happiness as the moral end. The fact that most Cyrenaics defined the moral end in terms of the bodily pleasure that one is experiencing at present, not as the pleasure achieved over a lifetime, might appear to support that conclusion.[27]

Nevertheless, there are good reasons for rejecting the hypothesis that the Cyrenaics entertained doubts about the nature of collections and our knowledge of them.

I have already said that there is not a trace of direct evidence at all that the Cyrenaics conceived of real objects and persons in compositional terms or that they voiced doubts about temporal identity. Nor is it plausible to draw that conclusion indirectly, on philosophical grounds. As I argued in chapters 6 and 7, the analysis of perception in terms of the *pathē* of the perceiver is effected at the level of single empirical properties, not of three-dimensional objects, and leaves untouched the fundamental ontological assumptions that real objects exist and that other people exist and have *pathē*. If so, it is not the case that the Cyrenaics deal with two subsets of *pathē*, *pathē* of qualities which are evident and irrefutable, and *pathē* of objects which are epistemically vulnerable. Hence there is no room for the hypothesis that the unreliability of the *pathē* coming from objects, such as a wall and a lump of honey, is due to the fact that they involve (or that they provide grounds for) judgements about collections of different impressions.[28]

What is more, the evidence goes some way towards affirming that the Cyrenaics conceive of perceivers as relatively stable entities. Aristocles,

---

[26] Irwin 1991 argues along similar lines. I cannot do justice to his admirably clear and subtle argument here, but I discuss it in detail in my article 'Is there an exception to Greek eudaemonism?' in M. Canto and P. Pellegrin (eds.) *Mélanges Jacques Brunschwig*, Paris (forthcoming).
[27] Again, see Irwin 1991.
[28] Compare Irwin 1991, pp. 64–5. Irwin is right, I believe, in maintaining that the fact that the Cyrenaics use expressions such as 'I am being whitened' or 'I am sweetened', but not 'I am walled' or 'I am manned', indicates that they do not analyse the perception of qualities and the perception of objects in the same way. But I disagree with him as to the reason why they do not apply parallel analyses in both cases.

quoted by Eusebius (XIV.18.32 [T5]), and Sextus (*M* VII.197–8 [T6b]) attest the Cyrenaic belief that each person has a certain physiological constitution which to an unknown extent determines the nature of his *pathē*. Thus, the stability and continuity of the body and perceptual apparatus of each perceiver may be contrasted with the passing nature of his experiences. And it may also provide a condition of the perceiver's identity over time: the *pathē* of each perceiver take place in a particular body, and this body can be considered a condition of the perceiver's temporal identity.

Further, there is some indication that the Cyrenaic theory contains materials for relating memory to temporal identity. Aristippus did not consider the memory (*mnēmē*) of past pleasures pertinent to the moral end because they are pleasures that *he has enjoyed* in the past, not pleasures that he is enjoying at present (Athenaeus, *Deipn.* XII.544a–b Kaibel); and his followers denied that pleasure consists in the memory of past goods, on the grounds that the movement of the soul that results in the pleasurable experiences of the past disappears with time and, presumably, cannot be recreated (D.L. II.89–90 [T7c]).[29] In these cases, the Cyrenaics appear to assume that *the same moral agent* has memory of past pleasures. So, if Aristippus has memory of past experiences both as being past and as being his own, this seems to presuppose[30] that he is the same Aristippus in different times and places.[31]

---

[29] See chapter 2, pp. 16–17.

[30] Compare Reid's criticism of Locke's thesis about memory as the necessary and sufficient condition of personal identity. Reid's argument is that you do not remember experiences; you remember *yourself* as experiencing, and therefore memory presupposes the identity of the self. See T. Reid, *Essays on the Intellectual Powers of Man* (1785), and especially the essay 'On memory', chapters 4 and 6. One may argue that you can remember a past experience *as if* it were your own; but then it would not be a memory.

[31] Compare Locke's much contested view that memory is the single necessary and sufficient condition of personal identity (see J. Locke, *An Essay Concerning Human Understanding*, II.27.1–29). See Reid's argument against Locke outlined in the previous note, as well as J. Butler's criticisms in the Appendix to *The Analogy of Religion* (Oxford 1897, vol. I, pp. 385ff.), and especially the objection that if personal identity does not require identity of substance (as Locke claims), then personal identity is not a case of identity, in the philosophical sense of the word. This is not the conclusion that Butler endorsed himself, but it was the conclusion that Hume appears to have reached. See the notorious section on personal identity in D. Hume, *Treatise of Human Nature*, 1.4.6. For an interesting interpretation of Hume's views, as well as a good outline of the debate on personal identity, see J. Perry, 'The problem of personal identity' in Perry 1975, pp. 3–30. For versions of the memory theory, see A. Quinton, 'The soul', in Perry 1975, pp. 53–72, and H. P. Grice, 'Personal identity', in Perry 1975, pp. 73–98. For further contributions, some of which contain criticisms of the memory theory, see S. Shoemaker, 'Personal identity and memory', in Perry 1975, pp. 119–34; Wiggins 1967; Strawson 1959, especially ch. 3, pp. 81–113; Parfit 1971; D. Lewis, 'Survival and identity', in Oksenberg Rorty 1976, pp. 17–40, and D. Dennet, 'Conditions of personhood', in the same volume, pp. 175–96, which sets out necessary conditions for personhood and emphasises the essentially normative character of the concept of a person. See also B. Williams, 'Personal identity and individuation', 'Bodily continuity and personal identity', and 'The self and the future', in Williams 1973, pp. 1–18, 19–25 and 46–63 respectively.

I come now to the idea that doubts about temporal identity, and in particular about the identity of persons over time, go hand in hand with the Cyrenaic rejection of eudaemonism and the substitution of bodily pleasure experienced in the present for happiness as the moral end. This is not the place to dwell on Cyrenaic ethics in detail, so I shall say what is directly relevant to the issue at hand and I shall argue for my position elsewhere.

In my view, the relation between eudaemonism and hedonism in Cyrenaic ethics is more complicated than is usually assumed. Aside from the founder of the school who, I believe, was straightforwardly a eudaemonist,[32] the ethical doctrines of most Cyrenaic philosophers appear to contain the following tension. They all determine the unitemporal pleasure of the present as the moral end, thus confining the moral end to pleasure while we are experiencing it. And yet they attribute ethical importance to something which is not the moral end, namely happiness and the achievement of a happy life. The evidence on the relation between pleasure and happiness indicates first that the Cyrenaics define happiness in compositional terms, as a particular collection of individual pleasures which retains the properties of its constituents;[33] and second, that they grant that the moral agent conceives of himself as a temporally extended person experiencing many particular pleasures and, as a result of them, feeling happy. If this is right, then the Cyrenaic position takes roughly the following shape. The *telos*, the moral end, is one, namely an individual feeling of pleasure resulting from a smooth motion of the flesh; this has value only while we are experiencing it. It is complete and self-sufficient[34] in the sense that one requires nothing else at the time when the pleasure is occurring. However, present pleasure is not the only thing we should aim at.[35]

---

[32] See the discussion of the evidence in my article 'The Socratic origins of the Cynics and Cyrenaics', in Vander Waerdt 1994, especially pp. 377–82.

[33] See D.L. II.91: 'It seems virtually impossible to them that the collection of pleasures would not amount to happiness.' The Cyrenaics consider this impossible, presumably because they reason that, since individual pleasures are goods, the collection of them will also be a good. A similar belief about collections, I think, underlies Hegesias' pessimism: 'Happiness is entirely impossible, for the body has been filled with many afflictions, while the soul shares in the sufferings of the body and is disturbed, and fortune is an obstacle to many of the things that we hope for. From these considerations, it follows that happiness cannot be realised' (D.L. II.94). Happiness is unattainable because there is no collection of experiences in a person's life which does not contain many pains as components. And no collection composed of pains can have the property of being a good, since many of its components do not have that property.

[34] On completeness and self-sufficiency as the criteria for considering something as the moral good, see Aristotle, *EN* I.7.

[35] It seems to me that there are two distinct senses in which we can speak about the *telos* in an ethical context: one in which the *telos* is the only thing aimed at (cf. the Stoic concept of the *telos*), and

Happiness is one other thing that we should seek – and it is a very important thing. One reason why we wish for it lies in the fact that, even though unitemporal pleasure can last for quite a long time,[36] it does not last for a lifetime. We wish to attain the moral end, and because it disappears, we wish to achieve it again and again. Thus, one pursues the particular collection which is one's happiness, because its achievement entails that one is having a complete fulfilment of good many times over during one's lifetime.[37]

On this interpretation, the Cyrenaics did not reject eudaemonism nearly as radically as some scholars claim.[38] And if they did not, they cannot have coherently postulated the importance of happiness unless they assumed that the moral agent preserves a stable identity through time.[39]

My conclusion is that the Cyrenaics do not have an ethical motivation for defending the non-identity thesis and for espousing the ontology of the 'subtler' philosophers. Instead, I suggest that they have good reasons *not* to adhere to the ontology of flux: not only is it counter-intuitive, but it is incompatible to an extent with important aspects of Cyrenaic ethics.

This difference in ontological commitments (or the lack thereof) is reflected on the linguistic and semantic level. The full-fledged relativism attributed to the 'subtler' philosophers entails drastic modifications of everyday language, i.e. the abolition of certain grammatical categories, of syntactical structures containing terms denoting substances, and of verbs which somehow imply that things stand still. On the other hand, as I suggested in chapter 8, the Cyrenaic remarks on language have a restricted scope, and there is no indication that our philosophers attempted to tailor the words people use to a Heraclitean view of reality.

Finally, on the epistemological level too, the differences between the

---

another in which *telos* primarily indicates fulfilment (cf., for example, Plato, *Charm.* 173d). If the Cyrenaics held that present pleasure is the *telos* in the former sense of '*telos*', their position would be incompatible, I think, with the eudaemonistic elements of their doctrines: if present pleasure is the only goal that we try to achieve, we should care for nothing else unless it is a means to present pleasure. On the other hand, if the Cyrenaic position is that having pleasure *now* is a complete fulfilment of the good, this is consistent with aiming at other things as well. Experiencing pleasure *now* means that I have got everything I need to get complete good *now*: past and future pleasures add nothing to it. But this does not mean that it is the only thing I should care for.

[36] See chapter 2, pp. 15–16.
[37] I argue for this interpretation in 'Is there an exception to Greek eudaemonism?' in M. Canto and P. Pellegrin (eds.) *Mélanges Jacques Brunschwig*, Paris (forthcoming).
[38] See, for example, Irwin 1991 and Annas 1993, especially pp. 230ff.
[39] On considerations about time and personal identity affecting ethical concerns, see Parfit 1984, especially pp. 117–86, 199ff. However, one might argue that happiness is a collection of pleasures, but not necessarily of *my* pleasures, if I keep changing my identity. On this topic, see Plato, *Symp.* 207ff.

two theories are considerable. On the one hand, although the 'subtler' philosophers maintain that in every perceptual act the perceiver and the perceived object are ever-changing processes, they still believe that at the time of perception there is *something* (what conventionally would be called an object) which appears to the perceiver to possess a certain quality (156d ff.). According to their theory, what the perceiver is incorrigibly aware of is *the object as he perceives it*. It is to that object that the Protagorean notion of truth primarily applies: when an act of perceiving occurs, what appears to the perceiver is true *for* him *of* the object which he perceives. Protagoras recasts the traditional notion of truth so that truth is of a constantly changing reality private to the perceiver. But it is truth of something ontologically separate from the perceiver, not merely awareness of the perceiver's condition.[40]

On the other hand, the Cyrenaics too reshape the notion of truth, but they reshape it differently from Protagoras. In contrast to Protagoras, their theory operates in fact with *two* concepts of truth. The one is the traditional, objective notion, according to which truth is of real, public objects: this they claim to be unattainable. The other is a subjective notion of truth and amounts to a kind of self-awareness.

Perhaps the relativism of the 'subtler' philosophers should be seen as cutting across the Cyrenaic thesis. What they maintain is that truth is about objects, but objects can only be private and momentary. There is no independent public object that one could be wrong about: what each perceiver knows incorrigibly is the only thing about which there is something to know. On the other hand, the Cyrenaics suggest that there is much more that we would wish to know in addition to our own *pathē*, namely truths about real objects.[41] But we shall never be able to reach them, because our perceptual apparatus does not possess the means to traverse the barrier between the *pathē*, which are usually created by our contact with the real objects, and the objects themselves.[42] The two

---

[40] This observation is limited to Plato's treatment of perceptual cases, and does not extend to practical and moral judgements.

[41] See the excellent discussion of relativism vs. scepticism in Annas and Barnes 1985, pp. 97–8.

[42] In relation to this point, consider how the Protagoreans and the Cyrenaics would respond to the problem of conflicting appearances. This problem is how to explain the ascription of opposite or different sensible properties to the same object: how can we explain the fact that to some people the wine is sweet, whereas to others it is bitter? On the one hand, the Protagoreans answer that however the wine appears to one, so it is for one: thus, the wine is both sweet and bitter, depending on the perceiver and on the conditions of perception, and no quality of the wine exists outside individual perceptual acts. On the other hand, the Cyrenaics would assume that there is an entity, the wine, and that we can have no access to its real properties. There is no way of settling the conflict of appearances, because what each of us perceives is not the wine, but his own *pathē* of it, and because there is no way of reaching beyond the *pathē* to the thing itself.

positions that I have been discussing come close to each other principally in so far as they both incorporate elements of subjectivism. The
same holds, I believe, for modern varieties of relativism and scepticism.
An interesting issue to explore is why subjectivism is so central to both
approaches and why it takes the specific forms it takes in either of them.
But this is a matter for another study.

A final comment concerns both parallels explored in this chapter and
the last. Philosophically rewarding as these may be, they can be pushed
only so far. We should not lose sight of the fact that, while the Epicureans and the Protagoreans in the *Theaetetus* considerably developed the
metaphysical, epistemological and semantic aspects of their doctrines,
the Cyrenaics did not – I think for the reasons outlined in chapter 1. So
there is something artificial in the ancient and modern discussions
comparing Cyrenaic views to the other two doctrines. Perhaps, then, we
should follow the Cyrenaic example: to dwell on the comparisons in
question only to the extent that this is useful for our purposes, and then
to drop the matter.

CHAPTER 11

# The Socratic connection

In the introductory chapter (chapter 1), I maintained that the Cyrenaics consider the exploration of epistemological issues instrumental to their hedonism and that this is partly dictated by their understanding of the Socratic project. They follow the model of Socrates (Cicero, *Tusc.* v.10–11) in that they consider ethics the only study worth pursuing, and commend other intellectual endeavours only in so far as these may help us lead the good life. Further, they espouse the Socratic idea that we should ground our choices on knowledge, limited as that may be, not on belief and conjecture. In the close of this study, I wish to take up a little further the topic of the Socratic identity of the school by asking a question which has less to do with the overall ethical project of the Cyrenaics and more with the character of Cyrenaic epistemology itself. Is there anything recognisably Socratic about it?

Historically, the preface to Sextus' presentation of the Cyrenaic doctrine in *M* vii.191–200 may indicate that in antiquity the doctrine was taken to have a Socratic affiliation: 'But now that an account of the Academic doctrine from Plato onwards has been rendered above, it is not perhaps out of place to go over the position of the Cyrenaics. It seems that the school of these men has sprung from the philosophy of Socrates, from which also emerged the succession of Plato's school' (190 [T6b]). This passage introduces an exposition of Cyrenaic philosophy neatly divided into two parts, an epistemological one focused on the criteria (*peri kritērion*: 191–8 [T6b]) and an ethical one discussing the moral end (*peri telōn*: 199–200 [T6b]). The statement concerning the Socratic origin of the doctrine may be intended to apply independently to the epistemology and to the ethics of the school, and to suggest that the former was considered an offshoot of the Socratic tradition in its own right.[1]

---

[1] See J. Brunschwig, 'La théorie cyrénaïque de la connaissance: quoi de socratique?', in Gourinat (forthcoming), in which the author proposes an alternative way of reading this passage.

Philosophically, before coming to the issue of the Socratic pedigree of the doctrine, I should like to make three preliminary observations. First, the question which I shall discuss is not what reasons the Cyrenaics *did* give for including themselves in the chorus of the Socratics, but what arguments they *could* have offered to that effect. I do not mean to preclude the possibility that they explained why their doctrine is faithful to the spirit of Socrates, but only to say that there is no direct evidence about it. Second, arguments that could have been intended to legitimise the doctrine as Socratic appear not to require much in the way of an overall interpretation of the teachings of Socrates. Mainly, they presuppose assumptions which could plausibly have been attributed to him on the strength of our main sources: the belief that it is important to have some kind of self-knowledge, Socrates' disclaimer that he has himself no knowledge,[2] and an ethical intellectualism centred on the idea that once people obtain the kind of knowledge that is relevant to moral action, not only will they be able to tell what things they should do, but they will also be able to do them.[3] Third, the issue of the generic origin of the doctrine is left open. Nothing that is said below is meant to confirm or preclude hypotheses such as that Aristippus of Cyrene influenced Pyrrho or that Pyrrho's Scepticism influenced Aristippus the Younger (a possibility about which there is little evidence, if any).[4]

The Cyrenaics could argue that, like Socrates, they obeyed the Delphic maxim 'Know thyself' and that, like Xenophon's Socrates (Xenophon, *Mem.* IV.2.24), they took it in an epistemological sense: they believed that no other knowledge can be attained unless one first acquires knowledge of oneself. Thus, both the description of the physical conditions related to the *pathē* and the epistemic analysis of the *pathē* themselves can be understood in the context of an effort to pursue further the Socratic example. Their enquiries into the nature and limits of self-knowledge led them a step further than Socrates, at least the Platonic Socrates. They realised that, in fact, the knowledge of the self, defined as the awareness of changes taking place in oneself, cannot serve as a necessary, let alone a sufficient condition for achieving objective knowledge. The emphasis on the lack of a common criterion and the doubts concerning knowledge of other minds were destined to stress that

---

[2] Perhaps one may include in the list of Socratic topics the problematisation of knowledge, if one is inclined to attribute to Socrates epistemological concerns. I suggest a way in which the Cyrenaics could attempt to legitimise their doctrine by appealing to Plato's *Theaetetus* in pp. 140–1.

[3] On the nature and limits of Socratic intellectualism, see the interpretations of Nehamas 1986 and, more recently, of Price 1995, pp. 8–29.

[4] See, however, Antoniades 1916, pp. 57ff. and Mannebach 1961, p.116.

the impossibility of achieving objective knowledge is definitional and structural, not merely factual, and thus to drive a wedge between the awareness of the self and the knowledge of external objects.

Further, they could appeal to Socrates' disavowal of knowledge in support of their position that one is necessarily bound to be ignorant about external objects, thus endorsing, or perhaps even inaugurating, the tradition which made Socrates the founder of scepticism.[5] Arcesilaus pointed out that Socrates' claim that he knows that he does not know (Plato, *Apol.* 21b and 21d) amounts to some kind of negative dogmatism.[6] But while, as the head of the Sceptical Academy, he considered it a flaw in an otherwise uncommitted enquirer, the Cyrenaics would not have found Socrates' profession of ignorance embarrassing if they chose to present their scepticism as deriving from it. In contrast with Arcesilaus and his followers,[7] their aim was not to suspend judgement about what is known and to keep searching for the truth, but to pronounce objective truth unreachable. The dogmatic character of their scepticism was emphasised by Sextus as one of the differences between Pyrrhonian and Cyrenaic scepticism: 'we suspend judgement about the external objects, so far as the arguments go. On the other hand, the Cyrenaics declare these objects have an inapprehensible nature' (Sextus, *PH* 1.215 [T6a]).

Another way in which the Cyrenaics could attempt to link their doctrine to Socrates would be to appeal to Plato's *Theaetetus* – a hypothesis that is plausible in view of the dialogue's remarkable influence in late Classical and Hellenistic thought. They could maintain that by bringing his interlocutors to see that the proposed definitions of knowledge entail absurdities and should be rejected, the Platonic Socrates insinuates that no definition of objective knowledge will prove adequate. The Cyrenaics could recommend themselves as Socratics on the grounds that they explored further the requirements for an objection-free defini-

---

[5] On this, see Cicero, *Acad.* 1.44; *Luc.* 74; *De or.* iii.67; *De fin.* ii.2. On Arcesilaus' argumentative techniques, see also Cicero, *Acad.* 1.45ff. and *Luc.*59, and Sextus, *PH* 1.232–4. It is contested whether Arcesilaus, who is traditionally considered the inventor of the sceptical Socrates, supported his claim by appealing to Socrates' profession of ignorance or by reviving what he took to be Socrates' practice of *ad hominem* arguing. I am inclined to side with those who maintain that, in the *Academica* at least, Socrates' assertion that he knows nothing is presented as *the reason why* he argues *ad hominem*. On the issue of Socrates and ancient scepticism, see Woodruff 1986; see also the contributions of J. Annas, 'Plato the Skeptic', and of C. Shields, 'Socrates among the Skeptics', in Vander Waerdt 1994, pp. 309–40 and 341–66 respectively.

[6] It is worth noticing that this interpretation of what Socrates says about his ignorance in Plato's *Apology* is by no means imposed by the text: he says that he knows nothing or that he is quite conscious of knowing nothing, but never claims *to know* that he knows nothing. On this point, see J. Annas, 'Plato the Skeptic', in Vander Waerdt 1994, p. 310.

[7] On the structure and aims of Academic Scepticism, see Striker 1981.

tion of knowledge and came to realise that, in order to secure it, they must redefine knowledge in terms of awareness of internal states.

Powerful reasons for including the Cyrenaics among the true heirs of Socrates can also be found in the intellectualist elements of their doctrines. Such elements link the epistemology of the school with its ethics,[8] and I cannot go into them in detail here. Perhaps it will suffice to say that the ethical doctrines of several Cyrenaic philosophers posit that correct moral behaviour is dependent on some kind of wisdom or understanding. This is a general and vague intellectualist stance which, however, becomes relevant to the school's epistemology in so far as the knowledge involved in the achievement of the moral end is defined in terms of self-awareness.

Such arguments invite a host of objections, some concerning the interpretations of the Socratic literature involved, others concerning philosophical coherence and persuasiveness. For example, one might retort that the interpretation of Socratic self-awareness in terms of consciousness of physical states is at best misleading; the Socratic profession of ignorance as witnessed in Plato's *Apology* does not amount to an epistemological claim; Socrates' intention in the *Theaetetus* is certainly not to suggest that no definition of knowledge is possible, but to explain why this task is important and to set down some conditions that would help to formulate a better answer to the question on which the dialogue is centred; and the ethical intellectualism traditionally ascribed to Socrates is unrelated to the idea that ethics should be backed up by an epistemological position. Besides, one might object, if the Cyrenaics drew a connection between these two aspects of their doctrine (and this is merely a conjecture), they would be open to the charge that moral properties such as goodness are not part of the self-evident content of the *pathē*; and even if the goodness of every individual *pathos* of pleasure were self-evident, it would not necessarily follow that a collection of such *pathē* must preserve the goodness of the pleasures constituting it.

Several of these criticisms may appear justified on philosophical grounds. However, they do not necessarily tell against the claim that the epistemology of the Cyrenaics can be considered faithful to the spirit of Socrates' teaching. Still, this claim may be thought illegitimate, precisely because it is based on misleading interpretations of the writings of Plato and other Socratics. A final remark may be made in reply.

The later Cyrenaics claimed to be themselves the true intellectual

---

[8] Notice, however, that Cyrenaic ethics is marked by an anti-intellectualist streak as well: see chapter 1, p. 4.

heirs of Socrates and probably based their interpretation of his thought on a tradition that was separate from that of the other Socratics, namely, the extensive writings of the founder of the school.⁹ Although they probably used the writings of Plato and Xenophon, as well as those of other Socratics, they must have assumed that these authors often got Socrates wrong. When they made use of these sources, their aim was not to interpret Plato's or Xenophon's picture of Socrates, but to find between the lines the elements that would allow them to recover and expound what they took to be the authentic Socrates.

⁹ See D.L. II.83–5, IV.40. Some ancient sources doubt the authenticity of Aristippus' writings. I believe that these doubts stem from a determination of some ancient authors to stress the affinity between Socrates and Aristippus by claiming that neither of them wrote anything.

# Sources and testimonies

The evidence on Cyrenaic epistemology comes from secondary sources and consists entirely of testimonies, not of fragments. None of the titles mentioned in the lists of the doxographers seems to be of an epistemological treatise. But the lists refer only to the works of Aristippus of Cyrene, Theodorus and Hegesias,[1] and none of them is known to have had detailed epistemological views. The epistemology of the school may have been developed in treatises of Aristippus the Younger and Anniceris, probably under the heading of ethics.[2]

Although the testimonies are second-hand and occur principally in polemical contexts, they are often based on good sources and constitute reliable evidence about the Cyrenaic positions. Also, the polemical arguments brought against these positions by ancient authors are frequently enlightening. In my selection of texts, I have included the epistemological testimonies, and also materials on psychology and ethics that have a bearing on the topics that I discuss.

## I    COLOTES AND PLUTARCH

Our earliest source on the Cyrenaic theory of knowledge is Colotes, a young contemporary of Epicurus. After Epicurus' death (271 BC) and Arcesilaus' ascent to the leadership of the Academy (some time in the 260s BC),[3] Colotes wrote a book entitled *On the Fact that it is not Possible even to Live according to the Doctrines of the Other Philosophers*, in which he criticised the doctrines of Parmenides, Empedocles, Socrates, Melissus, Plato,

---

[1] Regarding the writings of Aristippus of Cyrene, see *SSR* IV A 144–59; regarding Theodorus' works and especially his treatise *On the Gods*, see *SSR* IV H 1–2, 5, 13, 23; on Hegesias' book, see *SSR* IV F 4.

[2] See Sextus *M* VII.11 [T6d] and chapter 1 (p. 4).

[3] See T. Dorandi, *Filodemo. Storia dei filosofi [.]: Platone e l'Academia*, Naples 1991, pp. 53ff. According to the chronicle of Eusebius/Jerome (Arcesilaus T 4f Mette), Polemo died in 270 or 269 BC; he was succeeded by Crates before Arcesilaus took over, and Crates probably died in the period 268–264 BC.

Stilpo, and two schools which he does not name but which are easily identified as the Cyrenaics and the followers of Arcesilaus. His main aim was to prove that doctrines directly or indirectly undermining the credibility of the senses make life impossible. It is in this context that Colotes attempted to describe and ridicule the Cyrenaic theory of knowledge.

The evidence about Colotes' attack against the Cyrenaics comes from the first–second century AD writer Plutarch. In his work *Against Colotes*, Plutarch cited Colotes' criticisms, stated that they were grounded on a historically inaccurate rendering of the Cyrenaic doctrine, and gave what he claimed to be the true letter of this doctrine (1120b–f). Subsequently, he argued that the Cyrenaics and the Epicureans in fact held the same views concerning the truth of sense-impressions and that, therefore, by criticising the Cyrenaics Colotes contradicts himself (1120f–1121e). Thus, the passage from Plutarch's work contains two pieces of evidence about the epistemology of the Cyrenaics, which are both chronologically and philosophically distinct: a third-century BC version of the doctrine offered by an Epicurean writer of the same period and a first-century AD version given and commented upon by Plutarch.

Plutarch, *Against Colotes* 1120c–1121e
At any rate, after dealing with the philosophers of the past, [c] Colotes turns to the philosophers of his own time without mentioning the name of any of them; yet, the proper thing for him to do would have been to refute them too by naming them, or not to name the philosophers of the past either. And he, who so often criticised Socrates and Plato and Parmenides with his pen, obviously lost his nerve when he was to deal with the living philosophers; he was not moderate in his criticisms because he was respectful, or he would have shown respect to their betters (sc. the philosophers of the past). I guess he intends to refute the Cyrenaics in the first place and the Academy of Arcesilaus in the second place. The latter were the philosophers who suspended judgement about everything; but the former, placing all *pathē* and all sense-impressions within themselves, [d] believed that the evidence coming from them is not sufficient regarding assertions about external objects. Instead, distancing themselves from external objects, they shut themselves up within their *pathē* as in a state of siege, using the formula 'it appears' but refusing to affirm in addition that 'it is' with regard to external objects.

This is why, says Colotes, the Cyrenaics can neither live nor cope with things. In addition, he says, making fun of them, that 'these men do not say that a man or a horse or a wall is, but that they themselves are being walled or horsed or manned'. In the first place, he is using these expressions maliciously, just as a professional denouncer would. Doubtless, these consequences amongst others do follow from the teachings of these men. Yet he should have presented the doctrine in the form in which those philosophers teach it. [e] They say we are being sweetened and bittered and chilled and warmed and illuminated and darkened, each of these *pathē* having within itself its own evidence, which is intrinsic to it and irreversible. But whether the honey is sweet or the young olive-shoot bitter or the hail chilly or the unmixed wine warm or the sun luminous or the night air dark, is contested by many witnesses, [wild] animals and domesticated animals[4] and humans alike, for some dislike honey, others like olive-shoots or are burned off by hail or are chilled by the wine or go blind in the sunlight and see well at night. [f] So, when opinion stays close to the *pathē* it preserves its infallibility, but when it oversteps them and meddles with judgements and assertions about external objects, it often both disturbs itself and fights against other people who receive from the same objects contrary *pathē* and different sense-impressions.

It would seem that Colotes has the same trouble as boys who are just starting to learn how to read. While they are used to spelling the characters on their tablets, when they see these characters written on others things outside the tablets, they are doubtful and confused. (1121) And so with him: the views which he follows eagerly and treats with respect when they occur in the writings of Epicurus, he neither understands nor identifies when they are asserted by others. Those who maintain that when a film of atoms rounded at the corners, or again another one which is bent, comes into contact with our senses, the sensation is truly imprinted, but who do not allow us to affirm as well that the tower is round or the oar is bent, do establish as true their own *pathē* and sense-appearances but do not want to concede that the external objects have these characteristics. And just as those philosophers (sc. the Cyrenaics) are committed to speaking about being horsed or being walled but not about a horse or a wall, so these philosophers (sc. the Epicureans) must say that the eye is rounded or with rough angles [b] and not that the oar is bent or the tower round. The film of atoms from which the eye has been affected is bent, whereas the oar from which the film of atoms has come is not bent. Thus, since the *pathos* differs from the object, it is necessary for belief either to stick to the *pathos* or to be refuted whenever it asserts how things are in addition to how things appear. As to the fact that they protest aloud and are vexed on behalf of sensation, which is to say that they do not affirm that the external object is warm but only that the *pathos* inherent in sensation is warm, is that statement not the same as the [Cyrenaic] statement about taste, i.e. that they (sc. the Cyrenaics) do not say that the external object is sweet, but that a *pathos* or a movement of this kind related to taste has occurred? [c] But the person who says that he is receiving a man-like sense-impression but is not sensing whether there is a man, from where has he got his original idea? Was it not from the philosophers who claim that they receive a curve-like sense-

[4] De Lacy's σπερμάτων and the MS reading πραγμάτων do not make sense: grains do not perceive, nor do things. I supply, tentatively, προβάτων, tame or domesticated animals. See chapter 6, p. 84.

impression but that the sight does not go further to affirm that something is curved or round, but a sense-appearance or imprint of round form related to sight has occurred?

'Most certainly,' one will answer. 'But for my part, after I come close to the tower and after I touch the oar, I shall assert that the oar is straight and that the tower is angular; but this other person, even if he gets close he will admit what seems to be the case and what appears to him, but nothing more.' [d] Indeed, my dear friend, he will not, since he is better than you in observing and defending the logical consequences of his doctrine, that all sense-impressions alike are trustworthy about themselves and no sense-impression is trustworthy about anything else but all are equally good witnesses. And here is the end of your doctrine that all sense-impressions are true and none is unreliable or false, if indeed you think that this category of sense-impressions must state additional truths about the external objects, whereas you refused to trust that other category of sense-impressions in anything beyond the *pathos* itself. If they have an equal claim to trustworthiness, whether they occur as the result of observing an object closely or at a distance, it is only fair either to confer on all sense-impressions the power of making additional judgements about how things are, or to subtract that power from the former category of sense-impressions as well as from the latter. But if there is a difference in the *pathos* affecting one when one is at a distance and when one is close at hand, it is false to assert that no sense-impression and no sensation [e] is more evident than another. Likewise, what they call attestation and contestation have nothing to do with sensation but rather with belief. Thus, if they urge us to make assertions about the external objects by following these, they transfer the object of judgement from what is unfailingly true to what is often wrong. But why do we need to talk at present about views which are full of confusion and which contradict themselves?

## 2 PHILODEMUS (?)

Approximately two centuries after Colotes and one century before Plutarch, the Cyrenaic doctrine may be briefly mentioned in an anonymous incomplete text on Epicurean ethics, probably composed in the first half of the first century BC by the Epicurean philosopher Philodemus of Gadara. The text was found in a Herculaneum papyrus (PHerc. 1251), commonly known as 'the Comparetti Ethics' after the name of its first editor. The Cyrenaics are not named in it and their identification is conjectural. The evidence that appears to concern them occurs in the second and third columns of the papyrus, both of which are badly damaged. Their context is uncertain. But it is probable that in the first three columns of the text, the Epicurean author launched an attack against anti-rationalism, especially against positions undermining the belief that moral choices are performed according to rational calculation and on the basis of factual knowledge. His claim is, I think, that the epistemological views of the Cyrenaics dictated a kind of hedonism which precluded rational choice and rational justification of one's actions.[5] This text merits attention, since it is the only evidence that may refer explicitly to the philosophical relation between the epistemology and the ethics of the Cyrenaic school.

PHerc. 1251 [Philodemus] [*On Choices and Avoidances*]
Col. II . . . and they claim that in truth no (judgement) takes precedence over any other, being persuaded that the great *pathos* of the soul occurs as a result of pain and that thus we accomplish our choices and avoidances by observing both (sc. bodily and mental pain). It is not possible that the joys arise in us in the same way and all together, in accordance with some expectation . . .
Col. III . . . and some people[6] denied that it is possible to know anything. And, further, they added that if nothing is present on account of which one should make an immediate choice, then one should not choose immediately. Some other people, having selected the *pathē* of the soul as the moral ends and as not in need of additional judgement based on further criteria, granted to everybody an authority, which was not accountable, to take pleasure in whatever they cared to name and to do whatever contributed to it. And yet others held the doctrine that what our school calls grief or joy are totally empty notions because of the manifest indeterminacy of things . . .

### 3   THE ANONYMOUS THEAETETUS COMMENTATOR

Another Greek source is the commentary on Plato's *Theaetetus*, the only ancient commentary on that dialogue to survive to our days (Berlin papyrus 9782). Its author remains anonymous. He is probably a Middle Platonist, and his floruit may be anywhere between the first century BC and the second century AD.[7] The seventy-five columns of the papyrus cover a relatively short part of the dialogue, from its opening at 142a to the application of the theory of perpetual flux to sense-perception at 153d. The epistemological position of the Cyrenaics is mentioned in connection with Theaetetus' attempt to answer the question what is

---

[5] On the content and interpretation of PHerc. 1251 cols. I–III, see Indelli and Tsouna-McKirahan 1995, especially pp. 19–23, 81–2, 87–9, 115–28.
[6] This column mentions three different groups of thinkers, of which the second and the third groups are probably Cyrenaic sects.
[7] On the author and date of this text, see Diels and Schubart 1905; Tarrant 1983; Mansfeld 1991; and the recent edition of the commentary by Bastianini and Sedley 1995.

knowledge by defining knowledge as sense-perception.

The anonymous author comments on the Protagorean thesis that as things appear to one, so they are for one, and on the Heraclitean doctrine of flux brought in support of the epistemological relativism of Protagoras (62.1ff.): in a universe of perpetual flux, nothing has a stable identity, for neither the perceiving subject or faculty nor the perceived object exist in themselves, but only in so far as they are perceived (64.1–7); so, things are for me such as they affect me and they are for you such as they affect you (64.8–11) and, according to this hypothesis, man is the judge and measure of the affections or conditions which he experiences (64.12–16). Subsequently, the author attempts to clarify the application of the theory to the case of the perception of the wind by different people (152b). He stresses that, according to the Protagorean–Heraclitean theory, different perceivers are affected differently by the same wind, in the same place, at the same time (64.21–65.13). The proponents of the theory conclude that the wind causing these *pathē* is neither cold nor not cold, but that in reality it does not have such properties; for if a thing does have an intrinsic property, then it cannot produce different *pathē* in different perceivers in the same conditions and at the same time (65.14–25). The author's suggestion is that the Cyrenaic position, that only the *pathē* are apprehensible but the external objects are inapprehensible, is based on comparable grounds (cf. *hothen*: 65.29): we cannot tell whether the fire has the property of burning, because if it did, then all things that came into contact with it would be affected in the same way, i.e. they would burn.

The surviving commentary on the *Theaetetus* does not cover the part of the dialogue which contains the theory of the 'subtler' philosophers (156aff.). However, the claim of its author that there is a close philosophical relation between the Protagorean–Heraclitean doctrine in Plato's *Theaetetus* and the epistemological views of the Cyrenaics prefigures modern interpretations tending to identify these two doctrines.

Anonymous commentator on Plato's *Theaetetus* p.152b col. 65.29–39
Whence the Cyrenaics claim that the *pathē* alone are apprehensible but the external objects inapprehensible, for, they say, I apprehend that I am being burnt, but it is non-evident whether the fire is such as to burn. If it were such, all things would be burnt by it.

## 4 CICERO

The earliest and most important Latin author reporting physiological and psychological views of the Cyrenaics is Cicero, the Roman politician and intellectual of the first century BC, whose philosophical viewpoint is shaped by Academic scepticism. In his work *Lucullus*, three passages offer important evidence about the Cyrenaic doctrine: an argument defending the power of the senses to comprehend their peculiar objects, which mentions the so-called internal touch – the sensory channel through which, according to the Cyrenaics, we apprehend the *pathē* (18–20); an argument destined to undermine belief in the credibility of the senses, which contains, again, a brief reference to the Cyrenaic position that the only things which can be apprehended are those experienced by internal touch (75–6); and a set of remarks aiming to locate the position of Antiochus on the subject of the criterion of truth, where the criteria of Protagoras, the Cyrenaics and the Epicureans are grouped together in opposition to Plato's rationalistic criterion (142–3).

4a. Cicero, *Lucullus* 18–22

18. . . . Thus, the whole discourse against the Academy is undertaken by us in this manner, so that we preserve the definition which Philo wanted to subvert; unless we make it prevail, we concede that nothing can be perceived.

19. So, let us start from the senses, whose judgements are so clear and certain that if our nature were given the choice and were asked by some god whether she was satisfied with her senses when they are intact and uninjured or whether she asked for something better, I cannot see what more she could require. Nor indeed do I have to delay here while I respond to the examples of the bent oar or the pigeon's neck since I am not the one to say that whatever object is seen is such as it appears. Epicurus may reflect upon that and upon many other things. But, according to my judgement, the greatest truth lies in the senses, if they are healthy and powerful and if all obstacles and impediments are removed. This is why we often want to change the light and the position of the things which we are observing, and we either diminish or increase the distance between them and us, and we do many things until sheer sight acquires confidence in its own judgement. The same happens with sounds, smell or taste, so that there is none of us who wishes for a finer judgement in the senses, each in its own kind.

20. Indeed, when practice and skill are added in order for the eyes to comprehend a painting and the ears music, who is there who will not perceive how much power lies in the senses? How many things painters may see in shadows and in the light parts of the painting which we do not see! How many things which escape us in music are listened to by those trained in this kind of thing, who as soon as the flute-player blows the first note affirm that this is

*Antiope* or *Andromache*, while we do not even suspect it! There is no need to talk at all about taste and smell, in which there is a certain power of apprehension, albeit defective. Why should we speak of touch and indeed of what the philosophers call internal touch of either pleasure or pain, in which alone, the Cyrenaics believe, lies the criterion of the true because it (sc. the true) is sensed [through it]? So, can anybody say that there is no difference between the man who is in pain and the man who experiences pleasure, or is it that the person who thinks so is clearly insane?

21. But then, the things which we claim to be perceived by the senses are of the same kind as those which are said to be perceived not by the senses themselves but in some way through the senses, as for instance: 'This is white', 'This is sweet', 'This is harmonious', 'This is fragrant', 'This is rough.' Surely, these we believe to be grasped by the mind, not by the senses. Thus, 'This is a horse', 'This is a dog'. Then follows the rest of the series connecting more complex concepts, for instance those which include as it were a complete understanding of things: 'If one is a man, one is a rational mortal animal.' From this latter kind are imprinted upon us our primary notions of things, without which all understanding and enquiry and discussion are impossible.

22. Now, if there were false primary notions (for you seemed to render *ennoiai* by 'notions') – if, then, these were false or imprinted by appearances of such a kind that could not be distinguished from false ones, how would we make use of them after all? And how could we see what is consistent with any given thing and what is inconsistent with it? At any rate, no room at all is left for memory, which more than anything else sustains not only philosophy but also all practice of life and all the arts. How can there possibly be a memory of what is false? Or what can anyone remember that one does not understand and hold in one's mind? Indeed, what art can there be that does not consist, not of one or two, but of many mental percepts? And if you do away with it, how will you distinguish the expert from the ignorant? We shall not claim at random that this man is an expert and the other is not, unless we see the one remember what he has perceived and understood while the other does not. And just as one category of arts is such as to discern things only with the mind, and another such as to do or to construct something, how can the geometrician discern things that are either non-existent or cannot be distinguished from false ones, or how can the player of the harp perfect his rhythms and complete his verses? The same result will also occur in other arts of this kind, whose entire performance consists in making and doing; for what can be accomplished by an art unless the man who will exercise it has learned many mental percepts?

4b. Cicero, *Lucullus* 75–6

75. Do I not give you the impression that I do not simply mention the names of illustrious men, as Saturninus did, but also I always take as my model someone who is famous and noble? And yet, I could mention philosophers who are troublesome to your school but of small importance – Stilpo, Diodorus, Alexinus, the authors of certain intricate and cunning *sophismata* (for this is how deceitful and trifling riddles are called). But why should I bring them in, when I

have Chrysippus who is supposed to sustain the portico of the Stoics? How many arguments he produced against the senses and against everything that is approved in ordinary usage! But, you will retort, he also refuted them. In fact he does not seem to me to have done so. But suppose that he did: yet, surely, he would not have gathered so many arguments which might deceive us because of their great probability, had he not seen that they could not easily be resisted.

76. What do you think of the Cyrenaics, by no means contemptible philosophers? They deny that there is anything that can be perceived from the outside: the only things that they do perceive are those which they sense by internal touch, for instance pain or pleasure, and they do not know whether something has a particular colour or sound, but only sense that they are themselves affected in a certain way.

4c. Cicero, *Lucullus* 142–3

142. I come now to the third part of philosophy. One criterion is that of Protagoras, who holds that what appears to a person is true for that person, another is that of the Cyrenaics, who believe that there is no criterion whatsoever except the inmost affects, another is that of Epicurus, who places the whole criterion in the senses and in the primary notions of things and in pleasure. On the other hand, Plato believed that the whole criterion of truth and truth itself lies merely in reasoning and in the mind, detached from belief and from the senses.

143. Surely our friend Antiochus does not endorse any of this?

## 5  ARISTOCLES

Another Greek source is Aristocles of Messene, a second-century AD Peripatetic philosopher[8] whose work is partly preserved by Eusebius of Caesarea (*c.* AD 260–340) in his *Preparation for the Gospel* (XIV.18.31). The structure of this testimony has made scholars wonder whether Aristocles is Eusebius' source throughout the passage, or whether Eusebius drew from Aristocles' work only when he cited specific objections against Cyrenaic epistemology.

The passage is divided into two distinct parts. The first part opens with the observation that the criticisms against the Cyrenaic thesis that the *pathē* alone are apprehensible are similar to the objections raised against the Pyrrhonians, thus placing them in the broader context of an attack against scepticism in general.[9] This remark is followed by a parenthetical passage concerning the alleged hedonism of Aristippus of

---

[8] For a different dating of Aristocles, see the article of Simone Follet in the *Dictionnaire des philosophes antiques*, which places him in the first century BC.

[9] On Aristocles' polemic against various sceptics, see Trabucco 1960. Compare Aristocles' arguments against the sceptics with those against Protagoras and the Epicureans. On this, see Trabucco 1958–9.

Cyrene, the three initial stages of the Cyrenaic succession and the contribution of Aristippus the Younger to the psychological and ethical doctrines of the school. Then the text returns to the epistemology of the Cyrenaics, and in particular to the position of Aristippus the Younger concerning the three conditions of human constitution – pleasure, pain and the neutral condition. Regarding the authorship of this first part, it seems to me that Aristocles is its main source. Eusebius may have changed its original structure somewhat, but I doubt that he altered Aristocles' views in any significant respect. The parenthetical passage (whose authorship is controversial) may have been introduced by Aristocles in order to give some information about the school, including the psychological positions of Aristippus the Younger which are central to his epistemological views.[10]

The second part of the text (xiv.19.1–7) is an attack against the epistemological doctrine of the school and its original author is undoubtedly Aristocles. His discussion of Greek scepticism is probably based on Academic texts and it appears likely that both his account and his criticisms of the Cyrenaic doctrine also come from an Academic source.

Aristocles, quoted by Eusebius, *Preparation for the Gospel* xiv.18.31–19.7
So much for those who are believed to follow the philosophy of Pyrrho. The objections raised against the followers of Aristippus the Cyrenean, who claim that only the *pathē* are apprehensible, are of a similar kind. Aristippus was a companion of Socrates who formulated the Cyrenaic doctrine from which Epicurus took material for his own presentation of the moral end. Aristippus was very voluptuous and pleasure-loving. But he never lectured on the moral end in public. However, he said that the substance of happiness lies potentially in particular pleasures. And by speaking continuously about pleasure, he led his followers to the suspicion that he maintains that living pleasurably is the moral end. (18.32) One of his disciples was also his daughter, Arete. When she gave birth to a son she named him Aristippus, who was called The Mother-Taught because he was introduced to philosophy by her. He clearly defined the moral end as living pleasantly, introducing the concept of pleasure as motion. He said that there are three conditions regarding our own constitution: one in which we are in pain and which resembles the storm in the sea, another in which we experience pleasure and which is similar to smooth sea-waves (for pleasure is a smooth movement compared to a fair wind); as to the third state, it is an intermediate condition, nearly resembling a calm sea, in which we experience

---

[10] Other views about authorship are that the epistemological remarks at the beginning and at the end of the passage were copied from Aristocles, while the middle part was added by Eusebius; or that the whole first part of the text was composed by Eusebius, as an introduction to the criticisms of Aristocles that follow.

neither pain nor pleasure. Indeed, he said, we have the sensation of these *pathē* alone. The following objections are raised against these philosophers.

(19.1) Next would be those who claim that the *pathē* alone are apprehensible. This claim was made by some of the philosophers from Cyrene. These philosophers maintained that they know absolutely nothing, just as if a very deep sleep weighs down on them, unless somebody standing beside them struck or pricked them; for they said that when they are being burnt or cut, they know that they are undergoing something. But whether the thing which is burning them is fire or that which is cutting them is iron, they cannot tell. (19.2) But then one would immediately ask those who hold these views whether they know this at least, that they are undergoing and that they are sensing something. If they did not, they would not be able even to say that they know only the *pathos*; but again, if they do know this, then it is not true that only the *pathē* are apprehensible, for 'I am being burnt' is a locution, not a *pathos*. (19.3) At any rate, it is necessary that at least these three things exist together, the *pathos* itself, the thing that produced it and the subject undergoing it. Thus, the person apprehending the *pathos* would certainly sense the affected subject as well. It cannot be that, if one happens to be warmed, one will know that one is being warmed but will not know whether oneself or one's neighbour is the person who is being warmed. One will also know if this happens now or last year, if it happened in Athens or in Egypt, if one is alive or dead, and further, if one is a human being or a stone. (19.4) So, one will also know what one is affected by; for people are acquainted with each other and they know the streets, the towns and nourishment. Again, the craftsmen know their own tools, the doctors and the seamen infer by means of signs the things to come, and dogs discover the tracks of the wild animals. (19.5) Besides, the person who is undergoing a *pathos* must perceive it either as something welcome or as an unwelcome *pathos*. Then, by what means will one be able to tell that this is pleasure or this is pain? Or that one is undergoing something, when one is tasting or seeing or hearing? Or that one is tasting something with the tongue, seeing with the eyes or hearing with the ears? And how do they know that they ought to choose this thing but to avoid the other? In fact, if none of these things stirs them, they will have no impulse and no desire. But then they would not be animals either. It follows that they are ridiculous every time that they say that these things have happened to them, but that they do not know how or in what way. In that case, they would not be able to tell even whether they are human beings or whether they are alive. Consequently, neither could they tell whether they say or assert something. (19.6) At this point, what could one tell such people? Of course, it is surprising if they do not know whether they are on earth or in the heavens. And it would be much more surprising if they do not know whether indeed four is more than three or what one and two make, and yet they affirm that they practise philosophy, for they cannot even say how many fingers they have on their hands or whether each of them is one or many. (19.7) Thus, they would not know their own name or their fatherland or Aristippus. They would not know whom they love or hate, or what they desire. Nor will they be able to say whether they laughed or wept because one thing was funny and the other sad. So it is obvious that they also do not understand what we are talking about at this very moment. But then such people would not differ at all from peacocks or flies, although even they know the things which are in accordance with nature and the things which are not.

## 6 SEXTUS EMPIRICUS

The Sceptic and empiricist physician Sextus Empiricus (probably second century AD) is our best source on Cyrenaic epistemology. His main references to the doctrine occur in *The Outlines of Pyrrhonism* (1.215) and in his work *Against the Professors* (VII.191–200 and VI.52–3). His reference to the Cyrenaic doctrine in *PH* 1.215 is narrowly focused on some fundamental differences between the Pyrrhonian and the Cyrenaic versions of scepticism. On the other hand, his account in *M* VII.191–200 contains, arguably, the richest and most subtle presentation of the Cyrenaic position. It occurs in the context of a general survey of the views of the dogmatic philosophers on the subject of the criterion of truth and, more specifically, it is placed towards the middle of the final doxographical session of *M* VII (141–260), which is devoted to the doctrines of those dogmatic philosophers who maintained that the criterion lies in *enargeia* (whether accompanied by *logos* or not). There are good reasons for believing that the ultimate source of that passage is the work *Canonica* by Antiochus of Ascalon, a near contemporary of the founder of neo-Pyrrhonism, Aenesidemus (first century BC). Finally, Sextus' reference to the Cyrenaic doctrine in *M* VI.52–3 is found in the context of the dogmatic disagreement concerning the existence of sound.

6a. Sextus Empiricus, *Outlines of Pyrrhonism* 1.215
IN WHAT RESPECT SCEPTICISM DIFFERS FROM CYRENAIC PHILOSOPHY
Some people maintain that the Cyrenaic doctrine is the same as Scepticism, since it too says that only the *pathē* are apprehensible. In fact, it differs from Scepticism because the former maintains that the moral end is pleasure and the smooth movement of the flesh, whereas we say that it is tranquillity, wherefore it is opposed to their conception of the moral end. Whether pleasure is present or absent, the person who affirms that pleasure is the moral end submits to troubles, as I have concluded in the chapter about it. Besides, we suspend judgement about the external objects, as far as the arguments go. The Cyrenaics, on the other hand, affirm that the external objects have an inapprehensible nature.

6b. Sextus Empiricus, *Against the Professors* VII.190–200
(190) Now that an account of the Academic doctrine from Plato onwards has been rendered above, it is not perhaps out of place to go over the position of the Cyrenaics. It seems that the school of these men has sprung from the philos-

ophy of Socrates, from which also emerged the succession of Plato's school. (191) So, the Cyrenaics claim that the *pathē* are the criteria and that they alone are apprehended and are not deceitful, but that none of the things productive of the *pathē* is apprehensible or undeceitful. It is possible, they say, to assert infallibly and truly and firmly and incorrigibly that we are being whitened or sweetened, but it is impossible to affirm that the thing productive of the *pathos* in us is white or sweet, (192) because one may be disposed whitely even by something not-white or may be sweetened by something not-sweet. For just as the sufferer from vertigo or from jaundice is stirred by everything yellowly, and the one suffering from ophthalmia is reddened, and the person who presses down his eye is stirred as if by two objects, and the madman sees Thebes as if it were double and imagines the sun double, (193) and in all these cases it is true that people are undergoing this particular *pathos*, for instance they are being yellowed or reddened or doubled, but it is considered false that the thing which stirred them is yellow or red or double, likewise it is very plausible for us to assume that one can grasp nothing but one's own *pathē*. Hence, we must posit either that the *pathē* are *phainomena* or that the things productive of the *pathē* are *phainomena*. (194) And if we call the *pathē phainomena*, we must declare that all *phainomena* are true and apprehensible. But if we call the things productive of the *pathē phainomena*, all *phainomena* are false and inapprehensible. The *pathos* which occurs in us reveals to us nothing more than itself. Hence, if one must speak but the truth, only the *pathos* is actually a *phainomenon* to us; but what is external and productive of the *pathos* perhaps exists, but it is not a *phainomenon* to us. (195) And so, we are all unerring with regard to our own *pathē*, but we all make mistakes with regard to the external object; and those are apprehensible, but this is inapprehensible because the soul is too weak to distinguish it on account of the places, the distances, the motions, the changes, and numerous other causes. Hence they say that no criterion is common to mankind but that common names are assigned to objects. (196) All people in common call something white or sweet, but they do not have something common that is white or sweet. Each person is aware of his own private *pathos*, but whether this *pathos* occurs in oneself and in one's neighbour from a white object one cannot tell oneself, since one is not submitting to the *pathos* of the neighbour, nor can the neighbour tell, since he is not submitting to the *pathos* of that other person. (197) And since no *pathos* is common to us all, it is hasty to declare that what appears to me of a certain kind appears of this same kind to my neighbour as well; for perhaps I am constituted so as to be whitened by the external object when it comes into contact with my senses, while another person has the senses constructed so as to have been disposed differently. In any case, the *phainomenon* is assuredly not common to us all. (198) And that we really are not all stirred in the same way because of the different constructions of our senses is clear from the cases of people who suffer from jaundice or ophthalmia and from those who are in a normal condition. Just as some persons are affected yellowly, others redly and others whitely from one and the same object, likewise it is also probable that those who are in normal condition are not stirred in the same manner by the same things because of the different construction of their senses, but that the person with grey eyes is stirred in one way, the one with blue eyes in another, and the one with black eyes in another yet different way. It follows that the names which we assign to things are common, but that we have private *pathē*.

(199) What these philosophers say about the criteria seems to correspond to what they say about the moral ends, for the *pathē* do also extend to the moral ends. Some of the *pathē* are pleasant, others are painful and others are intermediate; and the painful ones are, they say, evils whose end is pain, the pleasant ones are goods, whose unmistakable end is pleasure, and the intermediates are neither goods nor evils, whose end is neither a good nor an evil, this being a *pathos* between pleasure and pain. (200) Thus, the *pathē* are the criteria and the ends of things, and we live, they say, by following these and by attending to evidence and to approval, to evidence regarding the other *pathē* and to approval in relation to pleasure.

Such are the teachings of the Cyrenaics, who restricted the criterion more than the school of Plato. The latter considered it a compound of evidence and reason, whereas the Cyrenaics confine it to the *enargeiai*, i.e., to the *pathē* alone.

6c. Sextus Empiricus, *Against the Professors* VI.52–3

(52) From these arguments, it is evident that the whole theory of the musicians about melody consisted essentially in nothing else but the musical notes. So, if these are done away with, music will be nothing. But how could one claim that the musical notes do not exist? Because, we will answer, they belong to the genus of sound and because it has been proven in the memoirs of Scepticism that sound does not exist, by appealing to the evidence of the Dogmatists. (53) And besides, the Cyrenaic philosophers claim that only the *pathē* exist, and nothing else. So, since sound is not a *pathos* but rather something capable of producing a *pathos*, it is not one of the things that exist. To be sure, by denying the existence of every sensory object, the schools of Democritus and of Plato deny the existence of sound as well, since sound is taken to be a sensory object.

6d. Sextus Empiricus, *Against the Professors* VII.11

According to some people the Cyrenaics too endorsed the ethical branch of philosophy only, and dismissed the physical and logical branches as contributing nothing to a happy life. However, some have thought that they (sc. the Cyrenaics) refute themselves from the way they divide ethics into headings – one dealing with objects of choice and avoidance, another with the *pathē*, yet another with actions, another with causes, and finally one with arguments. Among these, they say, the heading dealing with causes in fact is drawn from physics, while that dealing with arguments is drawn from logic.

## 7 DIOGENES LAERTIUS

Diogenes Laertius' work *Lives of Eminent Philosophers* may have been written in the third century AD. The Cyrenaic school is discussed in book II of that work, which also contains the Lives of Socrates and of several

Socratic philosophers in addition to the Cyrenaics. The structure of the testimony on the Cyrenaics comprises the Life of Aristippus of Cyrene (65–85a), followed by a passage on the successions of the Cyrenaic school (85b–86a), and then by the successive presentation of the doctrines of the Cyrenaics proper, i.e. 'those who remained attached to the sect of Aristippus and were known as Cyrenaics' (86b–93a), of Hegesias and his disciples (93b–96a), Anniceris and his disciples (96b–97a) and the sect of Theodorus (97b–104).

The account focuses on the ethical doctrines of the Cyrenaics, but parts of it are crucial for the interpretation of the epistemology of the school. It supplies information about the physiological features of the doctrine and it cites two tenets directly relevant to Cyrenaic epistemology. The first occurs at the end of Aristippus' Life and concerns his definition of the moral end as 'the smooth motion resulting in sensation' (85b). The second tenet is encountered towards the end of the section on the Cyrenaics proper: the *pathē* themselves are apprehensible, but not the things that cause them (92a). Although this is the central epistemological position of the Cyrenaics, it is not further analysed in this context. It may be mentioned in order to support the claim that the Cyrenaics held that things appear incomprehensible and for that reason abandoned the study of physics (92a).

Diogenes Laertius, *Lives of Eminent Philosophers*
7a. ii.85
He (sc. Aristippus of Cyrene) declared that the moral end is the smooth motion when it comes forth to consciousness.
7b. ii.86–7
(86) The philosophers who abode by the teaching of Aristippus and were called Cyrenaics had the following beliefs. There are two *pathē*, pain and pleasure, pleasure being a smooth motion and pain a rough motion. (87) One pleasure does not differ from another nor is one pleasure more pleasant than another in any respect. And pleasure is agreeable while pain is repulsive to all animals. However, notably according to Panaetius in his work *On the Philosophical Sects*, the bodily pleasure, which is the moral end, is not the static pleasure occurring after the removal of pain or, as it were, the freedom from discomfort, which Epicurus accepts and maintains to be the moral end.
7c. ii.88–90
(88) Individual pleasure is desirable for its own sake, whereas happiness is not desirable for its own sake but for the sake of individual pleasures. That pleasure is the moral end is proved by the fact that, from an early age onwards, we welcome it without making a deliberate choice, and once we obtain it, we seek for nothing more and avoid nothing so much as its opposite, pain. Pleasure is

good even if it comes from the most unseemly actions, as Hippobotus says in his book *On the Philosophical Sects*. Even if the action is inappropriate, still the pleasure that results from it is desirable for its own sake and is good. (89) However, the removal of pain, as it is defined by Epicurus, seems to them (sc. the Cyrenaics proper) not to be pleasure at all, nor the absence of pleasure pain; for they hold that both pleasure and pain are in motion, whereas the absence of pain or the absence of pleasure is not a motion, since the absence of pain resembles the condition of somebody who is asleep. They assert that some people may fail to choose pleasure because of some perversion. Not all psychic pleasures and pains are ultimately dependent on bodily pleasures and pains. We are disinterestedly delighted at the prosperity of our country as if it were our own prosperity. Again, they do not accept that pleasure consists in the memory of past goods or in the expectation of goods to come, as Epicurus held, (90) for the motion of the soul expires with time.

7d. II.92

They (sc. the Cyrenaics proper) said that the *pathē* are apprehensible themselves, not the things from which they derive. And they abandoned the study of nature because of its manifest uncertainty; but they engaged in logic because of its usefulness. However, Meleager in the second book of his work *On Philosophical Doctrines* and Clitomachus in the first book of his work *On the Philosophical Sects* attest that the Cyrenaics considered both physics and dialectic useless.

7e. II.93

They (sc. the Cyrenaics proper) maintain that the sorrow of one person exceeds that of another, and that the senses do not always tell the truth.

7f. II.94

They (sc. the Hegesians) also believed that there is nothing pleasant or unpleasant by nature. It is because of the lack of something or its rarity or its superabundance that some people feel pleasure while others feel disgust. Poverty and wealth have nothing to do with pleasure, for the rich and the poor do not feel pleasure in different ways. Slavery and freedom, noble birth or low birth, glory or dishonour, are also indifferent in measuring pleasure.

7g. II.95–6

They (sc. the Hegesians) refuted the senses, since they do not yield accurate knowledge. And they claimed to do whatever appeared reasonable. They also said that errors should be forgiven, for no person errs voluntarily, but because he is compelled by a *pathos*. And we must not hate the erring man, but we should teach him better. The wise man does not have so much privilege over other people in his choice of goods as he has in avoiding evils, positing as a goal to live without bodily or mental pain. (96) This is the advantage gained by those who have been indifferent about the things capable of producing pleasure.

7h. II.96

The Annicerians agreed in other respects with them (sc. the Hegesians, but also the Cyrenaics proper); but they admitted that friendship and gratitude and respect for parents exist in life, and that the wise man will act in some cases for the sake of his country.

7i. II.99

He (sc. Theodorus) said that the world was his country. Theft, adultery and sacrilege are allowed upon occasion; for none of these things is wrong by nature, once we remove the belief which is kept up in order to bind together the multitude.

The latest testimonies, only recently included in the evidence about Cyrenaic epistemology,[11] come from two Christian authors, well-versed in Greek and Roman culture: Eusebius of Caesarea (who appears to speak on his own account in this passage) and the fourth–fifth century AD. Latin author and Church Father, St Augustine.

## 8 EUSEBIUS

Eusebius cites the central epistemological thesis of the Cyrenaics in the same breath as the attitudes of the Pyrrhonians and the positions of Metrodorus and Protagoras, thus suggesting that their theory has affinities with scepticism, sensationalism and relativism.

8a. Eusebius, *Preparation for the Gospel* XIV.2.4

Aside from the philosophers that have been set forth by us, in this gymnastic contest the stadium will also contain, stripped of all truth, those from the opposite side who took up arms against all the dogmatic philosophers put together (I mean the school of Pyrrho), and who declared that nothing amongst men is apprehensible, and also the school of Aristippus, who maintain that only the *pathē* are apprehensible, and again the schools of Metrodorus and Protagoras who hold that we must trust only the sensations of the body.

8b. Eusebius, *Preparation for the Gospel* XV.62.7

After him (sc. Socrates) the school of Aristippus of Cyrene and then later the school of Aristo of Chios tried to claim that in doing philosophy we should study only ethics; for it is both possible and useful. In complete contrast, accounts of nature are neither apprehensible nor, even if it turns out that they are clearly understood, do they have any usefulness.

## 9 ST AUGUSTINE

St Augustine's testimony is crucial to our discussion. In the treatise *Contra Academicos* (III.11.26), he sets out to examine a hypothetical challenge that a sceptic might address to a person, namely that one is

---

[11] They are included in *SSR* IV A 210, 220, 221. I shall not translate the passages from Jerome (*Epist.* L 5) and from Clement of Alexandria (*Strom.* VII.7.41), which Giannantoni includes in the epistemological testimonies, for in fact they report religious rather than epistemological views.

deceived in believing that one is tasting something sweet while, in fact, one is dreaming. In his retort, St Augustine emphasises the irrefutability of subjective experience and mentions in that connection the doctrines of the Epicureans and of the Cyrenaics. The importance of this passage lies in the fact that it might be considered to raise the problem of the external world, and it also might appear to support Plutarch's claim that the Cyrenaics and the Epicureans held very similar positions regarding the reliability of the senses.

St Augustine, *Contra Academicos* iii.11.26
This I say, that a person, when he is tasting something, can swear with good faith that he knows through his own palate that this is sweet, or to the contrary, and he cannot be brought away from that knowledge by any Greek trickery. Who would be so shameless as to say to me when I am licking something with delight: 'maybe you are not tasting, but this is a dream'? Do I resist? But that would delight me even if I were asleep. And so, no likeness of false things confuses that which I said I know, and an Epicurean or the Cyrenaics may perhaps say many other things in favour of the senses, against which I have observed that nothing was said by the Academics.

# References

Alston, W. (1971) 'Varieties of privileged access', *American Philosophical Quarterly* 8: 223–41.

Annas, J. (1980) 'Truth and knowledge', in M. Schofield, M. Burnyeat and J. Barnes (eds.) *Doubt and Dogmatism* (Oxford) 84–104.

(1986) 'Doing without objective values', in M. Schofield and G. Striker (eds.) *The Norms of Nature* (Cambridge and Paris) 3–29.

(1990) 'Stoic epistemology', in S. Everson (ed.) *Companions to Ancient Thought. 1: Epistemology* (Cambridge) 184–203.

(1993) *The Morality of Happiness*, Oxford.

(1994) 'Plato the Skeptic', in P. A. Vander Waerdt (ed.) *The Socratic Movement* (Ithaca and London) 309–40.

Annas, J. and Barnes, J. (1985) *The Modes of Scepticism*, Cambridge.

Anscombe, G. E. M. (1994) 'The first person', in Q. Cassam (ed.) *Self-Knowledge* (Oxford) 140–59.

Anton, J. P. and Preus, A. (eds.) (1983) *Essays in Ancient Greek Philosophy*, Albany.

Antoniades, E. (1916) 'Aristipp und die Kyrenaiker', Dissertation, Göttingen.

Armstrong, D. M. (1968) *A Materialist Theory of the Mind*, London.

Asmis, E. (1984) *Epicurus' Scientific Method*, Ithaca and London.

Aune, B. (1967) *Knowledge, Mind and Nature*, New York.

Austin, J. L. (1961) 'Other Minds', in *Philosophical Papers* (Oxford) 76–116.

Ayer, A. J. (1958) *The Foundations of Empirical Knowledge*, London.

(1954) 'Can there be a private language?', *Proceedings of the Aristotelian Society* (suppl. vol.) 28: 63–76.

Bailey, C. (1928) *The Greek Atomists and Epicurus*, Oxford.

Barnes, J. (1982) 'The beliefs of a Pyrrhonist', *Proceedings of the Cambridge Philological Society* 28: 1–29.

(1989) 'Antiochus of Ascalon', in M. Griffin and J. Barnes (eds.) *Philosophia Togata* (Oxford) 51–96.

(1994) 'Scepticism and relativity', in A. Alberti (ed.) *Realta e Ragione. Studi di filosofia antica* (Florence).

Barnes, J. and Mignucci, M. (eds.) (1988) *Matter and Metaphysics*, Naples.

Bastianini, G. and Sedley, D. (1995) 'Commentarium in Platonis *Theaetetum*', *Corpus dei papiri filosofici greci e latini* III, Florence, 227–562.

Blank, D. L. (1982) *Ancient Philosophy and Grammar: The Syntax of Apollonius Dyscolus*, Berkeley and Los Angeles.

Boissonade, de Fontarabie, Jean François (ed.) (1920) *Ex Procli scholiis in Cratylum Platonis excerpta*, Leipzig and Leiden.

Bollack, J., Bollack M. et Wissmann H. (eds.) (1971) *La Lettre d'Epicure*, Paris.

Bonjour, L. (1986) *The Structure of Empirical Knowledge*, Cambridge, Mass.

Brentano, F. (1924) *Psychologie vom empirischen Standpunkte*, Leipzig.

Brunschwig, J. (1977) 'Epicure et le problème du langage privé', *Revue des Sciences humaines* 43: 157–77.

(1984) 'Remarques sur la théorie stoïcienne du nom propre', *Histoire epistémologie langage* 6: 287–310.

(1986) 'The Cradle Argument in Epicureanism and Stoicism', in M. Schofield and G. Striker (eds.) *The Norms of Nature* (Cambridge) 113–44.

(1988) 'Sextus Empiricus on the kritērion: the Skeptic as conceptual legatee', in J. M. Dillon and A. A. Long (eds.) *The Question of Eclecticism* (Berkeley and Los Angeles) 145–75.

(1994a) 'The ὅσον ἐπὶ τῷ λόγῳ formula in Sextus Empiricus', in *Papers in Hellenistic Philosophy* (Cambridge) 244–58.

(1994b) *Papers in Hellenistic Philosophy*, Cambridge.

(forthcoming) 'La théorie cyrénaïque de la connaissance: quoi de Socratique?', in J. B. Gourinat (ed.) *Socrate et les Socratiques* (Paris).

Brunschwig, J. and Nussbaum, M. C. (eds.) (1993) *Passions and Perceptions: Studies in Hellenistic Philosophy of Mind*, Paris and Cambridge.

Burge, T. (1988) 'Individualism and self-knowledge', *Journal of Philosophy* 85: 649–63.

Burnet, J. (1914) *Greek Philosophy*, London.

Burnyeat, M. F. (1976) 'Protagoras and self refutation in Plato's *Theaetetus*', *Philosophical Review* 85: 172–95.

(1979) 'Conflicting appearances', *Proceedings of the British Academy* 65: 69–111.

(1980) 'Can the Sceptic live his Scepticism?', in M. Schofield, M. Burnyeat and J. Barnes (eds.) *Doubt and Dogmatism* (Oxford) 20–53.

(1982) 'Idealism and Greek philosophy: what Descartes saw and Berkeley missed', *Philosophical Review* 91: 3–40.

(ed.) (1983) *The Sceptical Tradition*, Berkeley and Los Angeles.

(1984) 'The Skeptic in his place and time', in R. Rorty, J. B. Schneewind and Q. Skinner (eds.) *Philosophy in History* (Cambridge) 225–54.

(1990) *The Theaetetus of Plato*, Indianapolis.

Butler, R. J. (ed.) (1962) *Analytical Philosophy*, Oxford.

Cassam, Q. (ed.) (1994) *Self-Knowledge*, Oxford.

Caujolle-Zaslawsky, F. (1982) 'Qu'est-ce que la méthode sceptique?', Doctoral thesis, Paris.

Chisholm, R. (1941) 'Sextus Empiricus and modern empiricism', *Philosophy of Science* 8: 371–84.

(1957) *Perceiving*, Ithaca.

(1966) *Theory of Knowledge*, Englewood Cliffs, N.J.

(1969) 'On the observability of the self', *Philosophy and Phenomenological Research*

30: 7–21.

Clay, D. (1983) *Lucretius and Epicurus*, Ithaca and London.

Cornford, F. M. (1935) *Plato's Theory of Knowledge*, London.

Cornman, J. (1970) 'Sellars, scientific realism and *sensa*', *Review of Metaphysics* 23: 417–51.

(1971) *Materialism and Sensations*, New Haven and London.

(1975) *Perception, Common Sense and Science*, New Haven and London.

Couissin, P. (1983) 'The Stoicism of the New Academy', in M. F. Burnyeat (ed.) *The Skeptical Tradition* (Berkeley and Los Angeles) 31–63.

Dancy, J. (1985) *Introduction to Contemporary Epistemology*, Oxford.

Davidson, D. (1987) 'Knowing one's own mind', *Proceedings and Addresses of the American Philosophical Association* 60: 441–58.

de Witt, N. W. (1943) 'Epicurus: all sensations are true', *Transactions of the American Philological Association* 74: 19–32.

(1954) *Epicurus and his Philosophy*, Minneapolis.

Dennet, D. (1975) 'Conditions of personhood', in A. Rorty (ed.) *The Identities of Persons* (London) 175–96.

(1968) *Content and Consciousness*, London.

Denyer, N. (1991) *Language, Thought and Falsehood in Ancient Greek Philosophy*, London.

Detel, W. (1975) 'Αἴσθησις und λογισμός: zwei Probleme der epikureischen Methodologie', *Archiv für Geschichte der Philosophie* 57: 21–35.

Diels, H. and Schubart, W. (1905) 'Anonymer Kommentar zu Platons *Theaetet* (Papyrus 9782)', *Berliner Klassikertexte* 2, Berlin.

Dillon, J. and Long, A. A. (eds.) (1988) *The Question of Eclecticism*, Berkeley and Los Angeles.

Doering, K. (1988) *Der Sokratesschuler Aristipp und die Kyrenaiker*, Stuttgart.

Ducasse, C. J. (1942) 'Moore's refutation of idealism', in P. A. Schilpp (ed.) *The Philosophy of G. E. Moore*, Chicago.

(1949) *Nature, Mind and Death*, La Salle.

Dümmler, F. (1889) *Akademika*, Giessen.

Dumont, J.-P. (1972) *Le Scepticisme et le phénomène*, Paris.

Evans, E. (1969) 'Physiognomics in the ancient world', *Transactions of the American Philosophical Society* N.S. 59.

Evans, G. (1982) *The Varieties of Reference*, Oxford.

Everson, S. (ed.) (1990) *Companions to Ancient Thought. 1: Epistemology*, Cambridge.

(ed.) (1991a): *Companions to Ancient Thought. 2: Psychology*, Cambridge.

(1991b) 'The objective appearance of Pyrrhonism', in S. Everson (ed.) *Companions to Ancient Thought 2: Psychology* (Cambridge) 121–47.

(ed.) (1994) *Companions to Ancient Thought. 3: Language*, Cambridge.

Förster, R. (1893) *Scriptores Physiognomonici*, Leipzig.

Fraser, P. M. (1972) *Ptolemaic Alexandria*, Oxford.

Frede, M. (1987) *Essays in Ancient Philosophy*, Oxford.

(1990) 'An empiricist view of knowledge: memorism', in S. Everson (ed.) *Companions to Ancient Thought. 1: Epistemology* (Cambridge) 225–50.

Frischer, B. (1982) *The Sculpted Word*, Berkeley and Los Angeles.

Furley, D. J. (1967) *Two Studies in the Greek Atomists*, Princeton.
Gasking, D. (1962) 'Avowals', in R. J. Butler (ed.) *Analytical Philosophy* (Oxford) 154–69.
Giannantoni, G. (1958) *I Cirenaici*, Florence.
   (1990) *Socratis et Socraticorum reliquiae*, Rome.
Giannantoni, G. and Gigante, M. (eds.) (1996) *L'epicureismo greco e romano*, Naples.
Gigante, M. (1981) *Scetticismo e epicureismo*, Naples.
Glidden, D. K. (1975) 'Protagorean relativism and the Cyrenaics', in N. Rescher (ed.) *Studies in Epistemology* (Oxford) 113–40.
   (1988) 'Protagorean obliquity', *History of Philosophy Quarterly* 5: 321–40.
Glucker, J. (1978) *Antiochus and the Late Academy*, Hypomnemata 56, Göttingen.
Goldman, A. I. (1986) *Epistemology and Cognition*, Cambridge, Mass.
Goldschmidt, V. (1969) *Le système stoïcien et l'idée du temps*, Paris.
Gosling, J. C. B. and Taylor, C. C. W. (1982) *The Greeks on Pleasure*, Oxford.
Gourinat, J. B. (ed.) (forthcoming) *Socrate et les Socratiques*, Paris.
Grice, H. P. (1975) 'Personal identity', in J. Perry (ed.) *Personal Identity* (Berkeley and Los Angeles) 73–98.
Groarke, L. (1990) *Greek Scepticism: Anti-Realist Trends in Ancient Thought*, Montreal.
Grote, G. (1865) *Plato and Other Companions of Socrates*, London.
Guthrie, W. K. C. (1969) *A History of Greek Philosophy* (vol. III), Cambridge.
Hankinson, R. J. (1995) *The Sceptics*, London.
Harman, G. (1975) 'Moral relativism defended', *Philosophical Review* 84: 3–22.
Harris, H. (ed.) (1995) *Identity*, Oxford.
Heidelberger, H. (1966) 'On characterising the psychological', *Philosophy and Phenomenological Research* 26: 529–36.
Heiland, H. (1925) 'Aristoclis Messenii reliquiae', Dissertation, Giessen.
Hervey, H. (1957) 'The private language problem', *Philosophical Quarterly* 7: 63–79.
Hiley, D. (1988) *Philosophy in Question: Essays on a Pyrrhonian Theme*, Chicago and London.
Huby, P. M., and Neale, G. C. (eds.) (1987) *The Criterion of Truth: Studies in Honour of George Kerferd on his Seventieth Birthday*, Liverpool.
Humbert, J. (1967) *Les Petits Socratiques*, Paris.
Indelli, G. and Tsouna-McKirahan, V. (1995) [*Philodemus*] [*On Choices and Avoidances*], Naples.
Irwin, T. H. (1986) 'Socrates the Epicurean', *University of Illinois Classical Studies* 11: 85–112.
   (1991) 'Aristippus against happiness', *Monist* 74: 55–82.
Jackson, F. (1975) 'On the adverbial analysis of visual experience', *Metaphilosophy* 6: 195–225.
Kenny, A. (1966) 'Cartesian privacy', in G. Pitcher (ed.) *Wittgenstein: The Philosophical Investigations* (Garden City, N.Y.) 352–70.
Kerferd, G. B. (1949) 'Plato's account of the relativism of Protagoras', *Durham University Journal* 42: 20–6.

Konstan, D. (1982) 'Ancient atomism and its heritage: minimal parts', *Ancient Philosophy* 2: 60–75.

(1983) 'Problems in Epicurean physics', in J. P. Anton and A. Preus (eds.) *Essays in Ancient Greek Philosophy* II (Albany) 431–64.

Laks, A. (1993) 'Annicéris et les plaisirs psychiques', in J. Brunschwig and M. C. Nussbaum (eds.) *Passions and Perceptions: Studies in Hellenistic Philosophy of Mind* (Paris and Cambridge) 18–49.

Laks, A. and Schofield, M. (eds.) (1995) *Justice and Generosity*, Cambridge.

Laursen, J. C. (1992) *The Politics of Skepticism in the Ancients, Montaigne, Hume and Kant*, Leiden.

Leone, G. (1984) 'Epicuro, *Della natura*, libro XIV', *Cronache Ercolanesi* 14: 17–107.

Lewis, D. (1966) 'An argument for the Identity Theory', *Journal of Philosophy* 63: 17–25.

(1976) 'Survival and identity', in A. Rorty (ed.) *The Identities of Persons* (Berkeley and Los Angeles) 17–40.

Lloyd, A. C. (1971) 'Grammar and metaphysics in the Stoa', in A. A. Long (ed.) *Problems in Stoicism* (London) 58–74.

(1972) 'On Augustine's concept of a person', in R. A. Markus (ed.) *Augustine: A Collection of Critical Essays* (New York) 191–205.

Lloyd, G. E. R. (1966) *Polarity and Analogy*, Cambridge.

Long, A. A. (ed.) (1971a) *Problems in Stoicism*, London.

(1971b) '*Aisthēsis, prolēpsis* and linguistic theory in Epicurus', *Bulletin of the Institute of Classical Studies* 18: 114–33.

(1988) 'Ptolemy on the criterion', in J. Dillon and A. A. Long (eds.) *The Question of Eclecticism* (Berkeley and Los Angeles) 176–207.

Long, A. A. and Sedley, D. N. (1987) *The Hellenistic Philosophers*, Cambridge.

McGinn, C. (1989) *Mental Content*, Oxford.

McPherran, M. (1987) 'Skeptical homeopathy and self-refutation', *Phronesis* 32: 290–328.

Malcolm, N. (1958) 'Knowledge of other minds', *Journal of Philosophy* 55: 969–78.

Mannebach, E. (1961) *Aristippi et Cyrenaicorum fragmenta*, Leiden and Cologne.

Mansfeld, J. (1991) 'Two attributions', *Classical Quarterly* 41: 541–4.

Markus, R. A. (ed.) (1972) *Augustine: A Collection of Critical Essays*, New York.

Mates, B. (1981) *Skeptical Essays*, Chicago.

Matthews, G. B. (1977) 'Consciousness and life', *Philosophy* 52: 13–26.

Mellor, H. (1989) 'I and now', *Proceedings of the Aristotelian Society* 89: 79–94.

Misener, G. (1923) 'Loxus, physician and physiognomist', *Classical Philology* 18: 1–22.

Mitsis, P. (1988) *Epicurus' Ethical Theory*, Ithaca.

Mondolfo, R. (1953) 'I Cirenaici e i "raffinati" del *Teeteto* platonico', *Rivista di Filosofia* 44: 127–35.

(1958) *La comprensione del soggetto umano nell'antichità classica*, Florence.

Moore, G. E. (1924) 'A defence of common sense', in J. H. Muirhead (ed.) *Contemporary British Philosophy* (London) 193–223.

Muirhead, J. H. (ed.) (1924) *Contemporary British Philosophy*, London.

Nagel, T. (1974) 'What is it like to be a bat?', *Philosophical Review* 83: 435–50.

Natorp, P. (1890) 'Aristipp in Platons *Theaetet*', *Archiv für Geschichte der philosophie*, 347ff.

Nehamas, A. (1986) 'Socratic intellectualism', *Boston Area Colloquium in Ancient Philosophy* 2: 274–316.

Nussbaum, M. C. (1994) *The Therapy of Desire*, Princeton.

Obbink, D. (1992) ' "What all men believe – must be true": common conceptions and *consensio omnium* in Aristotle and Hellenistic philosophy', *Oxford Studies in Ancient Philosophy* 10: 193–231.

Oehler, K. (1961) 'Der Consensus omnium als Kriterium der Wahrheit in der antiken Philosophie und der Patristik', *Antike und Abendland* 10: 103–29.

Padel, R. (1992) *In and Out of the Mind*, Princeton.

Parfit, D. (1971) 'Personal identity', *Philosophical Review* 80: 3–27.

(1984) *Reasons and Persons*, Oxford.

Passmore, J. (1961) *Philosophical Reasoning*, London.

Perry, J. (ed.) (1975a) *Personal Identity*, Berkeley and Los Angeles.

(1975b) 'The problem of personal identity', in J. Perry (ed.) *Personal Identity* (Berkeley and Los Angeles) 3–30.

Pinborg, J. (1975) 'Historiography of linguistics. Classical antiquity: Greece', *Current Trends in Linguistics* 13: 65–126.

Pitcher, G. (ed.) (1966) *Wittgenstein: The Philosophical Investigations*, Garden City, N.Y.

Pollock, J. (1986) *Contemporary Theories of Knowledge*, London.

Price, A. W. (1995) *Mental Conflict*, London and New York.

Price, H. H. (1938) 'Our evidence for the existence of other minds', *Philosophy* 13: 425–56.

Putnam, H. (1983) *Realism and Reason*, Cambridge.

Quinton, A. (1975) 'The soul', in J. Perry (ed.) *Personal Identity* (Berkeley and Los Angeles) 53–72.

Reid, J. S. (1885) *The Academica of Cicero*, London.

Rist, J. (ed.) (1978) *The Stoics*, Berkeley and Los Angeles.

Robin, L. (1944) *Pyrrhon et le scepticisme grec*, Paris.

Rorty, A. O. (1976) *The Identities of Persons*, Berkeley and Los Angeles.

Rorty, R., Schneewind, J. B. and Skinner, Q. (eds.) (1984) *Philosophy in History*, Cambridge.

Ross, W. D. (1951) *Plato's Theory of Ideas*, Oxford.

Ryle, G. (1963) *The Concept of Mind*, Harmondsworth.

Sandbach, F. H. (1971) 'Phantasia katalēptikē', in A. A. Long (ed.) *Problems in Stoicism* (London) 9–21.

Schian, R. (1973) *Untersuchungen über das 'argumentum e consensu omnium'*, *Spudasmata* 28.

Schleiermacher, S. (1804–28) *Platons Werke*, Berlin.

Schmidt, R. T. (1979) *Die Grammatik der Stoiker*, Wiesbaden.

Schofield, M. (1988) 'The retrenchable present', in J. Barnes and M. Mignucci (eds.) *Matter and Metaphysics* (Naples) 329–74.

Schofield, M., Burnyeat, M. and Barnes, J. (eds.) (1980) *Doubt and Dogmatism*, Oxford.

Schofield, M. and Striker, G. (eds.) (1986) *The Norms of Nature: Studies in Hellenistic Ethics*, Cambridge.

Schwartz, E. (1951) *Ethik der Griechen*, Stuttgart.

Scott, D. (1989) 'Epicurean illusions', *Classical Quarterly* 39: 360–74.

Searle, J. R. (1980) 'Intrinsic intentionality', *Behavioural and Brain Science* 3: 450–6.

Sedley, D. N. (1973) 'Epicurus, *On Nature*, book xxviii', *Cronache Ercolanesi* 3: 5–83.

(1977) 'Diodorus Cronus and Hellenistic philosophy', *Proceedings of the Cambridge Philological Society* N.S. 23: 74–120.

(1982) 'The Stoic criterion of identity', *Phronesis* 27: 255–75.

(1987) 'Epicurus on the common sensibles', in P. M. Huby and G. C. Neale (eds.) *The Criterion of Truth* (Liverpool) 123–36.

(1988) 'Epicurean anti-reductionism', in J. Barnes and M. Mignucci (eds.) *Matter and Metaphysics* (Naples) 297–327.

(1992) 'Sextus Empiricus and the atomist criteria of truth', *Elenchos* 13: 24–56.

(1996) 'The inferential foundations of Epicurean ethics', in G. Giannantoni and M. Gigante (eds.) *Epicureismo greco et romano* (Naples) 303–39.

Sellars, W. (1963) *Science, Perception and Reality*, London.

(1964) 'Notes on intensionality', *Journal of Philosophy* 61: 655–65.

(1968) *Science and Metaphysics*, London.

(1971) 'Science, sense-impressions and sense: a reply to Cornman', *Review of Metaphysics* 24: 391–447.

(1975) 'On the objects of the adverbial theory of sensation', *Metaphilosophy* 6: 144–60.

Shields, C. (1994) 'Socrates among the Skeptics', in P. A. Vander Waerdt (ed.) *The Socratic Movement* (Ithaca) 341–66.

Shoemaker, S. (1975) 'Personal identity and memory', in J. Perry (ed.) *Personal Identity* (Berkeley and Los Angeles) 119–34.

Smart, J. J. C. (1963) *Philosophy and Scientific Realism*, London.

Solmsen, F. (1968) 'Αἴσθησις in Aristotelian and Epicurean thought', in *Kleine Schriften* I, 612–33.

(1977) 'Epicurus on void, matter and genesis', *Phronesis* 22: 263–81.

Sosa, E. (1988) 'Beyond Scepticism, to the best of our knowledge', *Mind* 97: 153–88.

Stough, C. (1984) 'Sextus Empiricus on non-assertion', *Phronesis* 29: 136–64.

Strawson, P. F. (1959) *Individuals*, London.

(1985) *Scepticism and Naturalism*, London.

Striker, G. (1974) "Κριτήριον τῆς ἀληθείας", *Nachrichten der Akademie der Wissenschaften in Göttingen*, Phil.-hist. Klasse 2.: 47–110.

(1977) 'Epicurus on the truth of sense impressions', *Archiv für Geschichte der Philosophie* 59: 125–42.

(1981) 'Über den Unterschied zwischen den Pyrrhonern und den

Akademikern', *Phronesis* 26: 153–71.

(1983) 'The ten Tropes of Aenesidemus', in M. F. Burnyeat (ed.) *The Skeptical Tradition* (Berkeley and Los Angeles) 95–115.

(1993) 'Epicurean hedonism', in J. Brunschwig and M. Nussbaum (eds.) *Passions and Perceptions* (Cambridge) 3–17.

Stroud, B. (1984) *The Significance of Philosophical Scepticism*, Oxford.

Tarrant, H. (1983) 'The date of Anon. In *Theaetetum*', *Classical Quarterly* 41: 161–87.

(1994) 'The *Hippias major* and Socratic theories of pleasure', in P. A. Vander Waerdt (ed.) *The Socratic Movement* (Ithaca), 107–26.

Taylor, C. C. W. (1980) 'All perceptions are true', in M. Schofield, M. Burnyeat and J. Barnes (eds.) *Doubt and Dogmatism* (Oxford) 105–24.

(1989) *Sources of Self: The Making of the Modern Identity*, Cambridge, Mass.

Trabucco, F. (1958/9) 'La polemica di Aristocle di Messene contro Protagora e Epicuro', *Atti dell' Accademia delle Scienze di Torino* 93: 1–43.

(1960) 'La polemica di Aristocle di Messene contro lo scetticismo e Aristippo e i Cirenaici', *Rivista critica di storia della filosofia* 15 (fasc. II): 115–40.

Tsouna, V. (1988) 'Les philosophes Cyrénaïques et leur théorie de la connaissance', Doctoral thesis, Paris.

(forthcoming) 'Is there an exception to Greek eudaemonism?'', in M. Canto and P. Pellegrin (eds.) *Mélanges Jacques Brunschwig*, Paris.

Tsouna-McKirahan, V. (1992) 'The Cyrenaic theory of knowledge', *Oxford Studies in Ancient Philosophy* 10: 161–92.

(1994) 'The Socratic origins of the Cynics and Cyrenaics', in P. A. Vander Waerdt (ed.) *The Socratic Movement* (Ithaca) 367–91.

(1995) 'Conservatism and Pyrrhonian Scepticism', *Syllecta Classica* 6: 69–86.

(1997) 'Doubts about Other Minds and the science of Physiognomics', *Classical Quarterly* 48 (no.i): 175–86.

(1998) 'Remarks about Other Minds in Greek philosophy', *Phronesis* XLIII/3, pp. 1–19.

Tye, M. (1984) 'The adverbial approach to visual experience', *Philosophical Review* 93: 195–225.

Urmson, J. O. and Warnock G. J. (1970) *Philosophical Papers*, Oxford.

Vander Waerdt, P. A. (1989) 'Colotes and the Epicurean refutation of Skepticism', *Greek, Roman and Byzantine Studies* 30: 225–67.

(ed.) (1994) *The Socratic Movement*, Ithaca.

Vlastos, G. (1991) *Socrates: Ironist and Moral Philosopher*, Ithaca.

Warnock, C. J. (1967) *Philosophy and Perception*, Oxford.

Waterlow, S. (1977) 'Protagoras and inconsistency', *Archiv für Geschichte der Philosophie* 59: 19–36.

Wiggins, D. (1967) *Identity and Spatio-Temporal Continuity*, Oxford.

Wilkes, K. V. (1988) *Real People: Personal Identity without Thought Experiments*, Oxford.

Williams, B. (1972) *Morality: An Introduction to Ethics*, Harmondsworth.

(1973) *Problems of the Self*, Cambridge.

(1978) *Descartes: The Project of Pure Enquiry*, Harmondsworth.

(1981) *Moral Luck*, Cambridge.

(1985) *Ethics and the Limits of Philosophy*, London.

Wilson, M. D. (1978) 'Cartesian dualism', in M. Hooker (ed.) *Descartes* (Baltimore).

Wisdom, J. (1952) *Other Minds*, Oxford.

Wittgenstein, L. (1953) (transl. by G. E. M. Anscombe) *Philosophical Investigations*, Oxford.

(1969) (transl. by Denis Paul and G. E. M. Anscombe) *On Certainty*, Oxford.

Woodruff, P. (1986) 'The skeptical side of Plato's method', *Revue internationale de philosophie* 156/7: 22–37.

Zeller, E. (1922) *Die Philosophie der Griechen* (5th edn), Leipzig, Part II, section I.

Zeyl, D. (1980) 'Socrates and hedonism', *Phronesis* 25: 250–69.

# Index of names

# Index locorum

Galen (ps.)
*Historia philosopha* (3) 4n
Heraclitus
(fr. 22B DK) 130n
Hesychius
*Onomatologos* (xc.6–9) 4n

Jerome (St)
*Epistulae* (L 5) 159n

Lactantius
*Divinae institutiones* (28.3) 15; (34.7) 15
Lucretius
*De natura rerum* (4.324–461) 79n; (r.353–63)
117n, 122n; (4.379–86) 122n; (4.469–521)
122n

Papyrus Herculanensis 19/698
106n; (XVII) 122n; (XVII.1–14) 20; (XVIII) 122n;
(XXIII) 122n; (XXV) 122n; (XXVI) 122n;
(XXVI.3–16) 19–20
Papyrus Herculanensis 1251
(I–III) 70n; (II–III) 147; (II.5–14) 70; (II.9)
27; (II.13) 27; (III.2–14) 71; (III.16) 27;
(III.17) 27
Plato
*Apology* (21b) 140, (21d) 140
*Charmides* (173d) 135n
*Phaedo* (78d) 16
*Philebus* (36c) 44n; (36c ff.) 44n; (36e) 44n
*Respublica* (580d ff.) 43–44n; (583b) 44n;
(584a) 44n bis; (612a) 16
*Symposium* (207 ff.) 135n; (207d) 130n; (211b)
16
*Theaetetus* (142a) 147; (142c) 129n; (143a–c)
129n; (152a) 126 bis; (152b) 148; (152d–e)
126; (152e) 130n; (153d) 147; (1553) 125 bis;
(156a) 125; (156a—157c) 126; (156a ff.) 148;
(156d ff.) 136; (157b) 130; (159a) 130;
(159a–160a) 130, 131n; (159c) 127; (160a–b)
127n; (160c) 127 ter; (160e–171e) 64; (178a
ff.) 68; (179c–183c) 127n; (181a–183b) 127n
*Timaeus* (59b) 16; (64b–c) 10n; (64d–65b)
10n; (86a) 130n
Plutarch
*Adversus Colotem* (1111td ff.) 81; (1120b–f) 84,
144; (1120c–f) 115; (1120c–1121e) 144–6;
(1120d) 26, 80n, 85, 85n, 86, 86n, 107, 119
bis; (1120d–3) 87, 190; (1120d–f) 121n;
(1120e) 23, 26, 29, 49, 76 bis, 80n, 108;
(1120e–f) 39; (1120e ff.) 87; (1120f–1212a)
115; (1120f–1121e) 115 bis, 177; (1121a) 116,
119; (1121a–b) 119; (1121b) 119; (1121b–c)
117; (1121c) 120n, 121; (1121d–e) 121; (1121e)
106n; (1123b–c) 116

Seneca
*Epistulae* (89.12) 4n
Sextus Empiricus
*Pyrrhoniae hypotyposes* (1.6) 43n; (1.13) 37, 59;
(1.13–15) 59; (1.15) 60 bis; (i.17) 60 bis;
(1.19) 37 bis, 60 ter; (1.20) 37; (1.22) 37;
(1.22–4) 36; (1.23) 37; (1.23–4) 60;
(1.40–79) 90n; (1.43–7) 90n; (i.44) 79n;
(1.79–90) 90n; (1.98) 37; (1.101) 79n;
(1.126) 58; (1.190) 59; (1.191) 58, 59;
(1.193) 59; (1.200) 59 bis; (1.201) 59 bis;
(1.215) 9, 54, 57 bis, 60, 76, 140, 154 ter;
(1.224–9) 39; (1.232–4) 140n; (II.7) 74n;
(II.96) 58; (II.99) 58; (II.107) 43n; (III.51)
58; (III.52) 58
*Adversus mathematicos* (I.117) 16; (I.226) 16;
(II.109) 43n; (VI.52–3) 80 bis, 81, 154, 156;
(VI.53) 81, 81n; (VII.111) 4n, 143n; (VII.15)
4n; (VII.61) 79n; (VII.141–260) 33n ter, 61,
154; (VII.151) 40; (VII.159) 54; (VII.161–2)
54; (VII.162) 79n; (VII.162–5) 54; (VII.166)
39n; (VII.174) 79n; (VII.176) 39n;
(VII.180–2) 39n; (VII.184) 39n; (VII.189)
39n; (VII.190) 138; (VII.190–200) 154–6;
(VII.191) 23, 26, 29, 32, 33, 38, 46, 77,
108; (VII.191–2) 47; (VII.191–5) 103;
(VII.191–8) 138; (VII.191–200) 38 bis, 55,
78, 80 bis, 138, 154 bis; (VII.192) 23, 24
bis, 26, 28, 29 bis; (VII.192–3) 28;
(VII.192–4) 80; (VII.193) 23, 24, 29 bis, 55,
77, 79; (VII.193–4) 65, 78 bis, 79;
(VII.193–5) 55; (VII.194) 47, 55 bis, 56, 57
bis, 60, 77, 78; (VII.195) 33, 55 bis, 76n,
100, 102, 103 ter, 106 ter, 108n;
(VII.195–6) 41, 102, 105; (VII.196–8) 90,
103 bis; (VII.196) 22, 41, 100, 102n, 103
bis, 108n; (VII.196–7) 47; (VII.196–8) 103;
(VII.197) 21, 26, 55n, 77, 100, 102 534;
(VII.197–8) 133; (VII.198) 24, 26–7, 29
bis, 52, 54, 77, 102 bis, 106, 108n; (VII.199)
10n, 11, 12, 12n, 27, 33; (VII.199–200) 138;
(VII.200) 27, 33, 61; (VII.206FF.) 122n;
(VII.209–10) 118; (VII.210) 117 bis, 122n;
(VII.210–16) 39; (VII.211FF.) 122n;
(VII.211–16) 123n; (VII.245) 102n;
(VII.248) 102n; (VII.248–51) 35; (VII.252)
35; (VIII.26) 43n; (VIII.63) 122n; (VIII.176)
58; (X.299) 58; (XI.143) 34 ter; (XI.144)
37; (XI.148) 37
Socrates et Socraticorum reliquiae
(IV A 144–59) 143n; (IV A 173) 10n; (IV A
185–7) 13n; (IV A 210) 159n; (IV A 220)
159n; (IV A 221) 159n; (IV F 4) 143n; (IV H
1–2) 143n; (IV H 5) 143n, (IV H 13) 143n.
(IV H 23) 143n

# Subject index